W9-BRI-924

Their
Ancient
Glittering
Eyes

Also by Donald Hall

PROSE

String Too Short to be Saved
Henry Moore
Dock Ellis and the Country of Baseball
Goatfoot Milktongue Twinbird
Remembering Poets
To Keep Moving
The Weather for Poetry
Fathers Playing Catch with Sons
The Ideal Bakery
Poetry and Ambition
Seasons at Eagle Pond
Here at Eagle Pond

POETRY

Exiles and Marriages

The Dark Houses

A Roof of Tiger Lilies

The Alligator Bride:
Poems New and Selected

The Yellow Room

The Town of Hill

Kicking the Leaves

The Happy Man

The One Day

Old and New Poems

Robert Frost

Dylan Thomas

T. S. Eliot

Archibald MacLeish

Yvor Winters

Marianne Moore

Ezra Pound

Their
Ancient
Glittering Eyes

Remembering Poets
and More
Poets

DONALD HALL

Ticknor & Fields
New York
1992

For information about permission to reproduce selections
from this book, write to Permissions, Ticknor & Fields,
215 Park Avenue South, New York, New York 10003.

Library of Congress Cataloging-in-Publication Data

Hall, Donald, date.
Their ancient glittering eyes : remembering poets and more poets :
Robert Frost, Dylan Thomas, Archibald MacLeish, T. S. Eliot,
Ezra Pound, Yvor Winters, Marianne Moore / Donald Hall.
p.   cm.
Enlarged ed. of: Remembering poets. © 1978.
Includes index.
ISBN 0-89919-979-8
1. Hall, Donald, 1928– — Friends and associates.
2. Poets, American — 20th century — Interviews.
3. Poets, American — 20th century — Biography. 4. Poetics.
I. Hall, Donald, date. Remembering poets. II. Title.
PS3515.A3152Z526 1992
811'.509 — dc20
[B]   92-889
CIP

Printed in the United States of America

HAD   10 9 8 7 6 5 4 3 2 1

Copyright acknowledgments appear on page 347.

Portions of this book previously appeared in *Commentary, Lear's,*
the *Paris Review,* and *American Poetry Review.*

Book design by Anne Chalmers

TO CHARLES CHRISTENSEN

We Poets in our youth begin in gladness;
But thereof come in the end despondency and madness.

> — William Wordsworth,
> "Resolution and Independence"

We work in the dark — we do what we can — we give what we have. Our doubt is our passion and our passion is our task. The rest is the madness of art.

> — Henry James,
> "The Middle Years"

I have long since made up my mind not to seek the acquaintance of poets.

> — Henry Adams,
> from a letter

There, on the mountain and the sky,
On all the tragic scene they stare.
One asks for mournful melodies;
Accomplished fingers begin to play.
Their eyes mid many wrinkles, their eyes,
Their ancient, glittering eyes, are gay.

> — William Butler Yeats,
> "Lapis Lazuli"

Contents

Preface

In 1975 and 1976, I tried writing a book of reminiscence called *Old Poets* — about Robert Frost, T. S. Eliot, and Ezra Pound. When it came up short, I added the asymmetrical Dylan Thomas and changed my title to *Remembering Poets;* the book appeared in 1978 and has been out of print for a decade. I didn't include Marianne Moore because I felt that my recollections added nothing to common knowledge; Archibald MacLeish was alive, and Yvor Winters by himself would not have fit. In the years since *Remembering Poets,* I've had further thoughts about Moore; MacLeish died, a prerequisite for inclusion in memoirs; I found myself thinking of Winters and MacLeish together, my old teachers so unlike each other. When I was invited to reprint *Remembering Poets,* I decided to tinker with the old essays and add three poets.

Tinkering: In *Their Ancient Glittering Eyes,* I revise phrases and passages of *Remembering Poets.* Many changes are small. I repair sentences, alter punctuation, and change "prone" to "supine" (thanks to a correspondent). Finding some old notes and letters, I add a few stories. But also: New biographies have corrected old assumptions, and from time to time I have changed my mind. "Omissions are not accidents," as Marianne Moore said when she revised her poems. When I have altered opinions or speculations, new words criticize old ones.

There is no obvious order for these essays, which by necessity overlap in time. *Remembering Poets* began with Dylan Thomas, as if to get him out of the way — the only poet not an American, the only one not to live a long life. This time I start with Frost

— the eldest, not a modernist, and whom I met when I was sixteen. Then come poets I met when I was an undergraduate, except that I intrude Winters to juxtapose him with MacLeish. My essay on Moore I place next to last in order to end with Pound, latest to die of the old ones. In an appendix I add the four interviews — Eliot, Pound, and Moore twice — that occasioned some encounters with these poets. A few late paragraphs about MacLeish are revised from an article in the *New York Times Book Review*.

Many people helped me with this book. George Plimpton commissioned three interviews. Jane Kenyon worked over my sentences. John Peck talked about Pound. Harry Levin gave permission to repeat an anecdote, and over many years — as teacher, tutor, and friend — helped me toward some historical sense. Pam Croome, who once lived there, recalled details about the Boat House. The Houghton Library at Harvard and the library at the University of New Hampshire allowed me access to papers I had deposited. Ben Mattison researched and made photocopies; Mark McCarthy checked facts with an avid resourcefulness. Louis Simpson gave me Robert Birley's *Sunk Without Trace*. James Laughlin read the essay on Pound, made corrections and argued with assumptions. Donald Davie helped avoid error in connection with Pound and Eliot, Jac Tharpe and William Sutton with Frost, and Ralph Maud with Thomas. Thom Gunn and Robert Pinsky read my remarks on Winters. Helen E. Ellis performed a similar kindness in connection with Archibald MacLeish, and Scott Donaldson generously allowed me to read his biography in manuscript. Patricia Willis of Yale's Beinecke Library helped me with Marianne Moore. Lewis Hyde's essay on John Berryman and alcoholism contributed to my understanding, not only in connection with Dylan Thomas. Frances McCullough's enthusiasm encouraged me from the start — and her criticism, together with Richard Ford's, improved *Remembering Poets*. Peter Davison continued the succor as editor of *Their Ancient Glittering Eyes*. Dorothy Foster, Sharon Giannotta, Susan Arnold, and especially Lois Fierro typed manuscript with compassion and finesse. I am indebted to many biographers and critics — Richard Poirier, William Pritchard, Stanley Burnshaw, Paul Ferris, Christopher Ricks, Lyndall Gordon, Scott Donaldson, Terry Comito, Thomas Parkinson, Charles Molesworth, Elizabeth Phillips, Hugh Kenner, and Humphrey Carpenter among others — for supplying information that stimulated speculation.

D. H.

23 May 1991

Their
Ancient
Glittering
Eyes

Introduction:
Old Poets

❧

GOSSIP AND CURIOSITY

There is a minor tradition in literature, or at the edges of literature, that occasionally finds room for a book like this one. This tradition derives from curiosity about writers we admire. I do not speak of literary biography, a scholar's task, but of literary gossip, reminiscences by friends and acquaintances of authors. Over centuries of print and literacy, readers have enjoyed such books: Boswell's *Johnson* is an ancestor but makes its own category. More to the point: A neighbor of E. A. Robinson's published *Next Door to a Poet;* William Dean Howells recollected *Literary Friends and Acquaintances;* Charles J. Woodberry assembled *Talks with Ralph Waldo Emerson;* Mark A. DeWolfe Howe edited *Memories of a Hostess,* drawn chiefly from the diaries of Mrs. James T. Fields. In *The Middle Years,* Henry James set down recollections of early meetings with George Eliot and Alfred Lord Tennyson. In recent decades, friends and neighbors — sometimes younger admirers — have reminisced about Willa Cather, Edmund Wilson, Ernest Hemingway, Allen Tate, Marianne Moore, Elizabeth Bishop, John Cheever.

An early example of the genre is a small triumph of literature, William Hazlitt's essay "My First Acquaintance with Poets." This piece of autobiography begins, "My father was a Dissenting minister at Wem, in Shropshire, and in the year 1798 . . ." Hazlitt turned twenty that year; he reminisces twenty-five years later about Coleridge's face:

> His forehead was broad and high, light as if built of ivory, with large projecting eyebrows, and his eyes rolling beneath them, like a sea with darkened luster. . . . His mouth was gross, voluptuous, open, eloquent; his chin good-humored and round; but his nose, the rudder of his face, the index of the will, was small, feeble, nothing — like what he has done.

I admire Hazlitt's willingness to judge, his courage, and his prose style. He continues his exploration of Coleridge's nautical face, "as if Columbus had launched his adventurous course for the New World in a scallop, without oars or compass."

Later, he describes a three-week visit to Coleridge during which Mr. Wordsworth put in an appearance. We make the acquaintance of Wordsworth without white whiskers, wearing something besides the blue-bound covers of the Oxford Standard Authors: "He was quaintly dressed . . . in a brown fustian jacket and striped pantaloons." And:

> There was a severe, worn pressure of thought around his temples, a fire in his eye, . . . an intense high narrow forehead, a Roman nose, cheeks furrowed by strong purpose and feeling, and a convulsive inclination to laughter about the mouth, a good deal at variance with the solemn, stately expression of the rest of his face.

Most, we hear Wordsworth's voice:

> He sat down and talked very naturally and freely, with a mixture of clear, gushing accents in his voice, a deep guttural intonation, and a strong tincture of the northern *burr*, like crust on wine.

Coleridge and Wordsworth wrote poems, which are words in books, and which are not human beings; but Hazlitt's memoir suggests that poems are written by people with small noses or Roman ones, voices that never stop talking or voices with northern *burrs*.

It goes without saying — or it ought to — that we love some poems and call them great. When I wrote *Remembering Poets* I felt unabashed in my admiration for great poems. I still do. In the early 1920s Robert Graves's examiners at Oxford reproved him for thinking that some poems were better than others. For decades, Graves's anecdote ridiculed dons who found quality irrelevant, or the assertion of quality presumptuous. Now, in academic America, some dons again find it unscrupulous or naïve or oppressive to claim that one poem is better than another. The idea of superiority comes into question. Surely superiority is an awkward idea, even oppressive; but so is death. "There is no order," said Samuel Johnson, "without subordination."

If we admire the poem, it is natural to be curious about the poet. This curiosity endured New Critical decades when it appeared vulgar to suggest that poems were made by poets. Because Roland Barthes pronounced the author dead, this fascination may now appear necrophiliac. Literary theory is the practice of philosophers, who know which side they are on, in the old war between the philosophers and the poets. (Of many strategies employed during the millennial struggle, the cleverest may be one army's assertion that the other *n'existe pas*.) Curiosity endures, surviving criticism or philosophy. The reader and critic Hazlitt as a young man was curious, devoted — and later felt betrayed by these men as they altered into the rigidities of age. I am grateful that he wrote his feelings and his recollections out.

When Ezra Pound collected his notes on Gaudier-Brzeska — the sculptor killed in the Great War at the age of twenty-three — he apologized:

In reading over what I have written, I find it full of conceit, or at least full of pronouns in the first person, and yet what do we, any of us, know of our friends and acquaintances save that on such and such a day we saw them, and that they did or said this, that or the other, to which words and acts we give witness.

If Pound felt apologetic about the first person singular in connection with his dead friend, then I should feel abject to associate my name with the old poets whom I knew so little. Yet I feel no shame. This book records a portion of my education. Whether my own poems look decent in retrospect is irrelevant: I grew up as a poet, for better or worse, among young poets and old, taking some poetic education from poet-siblings, most from poets dead for centuries, and less from father-teachers; Yvor Winters was an exception maybe because he spoke from an eccentric place. I learned from Richard Wilbur, a little, but he was only seven years older; it would have been dangerous to take more from him. But the grandparents! One can accept the jewels of Asia from old hands.

Yet from talking with Frost, Eliot, Moore, and Pound, I learned nothing directly about my own work. They were old enough to have detached from ongoing poetry, to feel alien to the ambitions of the grandchildren. Instead of advice, they provided the gift of their existence and endurance.

Many poets have taken courage from the old ones. Some have acknowledged the laying on of hands. Robert Graves told how Swinburne touched the infant Graves in his cradle, as if some magic moved from the diminutive elder to the poet in swaddling clothes. Of the poets here, Pound knew the grandfathers best. His attentions to the old are legend. He organized a tribute to Wilfrid Scawen Blunt; he wrote letters of homage to Thomas Hardy, whom he never met. And when Henry James died — Pound said in 1960, speaking of 1916 — "one felt there was no one to ask about anything. Up to then one felt someone knew."

REPUTATIONS

Eliot, Pound, Frost, and Moore were all bishops, if we speak in stereotype of the Establishment. For a time, one could accuse MacLeish and Thomas of the same preferment, but in death not even Eliot remains so elevated. Malcolm Cowley compared the shifting of writerly reputations to an institution more volatile than ecclesiastical governance; he spoke of the literary stock market, where this year's blue chip may become next year's penny stock. Writers with enormous followings in their own lifetimes go unread and unmentioned a generation later, not only best-selling novelists but poets. Reputations large at death always decline. When Pound had Propertius say that he would doubtless enjoy a boom after his funeral, his Propertius was unobservant: We saw a quick decline after death in the reputations of Thomas, Frost, and Eliot. (Pound is always another case; reputation finds it impossible to disentangle his poetic gift from his politics or pathology.) Their stock market prices declined — Eliot's because his living reputation was enforced by fear, Frost's because his fame was enhanced by mistaken rumors of benignity, Thomas's for other trivial reasons.

Reputations fluctuate in two directions. In the mid-nineteenth century John Greenleaf Whittier could refer casually to "the mad painter Blake." Andrew Marvell's ascent was late, who was rarely listed among the English poets for two centuries after his death, and whose "Horatian Ode" went uncollected for a hundred years. Wordsworth listed Marvell's name — for his politics. When Augustine Birrell wrote about Marvell, for the English Men of Letters series, he condescended to the poems. It took Eliot's tercentenary essay, decades after Palgrave collected "The Garden" and "To His Coy Mistress," to begin the discovery of a great English poet.

As I grew up, the young poet with the greatest reputation outside the academy was Stephen Vincent Benét, widely understood as successor to the farmer-poet Robert Frost. Lately, after a decade of swoon, Frost's stock has ascended again; Benét has disappeared from the board. Meanwhile, Eliot remains under attack, Pound is an obsession or an anathema, Cummings dwindles, H.D.'s reputation rises, and Stevens is deified. For some years after his death, an academic Dylan Thomas industry continued. A scholar surveying the market said, "The 1970s saw no letup . . ." — but admitted that in the 1980s a Thomas recession became a Thomas depression. After all, Thomas's life had been written, and the merry tales lost their freshness as new drunken or dopey poets took on the *maudit* role. The once ubiquitous *Collected Poems* turned up on the shelves of used book stores as poetry readers of the 1950s, divorced or crowded, sold off their libraries. Had the poet sunk without trace?

Robert Birley's *Sunk Without Trace,* the 1960–1961 Clark Lectures, recounts the rise and fall of six masterworks of their day — universally admired, no literate household without them — that rot in the Davey Jones's lockers of used and antiquarian booksellers: Edward Young's *Night Thoughts;* Thomas Moore's *Lalla Rookh;* William Warner's *Albion's England;* Nathaniel Lee's *The Rival Queens;* William Robertson's *The History of the Reign of Charles V;* Philip James Bailey's *Festus.* Or I think of the work that Samuel Johnson, writing *Lives of the Poets,* called the most popular English poem of all time — in the nation of Shakespeare, Milton, Dryden, and Pope: "Perhaps no composition in our language has been oftener perused than Pomfret's *Choice.*" Who today reads John Pomfret or "The Choice"? When a poet is vastly popular, the popularity always rises from sources partly silly, even when the poet is magnificent. Philip Larkin's English eminence derives partly from his insularity, xenophobia, and antipathy toward the modern; nevertheless he is a poet — and so is Robert Frost, although it was a kitsch Robert Frost who sold all those copies. Something about *Festus* propelled it into fame, something connected to its own time which proved not available to subsequent eras; it wanders the heavens like a dead spaceship, cold and dark. Thomas's brief eminence derived from his voice and from gossip about his escapades. The gossip is trivial; it does not inhabit the poems. The voice was partly Thomas's performance and partly the poetry's structures of rhythm and assonance, which inhere and will endure.

Thomas's reputation also suffers from a more serious if temporary swing in the fashion for language. The prevailing poem of the American moment, good and bad, is aggressively speech-like. Both current counter-motions, the language poets and the neo-formalists, push against this requirement, as indeed most English and American poetry over the centuries has done. Whitman is no more speech-like than Dickinson; both poets build their poems out of materials from contemporary speech, but neither remains uniformly colloquial. The diction master of the moment is William Carlos Williams, or the flat side of Ezra Pound — like his *Cathay* translations, which remain the most influential of his many styles. In the climate of plain speech, poets of lyric distortion look fussy, fancy, elitist, or fake. One doesn't hear much talk of Hopkins outside the academy, and Hart Crane remains a special taste; even W. B. Yeats, who moved from poetic diction toward passionate speech, seems inflated to many Americans.

But all things fall and are built again, and the unfashionable gyre of the word-crazy poet will return. It is sensible to assume that the taste of our own moment will come to seem fatuous, including your taste and mine. Excellent plain-speaking late twentieth century American poets will look boring for a while — as Dylan Thomas struts back from the grave.

WORK

There were other old poets I met briefly when I was young. In these pages I mention Stevens and Williams. I became acquainted with Edwin and Willa Muir when Edwin gave the Norton Lectures at Harvard in the mid-fifties, and saw him again, later in England, when he was dying. He was a lovable, frail, and passionate man, gentle and obdurate, who loathed academic talk about poetry. In my mid-twenties I improvised a definition of poetry in his presence that included the word "verbal." His mild eyes darkened: No definition of poetry might include such language! I delighted to hear his detailed and scrupulous praise for Wordsworth, as he cared deeply for poem and poet — and not for the figure he cut as he spoke.

Willa Muir loved Edwin with a querulous ferocity. He was Christian and she skeptical; when I last met them, I sensed her anger over Edwin's infidelity: The dying man looked forward to Paradise. It was Willa who planted a sentence in my head that helped direct or determine the life I have come to lead. When I knew them, I was about to take a teaching job, to support my writing. To make a living by free-lance writing was my fantasy, but it seemed as attractive and improbable as taking up piracy. I knew that Edwin wrote book reviews, that together they had translated Kafka, that they had worked for the British Council. When I asked Willa how they had managed, she uttered a phrase that raised the Jolly Roger and filled my sails: "We have lived by our wits."

Robert Graves directed me also, when he came to Ann Arbor during my second year of teaching. The day after his reading, as we drank coffee in the Michigan Union, I addressed him as "Mr. Graves." Sharply he asked me to call him Robert. He was alert, friendly, full of counsel — and suffered from the delusion that propriety was required of professors in American universities. In his rivalry he let me know that his Majorca was better than my Ann Arbor, as a poet's place. After two years in the classroom, I agreed with him. "I wish I could do what you do," I said, "and make my living writing prose." From the 1920s on, Graves had supported himself by writing novels, memoirs, crank anthropology, book reviews, *Punch* pieces, and poems. He looked me in the eye: "Have you ever tried?"

When I walked home from the Union, I started work on a memoir of summers in New Hampshire. Graves's question made its point. In my lazy twenties, I put in a couple of hours a day on poems, and rarely (summers, weekends) worked on essays or children's books. In my teens I had planned to write for a living, but after typing a couple of miserable novels — at seventeen, at nineteen — I gave up the idea. An academic job substituted the classroom for the desk, relatively an easy way to make a living, but I still daydreamed of free-lancing. Before we parted Graves contributed technical help. He was publishing three or four titles a year. "How do you have the energy?" I asked.

Robert never wanted for answers. "The twenty-minute nap," he said.

"I can't do that," I argued — so that he answered again with the question, "Have you ever tried?"

GLADNESS AND MADNESS

In the *Paris Review* interview, I reminded Eliot that he had written, seventeen years earlier, "No honest poet can ever feel quite sure of the permanent value of what he has written. He may have wasted his time and messed up his life for nothing." Eliot confirmed that he remained unsure of his work's value. All poets die without knowing what their work is worth; many fear not only that they have messed up their lives for nothing, but that they have harmed the lives of others.

Maybe no one ambitious, in any line of work, dies with conviction of accomplishment. Throughout their lives, dissatisfaction with work done drives ambitious people to try again. While they keep life and energy, the disparity between goal and achievement can be countered by plans for further work, but when death is imminent, or when old age drains ability and strength, depression over failure may become inexorable. Remember Leonardo's melancholy question at the end of his life: "Tell me if anything ever was done." In late letters, Henry James lamented the frailties of old age — because they prevented writing; he wanted to live and write the books that *now* he knew enough to write. Later, when he was dying — paralyzed by a stroke and demented — he dictated to his amanuensis as he had done for decades, the old habits remaining although the mind no longer controlled them. Much earlier he had written a short story called "The Middle Years," in which the novelist Dencombe was dying in middle age, convinced that his work has failed, and despairing that he lacks "the second chance" of a long life in which to do the great work of which he feels capable. During his last illness Dencombe meets a doctor who loves his published work, comforts him, and argues with him — finally convincing him that having done what he has done is "the only thing." If you've doubted, Dr. Hugh tells him, "if you've despaired, you've always 'done' it." Shortly before his death, Dencombe accepts this understanding: "A second chance — that's the delusion. There never was to be but one. We work in the dark — we do what we can — we give what we have. Our doubt is our passion and our passion is our task. The rest is the madness of art." In the madness of James's dying, this wisdom was unavailing.

To avoid ambition's despair, most of us follow simple maxims: Don't be too ambitious; take it easy; be a *good* father, mother, citizen, teacher, farmer, salesman, thief; settle for Thane of Cawdor. When I was a freshman at college John Ciardi was my teacher. He had published two books of poems, and I regarded him with awe. One night at his house I rambled on about poetic greatness. My pomposity irritated him, and I heard his sharp voice say, "Hall, why don't you stop trying to be *great,* and just be *good?*"

At the time I felt chagrin, but now I think that he was wrong. You will never be any good as a poet unless you arrange your life by the desire to write great poems, always knowing (and if you do not know it you are foolish) that you are likely to mess up your life for nothing. And probably you will feel that in pursuing your own desires you have messed up the lives of others. Some time ago Louis Simpson wrote a cautionary tale in "A Dream of Governors." When the Prince was young he killed the dragon and married the Princess; now the King is old and fat, and the land he rules is peaceful. Bored, lacking purpose or goal, he visits the witch who lives over the dragon's grave and begs her, "Bring evil on the land / That I may have a task." Of course this King is a monster; the narcissism of many artists is monstrous, as they sacrifice not only themselves for their art.

Whatever the reason, Wordsworth's couplet retains the truth of general observation: "We Poets in our youth begin in gladness; / But thereof come in the end despondency and madness." It is common to wonder: Why all this commotion — this struggle, suffering, elation, and despair — over an endeavor for which the rewards are so small? This question assumes that the currency of reward is money or power. For many poets, their ambition seems larger than the wish to become king of Scotland. Thus we value ourselves by valuing our products, and megalomania contributes to "the madness of art." Wordsworth's despondency and madness may come from despair of future ambition or from guilt over the results and products of ambition. Whatever the source of the trouble, some observers suggest not standing too close. Remember Henry Adams's wry resolution, recollecting a youthful meeting with Algernon Charles Swinburne: "I have long since made up my mind not to seek the acquaintance of poets."

As it appears, I sought their acquaintance, and *Their Ancient Glittering Eyes* records what I found. Dylan Thomas's eyes were hardly ancient, I grant, and neither his eyes nor the others' always glittered. But their presences glittered for me, and even Dylan Thomas seemed ancient enough, I was so young when I met him. Their presences have been emblems in my life, and I remember these poets as if I kept them carved in stone. My title comes from "Lapis Lazuli," where Yeats's phrase alludes not to the eyes of poets but to eyes reacting to the experience of art. Whatever old poets feel as they come toward the end of their lives, they have spent their lives trying to make antidotes to death; we honor this making when we attend to their lives and characters. Yeats's poem has been a favorite of mine since I heard Dylan Thomas read it in New Lecture Hall in 1949. The sculptural relief, carved in hard stone, shows three men climbing a mountain; Yeats describes the relief in order to make claims for art. As the observers look from their vantage on "the tragic scene" of our personal and historical lives, one of them calls for tragic art and a skillful artist responds. When "mournful melodies" are performed by "accomplished fingers," these "ancient glittering eyes" look upon the inevitable dissolution of nations and persons, and accept human fate even with joy: "Their ancient, glittering eyes, are gay."

Vanity, Fame, Love,
and Robert Frost

❧

LIFE, WORK, AND REPUTATION

When I grew up — in the suburbs, at suburban schools — I heard adults mention one living poet, and only one. Professors might prefer Eliot, young poets might imitate Auden, but for the reading public Robert Frost was the Great Living American Poet. His *Complete Poems*, like Longfellow's the century before, wedged among popular novels on middle-class bookshelves. Everyone knew him, and everyone loved him. With the aid of *Life*, we understood that Robert Frost was rustic, witty, avuncular, *benign*. Only a decade and a half after his death, his popular reputation changed totally. A consensus agreed that the old commonplaces were fraudulent. Reviewing a biography in the *New York Times Book Review*, one critic revealed that Frost was "a monster of egotism." Referring to the miseries that he and his family endured, she knew whom to blame: Frost left "behind him a wake of destroyed human lives." The same culture that applauded Frost as a simple farmer now reviled him as a simple monster. But he was not simple.

It was in the 1970s that a malign biographer persuaded critics and book reviewers, who were understandably eager to overthrow Luce's plaster cast of a rustic bard. Twenty years later, corrective biographies and memoirs have begun to set forth the complex man who wrote the poems. He was vain, he could be cruel, he was rivalrous with all other men; but he could also be generous and warm — when he could satisfy himself that his motives were dubious. He was a man possessed by guilt, by knowledge that he was *bad*, by the craving for love and the necessity to reject love offered — and by desire for fame which no amount of celebrity could satisfy.

When I was sixteen I met Frost the first time; I saw him last a few months before he died. Over the years he changed, for me, from a monument to a public fraud to something more human and complicated than either. When I look back now, with knowledge of the life he lived, I look at old scenes with new eyes.

To Robert Frost — I understood over the years — his family background seemed precarious or dangerous, and his adult life cursed. His father was a sometime drunk, dead at an early age. His mother endured a bad marriage, was widowed young, and failed as a schoolteacher when she returned to her native Massachusetts; yet she was a fond mother, kind to her children; and she wrote poems. Her son felt dangerously close to her, and followed that fondness into devotion to one young woman, Elinor White, whom he courted extravagantly, romantically, and doggedly. Appearing to lose her, he plunged into a fearful depression; later he hinted to friends that he had planned suicide. When Elinor and Robert finally married, they settled in Derry, New Hampshire, where they lived in poverty and began enduring an extraordinary series of family misfortunes. Their firstborn child, a son named Elliott, died of cholera infantum at the age of three; in later years, warning or bragging about his badness, Frost said that the doctor who attended Elliott blamed him for the death, for not having called sooner for help. The next child was Lesley, daughter and eldest survivor, celebrator and denouncer of her father. Then there was Irma, mad in middle life and institutionalized. Frost's only sister had been insane, and he feared madness for himself; he blamed his genes for his daughter's insanity. Then came Carroll, son, who killed himself at the age of thirty-eight. Youngest was Marjorie, dead after childbirth at twenty-nine.

When I speak of poverty in Derry, I speak of something rural, not so desperate as the poverty of cities. The family lived in natural beauty, among country pleasures, and Frost owned the farm; it was a gift from his grandfather, and he never needed to fear foreclosure. But the Frosts were almost destitute, keeping a few chickens, raising a garden, with nothing to provide income except poems that editors rejected. In the Derry years, only devotion or commitment as obdurate as granite could remain firm; for years, without encouragement from editors or critics, Frost worked at writing his poems, *instead* of weeding vegetables or milking the cow or tending his chickens properly or teaching school to support his family.

Finally he took a job teaching school, and earned thereby a small salary. Then he sold the farm, and with the capital took off with his family for England until the money ran out. There, by a stroke of luck, he found a publisher and started the trek toward fame. By the time he returned to the United States — to find magazines at last open to his poems, universities ready to hire him — he was almost forty years old and his children nearly grown. In guilty retrospect, he regretted that the children had grown up insecure, anxious, and poor. In retrospect, it seemed to him that out of selfish ambition he had mistreated his family, that from his family's suffering came madness, suicide, and early death. It needs to be said, in contradiction to Frost's guilty memory, that his daughter Lesley remembered her Derry years as idyllic. It needs to be said, also, that Elinor Frost cherished memories of the Derry years.

If Elinor White Frost was the onlie begettor of Robert's poems — as he insisted — she is little talked about, perhaps because she died in 1938, before biographers were taking notes. Perhaps she is the mystery and the source. Robert Frost's love for her, erotic and romantic, runs like a river through his work. Outside the work, we sense a consuming and volatile daily confrontation between this pair of lovers. Frost wrote about his "lover's quarrel with the world," and maybe lovers by his definition quarreled. If Robert was a difficult partner, he was not the only difficult member of the household. We know many small particulars of Elinor: she hated housekeeping; she celebrated *whim*, and wanted to go to England "to live under thatch"; she nagged Robert in Derry to milk the cow, more practical than he was. But later, when Robert prided himself on his honors — puffed up by the adulation that came with poetry readings — Elinor regretted the simplicity of Derry days, when the life had been truly poetical. (In her preference for the poetical life, even to poverty, she resembled no one so much as Caitlin Thomas.) Her politics were rabidly conservative and anti-Roosevelt, making her husband's Democratic conservatism look positively liberal. In the words of a close friend, Elinor was "sweet-severe"; she is described as beautiful, fierce, pessimistic, and wild. She was an atheist. (Sometimes she sounds so angry at God that she will not believe in Him.) She was unreconciled to Elliott's death, more extreme in grief even than her husband; and when Marjorie died, she said, "I long to die." As a mother she was devoted — and so was Robert as a father, who spent much time with his children; it went with not having a job.

If Robert's fathering was deleterious, it was not from cold neglect but from neglect's opposite; maybe he meddled too much. Shortly after her mother's death, Lesley told her father in bitterness that he should never have married; at the very least, he should never have had children. Whatever the justice of her anger, Frost felt guilty every minute he lived, and sought forgiveness everywhere, and accepted none of it. "When I am too full of joy," he told another poet, "I think how little good my health did anyone near me." He knew he was a bad man, however bad or good he was. How could he blame himself for Marjorie's septicemia? He could blame himself for anything. Writing a close friend, he said he "wondered about my past whether it had not been too cruel to those I dragged with me."

And this was before he watched his son slide into suicide — watched, and argued with Carroll, *argued* with his own son not to kill himself, and lost. Of course he found reason to blame himself for the suicide, as he did for everything else. In his guilt, his ego enjoyed the fantasy of omnipotence, but surely he felt true anguish, nearly to the point of madness. When he thought he was dying, in Florida in 1962, he told a friend that in his delirium he saw Lesley's vengeful face staring at him, finger pointing, "accusing, accusing." He told his friend, with a laugh unpleasant to hear, that the vision had terrified him back to life.

VAIN GRANITE

In August of 1945, when I was sixteen, I went to the Bread Loaf Writers' Conference at the old wooden inn outside Middlebury in Vermont. Frost had been associated with the Writers' Conference from the beginning, and he was my main reason for going. The year before, I had spent my first year at prep school, and I had met an English teacher named Hyde Cox who knew Robert Frost, who quoted his conversation, and who told me about Bread Loaf. Aspirant writers could spend two weeks there in the summer, listening to lectures, workshopping, sometimes being read and criticized by professionals; there, you could catch a glimpse of Robert Frost.

At fourteen, I had decided to become a poet; I worked on poems two or three hours every day after school. I collected rejection slips from *The New Yorker* and *The Atlantic,* and when I was sixteen began to publish in little magazines — very little magazines: *Trails, Matrix,* and *Experiment.* I was exhilarated; surely book publication and undying fame would follow as the night the day; Bread Loaf would accelerate matters.

My teacher's conversation not only made me want to go to Bread Loaf, it restored Robert Frost to me. My mother had read him to me when I was small. Then, as I began to write poetry myself, an eighth-grade teacher praised Frost to our class in terms that forced me to despise him: He was a lovable codger with a heart of gold. Because I was becoming a poet, I knew that poets were dangerous figures: revolutionary, bohemian, despised by ordinary society, *maudit*. For a while I dismissed Robert Frost as a poet that English teachers and parents promoted. With my new teacher's help, I read him again and recovered him. I remember finding "To Earthward," which became my favorite poem that year. I recited it to anyone who would listen. There was one stanza in particular I said for the tune's sake:

> I had the swirl and ache
> From sprays of honeysuckle
> That when they're gathered shake
> Dew on the knuckle.

The shape of this single sentence — deployed so artfully over four tightly rhymed lines — delighted me, the rhyme itself satisfying, almost amusing, and the rhythm an eloquent swoop of syntax. I loved especially the way the third line shaped itself like a saucer, a whole clause separating the first and last words which are themselves another clause.

By the time "To Earthward" finishes, however, it's a harsh journey. It starts, "Love at the lips was touch / As sweet as I could bear," but the poem is about aging, and about losing with age the ability to feel, except for the ability to feel pain. Frost ends by saying that he looks for pain in order to feel, and then he says that he looks forward to death — or he almost says it:

> When stiff and sore and scarred
> I take away my hand
> From leaning on it hard
> In grass and sand,
>
> The hurt is not enough:
> I long for weight and strength
> To feel the earth as rough
> To all my length.

I loved the pitch and roll of the sentences, and the rhymes, but I loved also the danger of these lines, the brave approach to forbidden feelings. I could not name the forbidden feelings then, but I felt them, and they made the lines scary, honest, and powerful. With the help of some friends, and years of aging, I know more about the poem now. When Frost longs for a "weight" to press down on him from above — the way his body presses his hand down — the weight could be six feet of dirt, and the body still sentient although dead; but the weight could also come from sexual assault, an imagined rape by an Amazon or a man. A poem that begins "Love at the lips" ends with rape or suicide, because if you long for strength to achieve this painful pressure, it must be strength of will to undertake the pain. This Robert Frost — masochistic, androgynous, suicidal — was not my eighth-grade teacher's Frost, nor a Bread Loaf Writers' Conference Frost, nor Frost's Frost either. But this Robert Frost was a real ambivalent human being: Trust the poem, not the poet.

The first night at Bread Loaf we heard a speech of welcome by the director, Theodore Morrison. We gathered in a large lecture hall where I sat next to a row of French doors. As Morrison talked — the history and purpose of Bread Loaf; what to expect in our two weeks — my eyes wandered over the listeners, wondering which of these people were writers I knew about. I was keeping my eyes out for Frost, hoping for a glance at the man who made great poems. Looking casually to my right, through the glass doors, I saw him. He was walking with two friends, Frost a little ahead, his mouth moving humorously as he talked. The ground outside sank away, and Frost, approaching the lecture hall uphill, appeared to be rising out of the ground. His face was strong and blocky, his white hair thick and rough. He looked like granite, some old carved stone like the menhirs in Ireland that I saw in *National Geographic,* but gifted to walk and speak. Through the window I watched as his mouth moved with talk, and the faces of his companions broke into laughter.

But I had no mind, at sixteen, for his companions. I had seen the great poet, maker of "To Earthward" and "After Apple-Picking." He was palpable, he was human, he was alive in my time. I felt light in my head and body. Merely seeing this man, merely laying startled eyes upon him, allowed me to feel enlarged. My dreams for my own life, for my own aging into stone, took on reality in the stern flesh of Robert Frost, who rose out of a hill in Vermont.

Frost attended some of the poetry workshops, conducted outdoors by Louis Untermeyer after lunch. When Frost was present we learned to tremble. Whatever poem was up for discussion that day, Frost was liable to be cutting, sarcastic, dismissive. The day when Untermeyer chose to read and discuss my poems was a day Frost didn't come; I was relieved. One day Frost took over the workshop all by himself. He chose a young woman's poem to read aloud, and asked for comments. A few people said a few fatuous things; only the brave or the stupid would lay themselves open to Frost's wit. He dismissed the fatuities with a cast of his forearm. Then he said, "Who *wrote* this poem?," his voice heavy with disgust. The young woman — I remember that she was small, attractive in the Cambridge manner, married to a Harvard graduate student — acknowledged authorship, looking deliberately stalwart. "*No*," said Frost, "I mean, who *really* wrote it?" There was silence, bewilderment. After a long pause, while Frost held to the sides of the podium with evident anger and stared at the audience as if he dared anyone to speak, the woman spoke again. "I wrote it," she said, "and I don't know what you're talking about."

"*You* didn't write it," Frost said, and waved the typed page in the air. "You know who wrote it?" His voice pronounced the name with the heaviest sarcasm he could summon, and he could summon sarcasm as well as anyone: "*T. S. Eliot!*"

That afternoon at the workshop, I gulped at Frost's asperity, but I accepted the notion that it was warranted. And it *was* warranted, I will argue now, if we take poetry more seriously than we take social smoothness. The poem *was* "written by T. S. Eliot" on a bad day, and if anyone imitates another author and makes it public — well, she gets what's coming to her. If we devote our lives to poetry, and take our lives seriously, we must praise and denounce with equal ferocity. People who follow the notion that praise alone is acceptable — "Boost, don't knock" — should sell Toyotas. To be a poet, as Frost was wont to say, you've got to have a snout for punishment.

But there was another side to his harshness. If the young woman had imitated Robert Frost instead of T. S. Eliot, Robert Frost would not have been so angry. He would have been scornful, if he had noticed, but he would not have been angry. Frost was angry because most of the professionals in the modern poetry business — teachers, critics, reviewers — preferred Eliot to Frost. In his competitive ambition, Frost was outraged. For him, as he liked to say, there was room for only one at the top of the steeple; he demanded to be the one. He was jealous of all other poets.

And not only of poets.

One day, talking with him on the porch, I sat with a young woman from Bryn Mawr and her mother, both good looking. Frost rocked and spoke laconically yet wittily, proud and strong, delighted to hold his audience. We sat in the breeze, late afternoon, late summer, three of us looking at one of us, waiting for the words he would utter, and I was aware — as at times of love, of triumph, and of catastrophe — of the moment as I lived it. He asked me about my school, and about where I would go to college. Then Frost, who had gone to Lawrence High School and fitfully to Dartmouth and Harvard, disparaged higher education. At the time I felt uncomfortable and did not know why: He was one-upping me, because *he* hadn't needed a diploma but *I* did. He could not help but make himself out to be better than any male around him, even if the male was sixteen.

PUBLIC FROST

I talked with Frost a few times during my four years at Harvard. He lived in Cambridge fall and spring. Around Harvard, Frost was cagey. America's foundation is possibly not so much freedom of religion as freedom of competition — or possibly the religion of competition; Harvard is its Vatican City. The only Americans more competitive than Harvard undergraduates are Harvard faculty members. When I saw Frost at Harvard, it was among undergraduates and faculty, and he kept his elbows close to his sides, and he saw to it that he sat in a corner of the room with his flanks covered. This was a sophisticated Robert Frost, suspicious, combative, happy; he was blessedly distant from the benign farmer, capable of verses, whom one met in the news magazines. The great competitor appeared to enjoy the schoolyard of competition. If he made a slip it would never be forgotten. He made no slips.

Here sits Robert Frost in a corner, his radar scanning the room for approaching missiles. Undergraduates ask questions about Yeats, Eliot, Pound. The corpses of Yeats, Eliot, and Pound litter the floor of the housemaster's living room. Someone mentions Robert Lowell's name. Frost says he guesses Lowell is pretty good. Of course he's a *convert*, he says, and he lays the word out like a frog in a biology lab. Then Frost remembers a story. Because he smiles when he remembers it, his audience understands that it is a malicious story. Frost tells us that Allen Tate's a convert too. Once he saw Tate at a party standing next to a Jesuit. He walked over to them and asked the Jesuit, "Are you a *convert?*" "No," said the Jesuit. "Well, neither am I," said Frost, and walked away. Telling his story he grins, and when he finishes he laughs a slow, long laugh.

Three years after graduation I spent a year at Stanford on a writing fellowship. When I heard that Frost would read his poems there, I was delighted. But the reading was horrid. It took place in a huge auditorium, packed full. Some faculty attended and some students; most of the listeners appeared to be Robert Frost's peculiar audience, who would not have attended a poetry reading by Wallace Stevens or William Carlos Williams but would have crossed flooded rivers and burning forests to hear Robert Frost. Many applauded and celebrated Frost for being what he was not, and to please them he fulfilled the stereo-type: He pretended to be what he was not. Finding himself with this audience, he cooed and chuckled, he trotted out country sayings, and he performed his tricks: Speaking one poem, he interrupted himself in the middle, smiled mischievously, and cackled, "Now, *that's* a good line." And Frost put down the professors, those fancy intellectuals who read all those hidden meanings into a simple old fellow's poems. Everybody laughed, everybody roared in delight. Almost everybody. I felt angry at his betrayal of himself and of poetry; he pretended to be the poet my grade school teacher had praised. He *performed* in order to be *loved*. He played Mortimer Snerd for these people; he played the combination of Edgar Bergen and Mortimer Snerd, making himself his own dummy.

Yet I went to Wallace Stegner's cocktail party afterward. Steg-ner was an old friend of Frost's from Bread Loaf who lived in a modern house fashioned neatly into the dry grass of California's low hills, great glass panels looking west toward sunsets. In the living room with its soft furniture, blond wood, and glass, Rob-ert Frost sat with a martini in his hand. But this was not the creature of an hour before, kindly and folksy, cuddly and chuckly. This Robert Frost held the stem of his martini glass neatly between thumb and forefinger, drank a few, held his liquor, and denounced other poets. I remember that he spoke of Yvor Winters — my teacher at Stanford, who had written un-favorably of Frost — as "clever," using the word as they use it at Oxford, to mean pretentious, shallow, callow, and meretri-cious.

On the same Stanford occasion, I had seen two versions of Frost: one a smooth performer who manipulated an audience by playing up to it, the other a jealous literary god blasting his enemies. Neither version seemed connected to the poet who had made great poems. I went home and read "Home Burial" again, that early narrative, better than "The Death of the Hired Man," sensitive to all measure of feeling. The wife has lost a child, and stands always at a special place on the stair from which she can see the grave. The practical husband says that the living have got to go on living, but the wife is irreconcilable. Frost has her say:

> . . . The nearest friends can go
> With anyone to death, comes so far short
> They might as well not try to go at all.
> No, from the time when one is sick to death,
> One is alone, and he dies more alone.
> Friends make pretense of following to the grave,
> But before one is in it, their minds are turned
> And making the best of their way back to life
> And living people, and things they understand.
> But the world's evil. I won't have grief so
> If I can change it. . . .

Frost and his wife Elinor were inconsolable over the losses of death; I think of "Out, out —" in which the boy loses his arm to a saw and then dies of shock. "And they," the poem ends, in a calm of outrage, "since they / Were not the one dead, turned to their affairs."

So what was this man doing, I asked myself, being a buffoon on the platform and a literary hit man at a cocktail party, when he had written such poems?

The question is silly. The man on the platform, the man at the cocktail party, was vain and vulnerable, needed adulation, needed victory. He was a man, not a monument. Because he had written great poems, I demanded greatness at all times and in all matters. "And I am not a demi-god," said Pound in a late *Canto*. The old poet has created — over decades of work, rejection, suffering, failure, and success — a *body* of work, not an edifice, not a monument, not an institution. If she or he is a great poet, then that body is an alternate to the mortal body; it is permanent and it contains the best. Poets in their skins will never equal their poems.

Still, the question bears asking another way: What purposes

did it serve Frost to mount and present, that day at Stanford and on many other days, a public character so far from his own? The deception, I think, served major purposes. The best of his poems represented his feelings with honesty and accuracy — and with terror. Robert Frost lived in terror of madness and suicide. (If a child dies, and you cannot go on, what is it that you plan to *do?*) When he wrote the poems that told the terror, and that summoned intelligence to control the terror, he suffered in the writing. When he retold his poems at poetry readings, or answered questions about them, he lied and lied and lied, in order not to repeat his ordeal. So his performance was the opposite of Anne Sexton's, and equally disturbing. She marketed her suffering, for a morbid audience; he denied his suffering, for a sentimental audience.

There was, I think, another reason as well: The need for love and applause was a need for forgiveness. I will return to this notion later.

When I was back at Harvard as a Junior Fellow, I helped Robert Pack and Louis Simpson edit *The New Poets of England and America,* and wrote Frost to ask if he would write an introduction for us. I did not think he would do it. For some months he did not answer. I wrote a second time; still no reply. At the publisher's impatient request, we tried another poet, and a few days later I had a letter from Robert Frost:

September 18, 1956

Dear Don Hall:

There would be no excuse in the world for my not writing you juniors a preface to your poetry unless it were the poor one that I try to keep a rule of not writing prefaces. But rules aren't meant to be kept. They're meant to break on impulse when you have any impulse left in you; before the evil days when fun ceases. So if you will let me see some of the poems to take off from I'm your cheerful victim. I'll be down in

Cambridge in a week or two now where I can see you to talk the matter over. I've been hoping to see you anyway.

Mind you I'm roused up to do this con amore and I'm not so lazy that I can't do it.

Ever yours
Robert Frost

I was surprised, and pleased for the book. We told Allen Tate, er, we won't be needing that introduction. I sent Frost some poems. I did not see him. Although his letter invited me to pay a visit, I waited for him to telephone, as if he should prove his invitation's sincerity by pursuing me with a lasso. After another wait, the brief and elegant introduction arrived. It was called "Maturity No Object," and did little dances among notions of poetry and growing older. The prose was typical of Frost in its eloquent tortuousness, epigram softened by idiom. Frost was concerned that almost all American poets were students or teachers and in his preface dealt with his doubts by promenading them without calling them doubts. And oh, he could make a sentence; he could make a pun and turn his heel on it for a transition.

In fact the poet and scholar have so much in common and live together so naturally that it is easy to make too much of a mystery about where they part company. Their material seems the same — perhaps differs a little in being differently come by and differently held in play. Thoroughness is the danger of the scholar, dredging to the dregs. He works on assignment and self-assignment with some sense of the value of what he is getting when he is getting it. He is perhaps too avid of knowledge. The poet's instinct is to shun or shed more knowledge than he can swing or sing. His most available knowledge is acquired unconsciously. Something warns him dogged determination however profound can only result in doggerel. His danger is rhyming trivia. His depth is the lightsome blue depth of the air.

It's the work of an older man. As I read it now, it talks to me more than it used to talk.

Now the book was ready, and I sent the introduction to New York. But I did something else — or I failed to do something else. I did not write Frost to tell him that we had received the introduction, that we admired it, that we were grateful. I was too cloddish to understand that Frost of all people would be waiting for our approval. Really, *anyone* would be waiting, but perhaps especially an artist in his seventies making connections with artists in their twenties. I could not conceive that "Robert Frost" could care for my opinion. Institutions do not have feelings and monuments do not need bolstering. In a week or two, an aggrieved Kathleen Morrison — Frost's friend who typed for him and acted as manager and protector — telephoned to wonder what was happening. I am sure she had heard certain grumblings.

When Frost wrote the introduction to our anthology, I know that he served himself. He wanted to stay in touch with the young; although he would be jealous of any of us whom he caught mounting the steeple, he wanted us to like him, to praise him. At the same time, perched where he was, it was generous of him to write for us at all, and he wrote a good small essay. Whatever the motives he acknowledged to himself, he would acknowledge only the selfish ones. When caught in the act of virtue, he would proclaim it vice. About the time he wrote the introduction, he began to involve himself in another act of generosity. Or rather, Archibald MacLeish saw to it that he became involved.

Everyone knows that Ezra Pound was locked up in Washington from 1945 to 1958, charged with treason. Almost everyone knows that Frost had a hand in the release. This good deed fit Frost's old reputation for benignity, but does not square with Frost's later, posthumous reputation. In truth, Frost's character wore at least three faces. He could show himself simple and sweet to masses of people, those years ago, while in private and to his literary acquaintances he avowed that he was selfish and cynical. A third and least obvious Frost was secretly magnanimous while accusing himself of being a saint at the Devil's prompting. To get Frost to do something good, you had to convince him he did it for a wicked reason.

Archibald MacLeish was leader among a circle of people who worked to free Ezra Pound. MacLeish was most effective of this group because his dedication was accompanied by political sophistication and by friends in Washington. Still, the push to release Pound needed strong public support and required a popular figurehead. Only Robert Frost was visible enough and respectable enough to influence Congress.

The first and essential move was to persuade Frost to act. Now, Frost never *liked* Pound. He owed Pound a debt of gratitude, which may account for initial dislike; they are rarely generous people who can forgive someone for helping them when they need help. Pound had nothing to do with Frost's original publication, but as soon as Pound read Frost's poems, he promoted them with Poundian zeal, reviewing them, recommending them, and bullying the American public about this neglected writer. Frost didn't like the bullying part, disliked Pound's ridicule of America for Philistinism, and was fearful that American editors and critics would associate him with Pound's rhetoric.

There were obvious disparities between the two men. Frost was older, New England, quiet, and private. Pound was young, noisy, flamboyant — it was the period when Pound wore trousers fabricated of green billiard table cloth — and Frost would not have taken to him under any circumstances. Then for forty years Pound was champion of modernism and free verse, while Frost wrote sonnets and took every occasion to ridicule verse without meter. "I'd just as soon play tennis without a net," he said twenty thousand times. While Pound, in his remarkable detachment, could praise Frost because Frost was excellent, even when Frost's excellence ran contrary to Pound's theories and advocacies, Frost resembled the common run of humanity and could not forgive the difference.

Finally, Frost was a patriot. Pound considered *himself* a patriot, for that matter, and found it ironic that he of all people should be called a traitor. But Frost shared the more conventional opinion that to broadcast for an enemy in time of war, and to ask American troops to lay down their arms, sounded like giving aid and comfort to an enemy. Frost was a patriot of an old fashion which it may be difficult for a reader to understand, if the reader has grown up after the Second World War — through Korea and Vietnam, through Chile and Panama and the Gulf, through assassinations and revelations of crookedness in high places. Frost came from the world of the Republic, when Fourth of July orators denounced the British Empire — and all other empires, ignoring our own adventures in Cuba, Panama, and the Philippines — and praised the independence and separation of this continent from the crowned heads of Europe and their wars. When the United States went to war, you *knew* that it was a righteous war, and you knew who would win. When Chinese troops overran the Americans in Korea, in the Yalu Valley, and Marines and the regular army made the most massive retreat in American history, Robert Frost wept for three days. When Frost returned from a USIA trip with Faulkner, and Faulkner had been drunk on foreign soil, he denounced Faulkner as "a disgrace to the colors."

So when MacLeish decided to convince Frost to help release Pound from St. Elizabeths, where he languished rather than stand trial for treason, it appeared a formidable charge. But MacLeish knew his man. I asked MacLeish how he planned to persuade Frost to intervene. Oh, he said, he would just tell Robert that Ezra was getting *too much attention,* locked up down there; if we get him out, people won't notice him so much.

So Frost talked to the attorney general on a couple of occasions, he called on some legislators, he talked with Sherman Adams, and his opinions were accepted in the newspapers as benign and fair-minded. MacLeish started the campaign, but once he was committed to help, Frost worked hard, making special trips to Washington, trying with his charm to influence the influential. Gradually Washington's attitudes toward Pound altered and the Justice Department was able to release him in 1958. Four years later, when I saw Frost next, I asked him how he had happened to work for Pound's release. He looked cunning, amused, and pleased with himself as he told me that Ezra was getting *too much attention,* being locked up down there; we got him out, now people don't notice him so much . . .

REMEMBER ME

At the inauguration of President Kennedy in 1961, Robert Frost read his old and fine poem about nationhood, "The Gift Outright," altering the tense of one verb, predicting great things by means of the future tense. He knew the poem by heart. Harsh sunlight kept him from reading aloud some chatty lines he had written for the occasion. For the first time in our history, a poet had taken part in an inauguration; and for the first time in our history, tens of millions of Americans heard a great American poet read a poem.

Frost was eighty-six, with only two more years to live. The inauguration changed his life, at the end of his life. He became famous, like a President or an athlete. When he flew to Russia and talked with Nikita Khrushchev, two books were written about his quick trip. When he went off to England for honorary degrees, and returned to his walkways of fifty years before, his voyage of return was photographed and reported on; his life became a series of media events.

He loved it.

I was teaching at Michigan, where Frost had been poet in residence briefly in the early twenties. He had planned to stay in Ann Arbor back then, but the university president who invited him died, and the new president asked Frost an indelicate question: The new president asked just exactly what he *did* around here. This insult gave Frost in his pride an excuse to pack up and return to New England, where he wanted to live anyway.

In 1962 the Student Union asked Robert Frost to fly to Ann Arbor and read his poems. He agreed to come, wanting to return to Ann Arbor on the tour he was making of places crucial to his life, the great goodbyes of an energetic ancient, goodbyes cherished and then repeated, the old man always retaining some confidence that he would, somehow, really be back *yet again.* The Union asked me to introduce him. I agreed, but I was nervous about it, half expecting him to say something rude about me, maybe one of his sallies about professors.

He would read on April 2, a Monday night. Student Union officers met him on Sunday at the airport and took him to Inglis House, a secluded estate willed to the university and used as a guest house. Then a small group of us — undergraduate officers of the Union and his old Ann Arbor friend Erich Walter and I — sat around with Frost for an hour, chatting while he drank a 7-Up. Walter talked old Ann Arbor times with him. I told Frost I had seen Pound two years before, and that Pound regretted what the newspapers had quoted him as saying — that Frost had taken long enough in helping him get out of St. Elizabeths — and Frost said, well, he *should* regret it.

Then he went on about Pound. During the campaign for Pound's release, Frost had seen a lot of people *about* Pound, he told us, but he never saw *Pound;* he didn't want to see him, because of all the crazy things he heard Pound quoted as saying; he didn't want to see him in that shape. Then he told us that he had never really liked Pound anyway, though he had things to be grateful for. In fact, he said, Pound was one of the reasons he moved from Beaconsfield, near London, down to a farm in Gloucester. He left Beaconsfield in order to avoid seeing Pound, at the same time not wanting to offend him; if he had stayed in Beaconsfield he would have had to refuse invitations all the time. Why did he dislike Pound? He warmed up his dislike. He found Pound *affected,* always looking for something new, trying to be new, trying to find what hadn't been done yet and doing it. Then he went on to say that he found Yeats affected too, and didn't like him either. He told how Yeats had once observed to George Russell, "I think we must absolve the stars." Old Robert

Frost — sitting in Inglis House surrounded by admirers, eighty-eight years old, in 1962 remembering fifty years back — roused himself to anger over the ancient blarney of William Butler Yeats.

"Bunk!" he roared in his best American. "Bunk!"

Monday, the day of his reading, began with a press conference at eleven. We picked Frost up at Inglis House and took him to the Regents' Room in the administration building. A man from the university's television studio showed Frost a drawing of himself made by a local artist for use in a television series. Frost signed the picture as requested, but grumbled. He didn't like the picture: It thickened his hair and made him look too solid; also, the artist had swept his hair romantically down over his forehead. "I don't wear my hair that way," he said. "They're trying to make me look like Sandburg." Then he remembered a story to tell on Carl Sandburg; as he told it, his malice cheered him up and his grumpiness vanished. I heard him tell the story twice later in the day, when he found new faces to tell the story to:

When Frost was in Ann Arbor, the year he lived out on Pontiac, he brought Sandburg to read his poems at the university. Before the reading, Frost, who was living alone, cooked Sandburg a lamb chop. As dinner was ready to serve, Sandburg went upstairs to the bathroom and didn't come downstairs for an hour and a half. Frost was furious, the dinner ruined. "What were you *doing* there?" he asked Sandburg. "I had to do my hair," Sandburg said, "for the boys." Or that's what Frost *said* Sandburg said.

At the press conference, Frost sat at the head of a long table, the television lights bright in his eyes and three cameras cranking. I sat beside him, my job to bellow repetition of questions into his ear, on account of his deafness. Frost was funny and lively, repeating things he had said before, happy, the center of everything. Then he signed some books, and we went back to Inglis House for lunch. Now he talked politics. We should have settled the Cuban problem a long time ago, he said, but he didn't tell us how. He ridiculed welfare, which he had been doing for thirty years. He told about an argument he had with Justice Black. Frost met Black at Frost's eighty-eighth birthday party, just a few days before, and Frost had immediately launched into a hymn of praise for the Supreme Court: One of the greatest institutions the world has ever known, he'd said, and above partisanship. Black disputed the point, perhaps out of modesty. Frost's praise, Black said, was sentimental. Black avowed that *he* was not removed from partisanship; he was a labor man and he had always been a labor man. As Frost told the story, he became angry; he told us that he told Black the Court should put "patriotism above party."

After lunch someone drove us back to my house. In my living room he signed books — "from his old friend Robert Frost with high regard"; "remembering old Bread Loaf Days" — and told stories. My wife Kirby and I drove him around Ann Arbor, at his request, to look for the houses he had lived in and the streets where he had walked. On Pontiac we passed the lot where his house had been; Henry Ford had bought it and hauled it to Greenfield Village, not because "Robert Frost Slept Here" but because it was an historic building made of walnut. We drove out Broadway where he said he had walked for hours and hours. We looked for the house where he had lived on Washtenaw Avenue. Something reminded him of a story from the early twenties when he lived in the Washtenaw house. People do strange things, he said, and the corners of his mouth puckered with amusement or deviltry. One time there was a professor here who was "caught doing something strange," Frost said. The man identified himself to the police, who called the university to confirm the existence of a professor by this name; they said they'd caught this man who claimed to be a professor, but they couldn't tell — because he didn't have any clothes on. When Frost finished his story, and chuckled his slow chuckle, he glanced toward Kirby in the back seat, saying, "I probably shouldn't be saying this."

Talking about the Kennedys, Frost brought up Teddy's cheating on an examination at Harvard. Then he said that he never cheated in school, he *wouldn't* have done such a thing; but his virtue, he hastened to assure me, was a byproduct of vice: He would not cheat because he was proud. He looked at me shrewdly — aware of giving himself away, delightedly giving himself away — and said that when he had gone to Lawrence High School he had been good at Latin; that he would come to school and hide in the bushes until the bell rang, then dash inside. When he had told me so much he stopped, and watched to see if I got the point. It took me a moment but I did: He hid in the bushes with his Latin homework done all by himself. He would take no help on his homework — and he would give none either.

He wanted to see some classrooms, he said. We parked and walked through Mason and Angell halls. Passing one lecture hall, I mentioned that I taught a class in it. "How much do they make you teach?" he asked.

My teaching schedule was light. I taught the same number of classes as anyone else, but they were jammed together into two afternoons; morning is always my best time for work. "Tuesday and Thursday afternoons," I said. "One to four."

His face changed; we might have been rivals for team captain, or for a girl, or for a last piece of chicken tetrazzini. Smug and powerful, he said, "They didn't make me teach that much."

He grew tired after half an hour, and I took him back to Inglis House. He asked me what I had written lately, and said he wasn't always sure what people were up to. I told him about a prose book called *String Too Short to Be Saved*, a memoir about summers on the New Hampshire place that my grandfather farmed. He asked if he could see it; maybe he could read in it before his afternoon nap. After we left him at Inglis House, I went home and picked up a copy and took it back to the house-keeper for him. I was anxious that he like it. It was a book of love for my grandparents, and other old people of the country, and for the culture they had known when they were young — culture of lyceum and political debate, fairs, and baseball games that pitted married men against single men.

When we picked him up that night, Frost wanted to know how tickets had gone, and when he discovered that Hill Auditorium was sold out, his pleasure filled up the limousine that the Union had rented for the occasion. Four thousand seats; standing room only. His pleasure in a crowd found its counterpart if ever he lacked a crowd. Betty Kray, who ran the Poetry Center in New York, told me about Frost's "madness of old age" — though I suspect that old age only made manifest what had earlier been lightly disguised. When Frost read in the Poetry Center series, she told me, she could allow no empty seat visible from the platform. If there were empty seats, the old poet would be inconsolable, would rage and fume, would invoke conspiracy and intrigue. In desperation, when she lacked a full house, she and her assistants dredged additional bodies from offices nearby — free tickets, *please* come, just sit there. . .

Arrived at Hill Auditorium, we walked to the green room behind the stage so that Frost could rest for a moment. He told me he had been reading my book; it was good, he told me, and his eyes took on that amusement which let me know he had a wisecrack. "You talk about the *decay* of New England," he said. Of course he wouldn't like that part so much, although he was the poet of deserted villages and abandoned farms. "It's a *compost heap*," he said.

When I left him backstage, to go out to introduce him, he said, "You know I can't hear you. You can abuse me all you like." Of course it was a joke; of course it expressed the same distrust that *I* felt. When he shuffled onstage, to immense and prolonged applause, I stayed long enough to hook the lavaliere microphone around his neck. Then I went backstage and watched the reading for a while on the television monitors; then I snuck out front and stood against the wall to watch him read for the last time. Bread Loaf, Stanford, Ann Arbor. It was the best reading of the three. He was triumphant, utterly happy, as he returned to a scene of his struggling middle age. In his triumph, he read with energy and conviction, stopping to make jokes on occasion, but not jokes to humiliate poetry or the professors who looked for hidden meanings. And I, who had been afraid that he would belittle me, heard him speak of me with affection. He said he wanted to come to Ann Arbor, despite his recent illness, for a number of reasons, and one of them was to see a young poet he had helped to bring up. He left the audience with the impression that he had supervised my writing from the age of sixteen. He referred to me as a son. He started to mention *String Too Short to Be Saved*, but he couldn't remember the title, so he changed the subject. Then he said that New England was in decay, all right; it was a compost heap from which had come five Presidents and Donald Hall and himself, so it wasn't so bad.

After reading for an hour he looked as tired as he looked pleased, and he slowed himself down and stopped. I climbed onto the stage and undid his microphone. The audience applauded and stood up. He waved them off and, holding the microphone in his hand, said one more poem. Then he followed me from the stage — the audience standing and applauding again, determined to stand and applaud forever — and when we stood in the dark corridor behind the stage, he said, "It's a pity not to let them have more when they are like that. Why don't you go out and ask them if they want any more?" There was no stopping him. I told him that the question was unnecessary, that if he felt strong enough he should go out and do another.

After the second encore I led him back to the green room again — exhausted, gray looking, but his eyes bright with triumph. Ten minutes restored him, and he was ready to return to Inglis House for scrambled eggs and 7-Up. When we opened the green room door, we found hundreds of students crowded into the backstage corridors, waiting for sight of the old poet. The white hair behind me drew cheers, and there was movement through the crowd as people pushed to see him. Hands held out copies of books for signing, autograph books, scraps of paper. We moved toward the car, Jim Seff and I running interference. Behind us Frost was saying thank you, thank you, and refusing to sign anything. Looking ahead, I could see that the doors were open and the limousine waiting. Hundreds more people milled outside around the car. He had dreamed his entire life of moments like this, and when the dreams came true they were every bit as good as he had expected them to be. At the same time, there was something in Frost that needed to reject the adulation when it took concrete form. In front of me as I struggled through the crowd I saw two girls; one of them looked shy, and held a piece of paper; the other, her bold friend, was urging her, "Go ahead. Give it to him." So the shy one handed Frost a drawing she had made of him during the reading; the old poet squinted and shoved it back at her, still shuffling forward, growling, "What do I want with that?"

When we reached the car, he turned back to the crowd for a moment, before negotiating his way into the back seat, raised his arms above his shoulders like Eisenhower giving the victory sign, and said in a loud, tremulous voice, "Remember me."

"We will," said the many voices around us and in back of us. "We will."

Wedged into the back seat, Frost spoke slowly as the car moved cautiously out into the crowd, turning into the street. Oh, it was wonderful — to come back in this way, to have this kind of tribute. And it was so strange, he said, because even as late as when he was forty-five years old, he had never expected real recognition. He only hoped, he only felt able to hope, that he might make a couple of little poems that would stick. Stick in an anthology somewhere.

I listened to him, moved, and feeling closer to him than I had ever felt or dared to feel. Many times I had found myself amused or aghast at a poet's vanity — since I first discovered it at Bread Loaf: Frost's or my own or another's. But vanity is a word used for the light side of a heavy thing. "Fame is the spur," said

Milton, in lines that faintly embarrass people. "That last infirmity of noble mind." The notion of fame embarrasses us because we confuse it with mere lightness, like preening before a mirror; or we confuse it with celebrity, as if Milton confessed his desire to resemble Johnny Carson. Fame is a word for the love that everyone wants, impersonal love, love from strangers for what we are, what we do or make. People write poems when they are ten so that their mothers will love them; when they are sixteen so that their peers will love them; when they are thirty (and eighty-eight) so that the Muse will love them, and ages to come, and *all* men and women, universally, forever and ever, as long as the language exists and maybe longer. Although Frost had become a contemporary celebrity, and although the people of Hill Auditorium resembled Johnny Carson's audience more than Milton's, Frost's response to applause came from his deep and vast ambition to become a great poet, to be immortal, to write poems that would *stick*. His ambition was never merely to be a celebrated poet; it was larger and more serious than that, for he knew that to write great poems he had to make perfect works of art which embodied wisdom and knowledge beyond the perfection of art. In pursuit of such ambition you may become pitiless and harsh to those around you. Like Orpheus you kill your wife a second time, when you turn around to see if she *really* likes this new song; then perhaps you deserve to be torn apart by the Thracean women.

Or you think you deserve it; the poet sees to his own punishment. I was watching Frost in the faint light of the back seat, and suddenly his face turned dark. "But it's sad too," he said. He said "sad," which is a faint and crepuscular word, but his face looked more like "despair" or "agony" than sadness. "It has a sad side too," he said. For a while he said nothing; I did not know what he meant. "We were so poor," he said. I remembered the years of poverty at Derry, the deaths of children, suicide, madness.

He was a guilty man, guilty over the wrongs he felt he had done to people he loved — the same guilt that Ezra Pound lived with; the same guilt, I suppose, that tormented T. S. Eliot in middle life. Therefore, perhaps, he courted love, *any* love, even the kind he took from his Stanford audience, to assuage his conviction that he was bad. The need for love and applause was a need for forgiveness. And when he received the love he asked for, he rejected it, and then he asked for more.

I left him at Inglis House, to eat his supper with undergraduates. He asked if he would see me the next day, and I told him that I hadn't planned on it. He asked if I could visit him in Vermont next summer, and I told him I could.

The next morning I had an errand in Detroit, so I wasn't there when he telephoned. He wanted me to come over and talk with him, he told my wife. He had been reading *String* when he went to bed, he told her, and he wanted to talk to me about it. He asked if I could come over in the afternoon before he left for the airport. No, she said, I was teaching then, but she'd ask me to telephone him when I got back for lunch. Then she told him that she liked his reading the night before. The compliment allowed him to ask a question that had been troubling him: He had brought two different black suits with him, he told her, and while he was out on the platform last night he had realized that he was wearing the pants from one suit and the coat from the other; could she tell? could she notice? did she think anyone noticed? She could tell him without hypocrisy that she had noticed nothing, and he seemed relieved; well, he said, he guessed they were pretty much the same color.

When I called him, we made it definite about Vermont next summer. "I want to see a lot more of you," he said, and referred to me again in metaphor as his son. "I hardly recognized you," he said, "when we first met. I didn't remember you were so tall." On the way to the press conference he had said, "You're getting taller every time I look at you." When I was sixteen at Bread Loaf I had my full height; it was as if Frost had to invent a new, larger body to explain his interest. Then on the telephone he returned to *String Too Short to Be Saved.* "So much more happened to you than ever happened to me," he said, about a book in which little happened. "There is nothing precious about you," he said. Then he said something I carry with me: "You can do anything in poetry you want to do." I took it, correctly, that he meant to say that by 1962, when I would turn thirty-four, I had not done a great deal.

LAST VERSIONS

In June, on our way from New Hampshire back to Michigan, we stopped at Frost's cabin on the Homer Noble Farm at Ripton in Vermont, near Bread Loaf. We were to arrive midmorning. First we called at the old farmhouse, where Kathleen and Ted Morrison spent their summers, about two hundred yards downhill from Frost's cabin. Mrs. Morrison telephoned uphill to the cabin, and told us that Robert would be ready for us in fifteen or twenty minutes. I felt annoyed — ungenerous, suspicious — as if someone with power kept me waiting in order to assert power. We passed the time of day with Mrs. Morrison — who must have spent so many hours like this, as doorkeeper or receptionist — until the phone rang and we were directed toward the cabin. It was a cool, sharp day, little sparks of rain in our eyes, a quick wind, as Kirby and I struggled uphill with our children. The log cabin appeared before us, not beautiful but comfortable, and the old man opened the door, smiling and handsome and vigorous. Behind him a fierce fire of birch logs blazed in the living room fireplace. He had kept us waiting, he told us when he let us in, because it was such a raw and rainy day; he wanted to have a good fire going.

We visited for two hours, five of us, and the children — Philippa was three, Andrew eight — were attentive and quiet. Frost monologued most of the time, out of his deafness. He wore a white shirt, dark trousers, and canvas shoes with thick rubber soles which comforted his feet. The flap of his belt — the loose part that sticks out past the buckle — incompletely fitted into the leather loop that was supposed to restrain it; this incompleteness bothered Philippa, who spent two hours attempting to straighten the belt through the loop and smooth it flat. Frost accepted her ministry without complaint. Late in the visit, Philippa made her only show of boredom. "Do you have a TV?" she asked him. There was no set visible in the cabin. Frost would accept adulation from anyone. He looked down on the three-year-old, smiling from his deaf tower, and acknowledged: "You've seen me on TV?"

He rambled on, friendly and impersonal. He talked about the prejudice against Roman Catholics in the Lawrence of his youth; there was one Catholic teacher at his high school — a startling liberalism. He grumbled that Amy Lowell had claimed that he could write only about maniacs. He said that he didn't feel that way about the people in his poems. He talked about old Homer Noble, the original farmer of this place, and how Homer Noble had grubbed to make a living: In the winter he held sugaring-off parties for Middlebury students; in July and August he rented space to teachers attending summer school. Frost told us that he had just turned down an invitation from Robert and Ethel Kennedy that very day: They had asked him to a dinner dance, and he told us about it, bragging and making fun of himself. "I never been to a dinner dance," he said. "That's not my sort of thing, a dinner dance. They throw each other in the pool. I would have been ashamed. Not for them, for myself." He told about Ethel showing him around the grounds, which were "affluent," he said. "We live like Republicans," Ethel told him, "and act like Democrats." Then maybe Frost felt he had gone far enough, showing fondness for the Kennedys. Just the other day, he told us, a Philadelphia newspaper had asked him to write a short patriotic essay, two hundred and fifty or three hundred words, on how the country had changed after Kennedy's election. The notion made Frost impatient. "That's *bunk,*" he said. "It's not the administration. It was always there."

So his talk went, in June of 1962, with this strange and happy audience. And all the time, as I sat listening and relaxed, I was aware that I would almost certainly never see him again, aware that this eighty-eight-year-old complexity — that I had seen walk out of the ground when I was sixteen, that I had admired, despised, feared, and loved — would go into the ground forever before I could see him again. I could almost look ahead to a morning next winter, when we turned on the radio at breakfast and heard that Robert Frost had died at Peter Bent Brigham Hospital in Boston. And I could feel the loss as I would not have felt it a year earlier. I would feel, after years of fear and defense, that I had lost a model of survival, endurance: a model you need not so much at sixteen as at thirty-five. Not to mention sixty-three.

That morning in the cabin Frost was vigorous and many-sided, determined to survive, complex and energetic. He talked about other poets; while we had visited New Hampshire, Frost had returned to Ann Arbor — *yet again* — to receive an honorary degree along with Theodore Roethke. Frost had known Roethke before, and spoke of him tolerantly, but criticized him, of all things, for being so competitive with other poets. Perhaps it was Roethke's style that bothered Frost; Roethke made his competitiveness obvious with a boyish enthusiasm. A few months after Frost's death I saw Roethke in Seattle — not long before Roethke died, as it happened. He met me as I came into a house for a party, pulled me aside, dragged yards of galley out of the pockets of his jacket, and sat me down to read *The Far Field,* saying, "I've got a book coming out that's going to drive Wilbur and Lowell *into the shadows.*" This announcement was made without malice toward Wilbur or Lowell.

Frost asked me as well if I knew a poet from the Midwest, a man I'll call Harry Dutcher, who was writing a book on him. Frost had met him and liked him, he told me. Was Harry Dutcher a good poet? I said he was, and tried to characterize his poetry. Frost listened intently, and I felt that I could follow a trail of feelings across his face. I could see Frost the schemer, wanting Dutcher to write a favorable book, eager that I should carry Frost's approval back to Dutcher. On the other hand, I felt that his liking for Dutcher was genuine. And when Frost asked me the quality of Dutcher's poems, he wanted to hear two distinct answers: One Robert Frost wanted to hear that Dutcher was good, because Frost liked him; another wanted to hear that Dutcher was bad, and be rid of the potential steeple climber.

As we chatted I looked around his room, at the lapboard he used for writing, at the books he was reading, notes sticking out of them; Robinson's new edition of Chaucer was there, and a volume of Horace. I remember him attacking the idea that there was an American language. That notion was silly, he said; at least the notion that American and English poets were writing their poems in different languages was silly. Then with his usual doubleness he contradicted himself: He said he wrote the way he talked, and it was an American way; he preferred the way he talked to the way Englishmen talked. "You went over there too," he told me. I had spent three years in England and would return a year later. "I'm glad you didn't stay over there and turn into an Englishman." I don't know if Frost knew that I had thought about it; he sounded as if he knew. Then he said something astonishing that reflected his new amiability. "I like Eliot and I like Pound" — these clauses necessarily led into "but" — "I like Eliot and I like Pound," he told us, "but they left us behind. They should have stayed over here." He meant what he said; still, the old mind needed to flip again: "Of course, I heard an Englishman say, 'What's there to stay for?' "

It was late in the morning. He walked to the door and looked out at the sun beginning to shine through the damp air. "It's done rainin', ain't it?" he said. It was time to go. We shook hands all around and talked about when we would see each other again. With eighty-eight years on one of us, we agreed to make this Vermont summer visit an annual occasion, and to stay longer next time.

We said these things as Frost walked us to our car. As we started off I watched him in the rearview mirror, and saw him begin to run after us. I stopped, and he caught up with us. He leaned in the window on the driver's side and reminded me to give his good wishes to Harry Dutcher when I saw him; he repeated that he hoped he was a good poet. We said goodbye again and I started up. This time I didn't look in the mirror, but slowed down because of a hole in the driveway, when I realized that he had run after us again — eighty-eight years old, with sore feet, jogging after the car — because his face suddenly appeared at my window. He had thought of one more thing. I would please *not* tell Harry that Frost had hoped he was a good poet, because that would reveal that Frost had not read his work.

Dylan Thomas
and Public Suicide

⟡

SCOTCH AT THE ADVOCATE

Everyone knew Dylan Thomas. I knew him only the way everyone did — in pubs, late in his short life, drinking, laughing, telling stories. He was the most gregarious man in the world when he was drinking, which means that he was often gregarious. Drinking, he took pleasure in talking with strangers, who were treated as friends if he liked them at all. His real friends — Swansea people, or friends from the first years in London — watched him perform with strangers and spoke of Instant Dylan. I suppose that his gregariousness was another refuge from pain, the anesthesia of promiscuous acquaintance, like drink's anesthesia that slid toward death. I suppose that Dylan knew what he was doing: laughter and death and public suicide.

It was February of 1950 when I first met him. I was a junior in college, and I had known for some months that Dylan Thomas would come to Harvard to read his poems. The fad or fashion for Thomas had not begun — it was his first reading tour in the United States — but I knew about the quality of his reading. The Caedmon recordings did not yet exist, but I heard his astonishing voice on an LP called *Pleasure Dome*. I had known his poetry for years, first in an Oscar Williams anthology, then in a *Selected Writings* that New Directions brought out, edited by John L. Sweeney, who ran the Poetry Room at Harvard. I loved his poems. A few weeks before he was due to arrive, F. O. Matthiessen, literary critic and Harvard professor of English, telephoned us at the *Advocate,* the student literary magazine, to ask if we would like to give Thomas a party after his reading. It was generous of Matthiessen to offer the poet to undergraduates; at most colleges, English professors eat the poet all by themselves.

Thomas read in New Lecture Hall at four o'clock. First he read poems by other poets: Hardy, W. H. Davies, Henry Reed, Yeats. We were spellbound, and we were an audience determined not to be spellbound. Behind the lectern stood a small unsmiling figure — big belly, pudgy face, nose like the bulb on a Klaxon horn, chinless, red-faced, pop-eyed, curly-haired, with an expression at once frightened and insolent. Out of this silly body rolled a voice like Jehovah's, or Ocean's, or Firmament's. R's rolled, vowels rose and fell — he had a range like Yma Sumac's — consonants thudded and crashed and leapt to their feet again. When he performed Hardy I was astonished. I had never known Hardy's best poems. He spoke "The Naming of Parts" by Henry Reed, and the same author's parody of T. S. Eliot, "Chard Whitlow." When he read the Reed/Eliot, he parodied Eliot's accent, which he defined as Church-of-English, producing a Thomas/Reed/Eliot three-decker. He read some Yeats poems I loved. Yeats had been my favorite poet for two years, but early in 1950 the Yeats *Collected Poems* was still the 1933 edition; the posthumous *Last Poems* remained locked in the rare book room. Therefore, when Thomas read "News for the Delphic Oracle" it was news to us; when he read "Lapis Lazuli," he introduced us to the poem. The glorious voice stretched long syllables out on the air:

> Their eyes mid many wrinkles, their eyes,
> Their ancient, glittering eyes, are gay.

I hovered five inches above my uncomfortable chair in New Lecture Hall, stunned by the beauty of poem and reading. Although I was later to meet him under different guises, I remember the first Dylan Thomas I saw: a small and disheveled figure bodying forth great poetry in great performance, an act of homage to poetry, an act of love for magnificent words.

When he had finished reading other poets he made a deprecating remark, which seemed perfunctory but wasn't, and read several of his own poems, ending with "Poem in October," spoken with force and sweetness. We applauded mightily. The little man on the platform nodded in response, looking nervous or diffident now, and lit up a cigarette. I approached him, along with Sweeney and Matthiessen, to pick him up and take him to the *Advocate*. As I came near, I saw a janitor walk over to him, where he stood below the stage talking with students, and snarl, "Put out that cigarette. Can't you read?" Thomas already seemed diminished, but now he shrank like Alice; he pretended to stomp out the cigarette, looked sullen, and didn't; he continued to sneak his drags.

We drove the short distance to the *Advocate*. Someone mentioned his reading of "News for the Delphic Oracle" and he told a story. His voice rose, mellifluous and unnatural, filling the small car like a blast from Aeolus; as I would later understand, he was intolerably uncomfortable when surrounded by academic politeness and deference. The story told about someone visiting Yeats in Ireland not long before Yeats's death, when the old poet was making "News for the Delphic Oracle." The poem ends, ". . . nymphs and satyrs / Copulate in the foam." Yeats showed Dylan's friend the poem in a draft ending, "nymphs and satyrs / Fuck in the foam." Then Dylan told us, "And I think it's a fine thing that Yeats changed it. Otherwise, it would only be known as a poem with the word 'fuck' in it. We're not intelligent enough for that." All the while he told the story, I knew he was telling it for effect. Harvard was not ready for "fuck" in 1950.

In a moment I heard the great voice open itself up again, like a bag of tricks: "Will there be anything to drink at this party?" Matthiessen answered: "Why, yes. The boys usually have only martinis, but I'm sure they can get you some beer." (Thomas had drunk beer all day.) "Oh, no," said Thomas. "Now that I've done my work, I can get down to the serious stuff." How well he said it. His accent parodied upper-class speech and made it obvious that he was acting. After a moment's delicate pause, he added in a whine — now doing a character long suffering from deprivation — "Scotch will do for me."

We sent out for some Scotch, and it did for him. He roared and raved, he teetered and tottered. He would approach a young man, say, "There's a long street where I live, fucked every woman on it, fucked their mothers too," and then weave on, often to a young woman whom he would pretend to desire. Sometimes he was funny. Much of the time he wasn't. After a while I was annoyed; I decided that Dylan Thomas was an ass playing the role of The Poet. I saw pretense; I saw premeditation trying to pass itself off as spontaneity; I saw nastiness: It was not from love of women that he suggested bed.

Everyone knows these stories: Dylan the Drunken Boor, Dylan the Roaring Boy. I will add only one to the world's store; it was typical — mildly funny, mildly cruel. There was at the party a young woman I will call Rachel, who was a Radcliffe freshman. After Dylan's reading, she had changed clothes in her boyfriend's room because she wanted to wear her best dress unwrinkled to the party. Her best dress was cut low. Dylan approached her, as she stood next to her boyfriend, peered down her dress, put his hands on her waist, and rocked from side to side. Embarrassed, eighteen years old, Rachel tried making conversation; she asked him when he was going back to England. "Now," he boomed. "Immediately," he crooned. "*Now.*"

"When did you get here?" she asked.

"This afternoon," he said. As he spoke or sang, he rocked back and forth and gazed into her eyes. "I will write sensual poems to you," he went on. "They will begin —" and he made a low, throaty whistle. "They will be the only poems in the language that begin —" and he gave the whistle again.

Blushing, Rachel struggled to speak, telling him that she had liked his reading very, very much. In low and velvet tones, looking deep into her blinking eyes, Dylan intoned, "Did you wear — that dress — to my reading?" Then he bent forward to make it obvious to everyone — spectators followed him around — that he looked down her dress; he exaggerated like a burlesque comedian. His rhetorical question brought Rachel nearly to tears. As she stumbled to answer his question, Dylan interrupted her to intone his curtain line, delivered with the sonority of a provincial Prospero: "I would rather — suckle those paps — than go back — to my old wife — in Wales." As the long diphthong of "Wales" slid past the *l* into a terminal *z*, Dylan forgot his passion for Rachel, turned on his heel, and looked for someone new.

When I went home I wrote about Dylan in a journal I kept for a while; I did not like him. The next week or two I kept hearing more stories: how he had rolled on the floor at Matty's later in the evening, his shirt open and his belly showing; how Charlee Wilbur and Betty Eberhart had put him to bed, early in the following morning, in the Faculty Club where he had a room; how he had drunk his way to Mount Holyoke the next day, and what he said to the woman there who asked him about modern poetry.

BITTER IN LONDON

Two years later, when I was studying at Oxford, I went to London to find Dylan Thomas. Two years had diminished my annoyance; I loved his poems more than ever, and in my own work I tried to achieve those sensuous textures. Besides, I was doing what I was told: The Oxford University Poetry Society, of which I was secretary, wanted Thomas to read his poems.

We sold membership cards for fifty cents, out of which we bought sherry and dinner for visiting poets, and paid their train fares to Oxford. That's all we paid, and poets came from all over England to read for nothing at Oxford; generally, they charged us first class railroad fare. The secretary of OUPS made the arrangements with poets, reservations for dinner and hotel room, and held a sherry party in his own rooms. The duties were not onerous, and one was rewarded by becoming president of OUPS the following term.

From someone I heard that Dylan and Caitlin had left Wales for London, and were living in Camden Town not far from the Regent's Park zoo. Because Dylan was doing some BBC work — as actor, writer, poet, talker — it was convenient to live in London for a while rather than Wales. I wrote him letters at an address supplied. No answer. I decided to take a train up to London and look for him. So I arrived at Paddington at nine o'clock on the morning of December 5, 1951, and took the tube to Camden Town. I found the road I had written to, I found the number, I knocked on the door and was directed elsewhere: Yes, they had lived out back, but they had moved a few blocks away. I continued my search, and a few blocks away I found an African at the new address I had been given who knew nothing of people named Thomas. I tried at the corner sweetshop; the old woman shook her head. I ran after the postman; there was no Dylan Thomas on his route.

By ten-thirty in the morning, I had exhausted my leads. I wondered if I should call Louis MacNeice at the BBC; I had met him briefly at Oxford. Shy about calling MacNeice, I decided to postpone the question with a pint of bitter; the hour of ten-thirty opened the pubs and made postponement attractive. Near the tube was a great nineteenth-century gin palace, which I entered when the landlord opened the doors. I stood near the porcelain beer engines, studying my Bass, when I felt a minor commotion at the level of my shoulder. I looked down and caught Dylan's face looking up — he was "above medium height for Wales," as he liked to put it — and in my surprise I blurted out his name. To my greater surprise he recognized me, enough to remember where he had seen me before. "Oh, God," he said, "you were at the *Advocate*. You must hate me."

We spent the day drinking together all over London. After the first flush of alcoholic guilt, Dylan settled down to quiet drinking and talking. I began to see the everyday Dylan — sober at first, then mildly drunk, friendly, gradually more gregarious, generous, funny, and opinionated. The night before, Dylan and Caitlin had gone to the Swedish film of Strindberg's *Miss Julie*, a devastating movie that I had seen the summer before — a nightmare of gynophobia, in which a young woman demonstrates sexual power over her valet, a social inferior and sexual enemy. Dylan and Caitlin had been disturbed by the film, as well they might have been, and walked around London half the night, unable to quiet down to sleep. This morning he needed a drink. He thought he intended to have a pint or two and go back home to work. He never did. John Davenport dropped in, we went to an exhibition, we went to the Mandrake Club — and one thing led to another. On that particular lost day, in Dylan's life of lost days, I was the original hanger-on who provided the excuse to drink another and then another.

In the pub that morning we talked politics and money. Dylan was an anarchist that morning — and frequently, so far as he was political; he was anarchist by nature. At Harvard, he told me, he had liked everybody except for Archibald MacLeish, because MacLeish had been in government. I remembered MacLeish telling me of an encounter with Dylan late at night after the reading. MacLeish had asked him, "We all know what you've done with the first thirty-five years of your life. What will you do with the next thirty-five years of your life?" Dylan drew himself up and boomed, "I will write poems, fuck women, and annoy my friends."

Dylan spoke of F. O. Matthiessen's party, where he had rolled on the floor, and I mentioned that it was a month later — April Fool's Day, 1950 — that Matty had jumped from the high window of a Boston hotel. "Oh, God," said Dylan, "was I *that* bad?"

And Dylan talked money, or at least his lack of it; tax men were after him, and books were unfinished. Worry about money worked its way through his speech like a thread in tweed. Also we talked poetry-gossip and poetry-business. He agreed instantly to come to the Poetry Society in May, we settled on a date, and he gave me a current address. (No help to money problems from OUPS.) He talked about American poets he had met on his tour. Mostly he was funny about them, and put down their work, but his dismissals were strangely unmalicious or impersonal, maybe even disinterested: He was a hard and serious judge. I remember his distaste for Kenneth Patchen, whom he dismissed as fake-tough. He dredged up lines of Patchen that fit the description, which he carried around with him like a cartoon to laugh at: "Cold stars watch us, chum / Cold stars, and the whores." The pauses around "chum," in his performance, made the lines precious. As Dylan quoted them all day long, his accent became tougher and tougher, moving through James Cagney past George Raft to John Garfield.

Friends of Dylan joined us in the pub, had a pint, and left. By this time I was his "American friend, Don." I allowed myself to believe him; his laughter when I joked seemed genuine enough, and his amusement at Oxford stories. This man was not the cruel show-off I had met at Harvard. Laughing and friendly, he put me up to chug-a-lugging pints, one after the other, telling me that at *my* age, *he* could . . . (That day in 1951, Dylan was thirty-seven, I was twenty-three.) I don't believe that we ate lunch but I may have swallowed a sausage or two. Toward closing time in midafternoon, John Davenport came in: good friend of Dylan's, drinker, one of those brilliant men who whirl around literary London *just about* to write something great, and never do. Davenport had invitations to the *vernissage* of a Dali exhibition, the show in which Dali revealed his new piety by painting virgins with holes through their stomachs. Neither Davenport nor Dylan nor I — I was volunteering opinions by this time — admired Dali, but for some reason we decided to go. From Davenport I discovered the hotel where Dali was staying, and later in the day I telephoned and talked with Gala; maybe Salvador Dali would also address the Oxford University Poetry Society. When I answered Gala's question about our usual fee, I had my answer. It was André Breton who made the anagram for Dali: "Avida Dollars."

The *vernissage* was crowded, stuffy, smoky, filled with people calling "Dylan!" — and he knew them all, and grinned at them out of his fond friendly absurd face, and in ten minutes we pulled ourselves out to the street and looked for a taxi. I didn't know where we were going; I didn't care, I was lurching around London with Dylan Thomas, my *friend* Dylan Thomas, drunk as a lark and happy as a lord. Opening the door of the taxi, I heard the cry of "Dylan!" again. A young man with long blond hair flopping ran toward us down the street and exchanged a word with Dylan, who introduced his American friend Don from Oxford to Ken Tynan just down from Oxford, and Tynan ran off, we entered the taxi, and Dylan directed the driver to the Mandrake. Then he told me where we were going. Licensing laws had sponsored the growth of such establishments throughout England, nominally social clubs exempt from laws governing pubs, really nothing but off-hour drinking places that thrived during the hours when pubs were closed. The Mandrake was a legal speakeasy patronized especially by BBC people and artistic sorts. When we entered the establishment, subdued "Dylan!"s arose from various patrons, and soon Dylan stood at some distance from the bar, a glass in each hand and a cigarette in the corner of his mouth, contriving a semicircle of listeners as he monologued and everyone bought him drinks. I remember Dylan's long rendition of an American movie, which he made up as he went along, a gangster movie in which he played all the parts, doing a sampler of American accents, each of them exaggerated, accurate enough, and hilarious.

When it turned six we migrated to a pub. Dylan met a Communist friend accompanied by a young woman with long hair and long legs. I watched them speak in low voices, drawn aside. Then Dylan beckoned me off, saying we had to go somewhere, and walked me a few blocks; then he told me he had to meet someone, an appointment. I was dumped. I think I didn't care, for I knew I was out of my mind.

Nonetheless, I telephoned the Dali suite. Nonetheless, from my hotel room I wrote a letter to my parents in Connecticut, squeezing illegible sentences onto a blue air letter from 8 Tavestock Place, London WC1. When I wrote of Dylan that "we have become bosom friends," I can hope that I used the cliché to indicate exaggeration by irony. In any event, one's letter at twenty-three to one's parents remains unreliable. "Dylan is fine," I wrote my parents, "though he drinks a bit heavily."

As the day approached when Dylan would read at Oxford, I wrote him at his London address about arrangements. No answer. I had been afraid that he might forget a date set in a pub. I wrote again. I telegraphed. A few hours before he was supposed to read, I thought to telephone Wales. Yes, he was there, Caitlin said; no, he would not be in Oxford that evening; no, he could not come to the phone; no, she would not ask him to.

I posted a notice on the door of the lecture hall that Dylan Thomas had been forced to postpone his reading.

BITTER IN WALES

That summer I flew back to the United States and married before I returned for my final Oxford year. Now I was president of the Poetry Society, with a secretary named George MacBeth carrying my old burdens. I determined to see that Dylan would read his poems during my term as president. I wrote him in Wales and proposed that if he could read at Oxford in October, at the beginning of term, we would drive to Laugharne in our wedding-present car and fetch him back to the reading. I presented the notion as a convenience to him; of course it was an adventure for me, but it was also a considerable convenience: If I drove him myself, I could make sure he got there; if I counted on him to catch a train for Oxford, I would never be sure until I saw him waddle out of first class.

On blue stationery, in a small and delicate hand, he wrote to apologize for missing the previous engagement — he had no memory of it — and to agree to the date I suggested.

We drove from Oxford to Wales, and to Dylan's village. Laugharne was the place we had heard of: with a ruined castle and small stone cottages, tidy and miniature, as if a toy train might hoot through at any moment. From an old man on the street I asked directions to the Boat House, where Dylan and Caitlin lived. I learned where to park the car in order to walk there; we left the Morris Minor and set off together — my wife Kirby twenty years old in her muskrat coat — along a dirt cliff over Carmarthen Bay, seagulls swooping and honking above us. Unknowing, we passed Dylan's workshed — Dylan inside it writing *Under Milk Wood* — before we came suddenly upon the Boat House, which dropped to our right down to water level and the bay. From the lane where we walked, a gate opened to a path that swooped down to the front door of the house built from water to cliff top, house made of stone washed a pale pink. It had been the ferryman's house, and the backyard at bay level was the boatyard, complete with a disused landing stage and a used outhouse; there was no running water in the Boat House. The kitchen was one story up from water level, next to it a dining room with one wall of cliff rock. At the third level — where we entered as we walked from Laugharne — was a tiny hallway, a bedroom, and a sitting room with a veranda overlooking the bay. A staircase led to two children's bedrooms on a fourth story. It was a house as awkward and as beautiful as I have ever seen.

Caitlin greeted us, looking tired and pretty, fierce, struggling with a head cold. When she led us to the bedroom she took sarcastic notice of Kirby's muskrat coat; then she asked, "How long have you been married?" About six weeks, she was told, and when Caitlin heard the length of time, she snorted, "I suppose that accounts for the rosy glow."

Caitlin had small reason to care for her husband's admirers; people married to anyone famous learn quickly to loathe the followers, and Caitlin had considerable injury to complain of. When Dylan went up to London — where he would entrain from Oxford, day after tomorrow, to perform for the BBC — he would disappear when he had done his work. Hangers-on would buy him drinks and be audience to the perpetual performance; a woman would take him home to bed. To vomit with Dylan, or to sleep with him, brought forms of glory. After Dylan had not turned up for a few days, Caitlin would carry herself to London, check through familiar clubs and pubs and girls, find Dylan and take him back to Laugharne. There, he would undergo a hangover like withdrawal from heroin. Both Dylan and Caitlin described these hangovers, Dylan with attempted humor, for it turned out that when I had called the spring before he had been enduring a bad one. Not only could he not come to the telephone, the distant ringing of the phone was agony to him. If his eyes admitted a flick of light from the curtained windows, they rasped in agony. His stomach burned and he could keep nothing on it, not milk nor medicine. These hangovers lasted four days, or five. When he went to the United States everything was worse. He stayed longer, threw away more money, and she could not fetch him home. In addition, he tended to fall in love with someone when he visited the United States. If Caitlin was sarcastic to the smiling American twenty-year-old bride, it is small wonder.

We put our bags in their bedroom. Dylan was still working, Caitlin told us, but it was almost six o'clock. He quit work when the pubs opened. In a few moments the familiar figure puffed down the lane and turned in at the Boat House gate. He looked as bloated as ever — Dylan resembled those little fish that blow themselves up with air, by way of protection; and his chin was as weak as a fish's; and his strong eyes glittered like a mackerel's cold on a marble slab — but there was something unfamiliar about him also, to me who had seen him in America and in London. After a moment's shyness, he was cheerful and funny without the help of a pint of bitter. He was the healthy and happy Dylan of Laugharne, who had just worked four hours straight on his play. He looked at his watch and said it was time to walk to town. The pubs would be open by the time we got there.

Caitlin stayed behind to start the risotto that would make our supper when we returned. When she had put the two young children to bed — their eldest Llewelyn was away at school — she would join us in town.

We left behind us the pink-washed stone of the Boat House and walked slowly along the lane back to town. Dylan told us about his day — this day in particular, and his ideal day of work in Wales. He had written two lines today, for *Under Milk Wood,* and two lines a day was what he had learned to expect of himself. Dylan would use many sheets of scratch paper, digging out his two lines, and when he had made them he would add them to the ongoing manuscript of the work. Most writers write whole drafts, over and over again, but Dylan's first whole draft was generally his last, not counting the scratch sheets he filled as he went along. Today it was not a poem he was making but a play; yet it was a play in verse and he wrote it as he made a poem. He still called it "Llareggub," the title under which it first appeared, and it delighted him to have invented the Welsh-looking town's name which was "bugger all" spelled backwards.

Typically in Wales, as he told it, Dylan would arise about nine o'clock, eat a huge breakfast — he was an eater when he was not drunk, and his belly was composed not only of beer — and then read for a spell in the outhouse. At ten or ten-thirty he would walk into town for his mail, drink a couple of morning pints, have a gossip, do the crossword with his dying father who lived in a Laugharne cottage, and saunter back to the Boat House for a large lunch. From two to six he wrote in his shack, which had begun life as somebody's bicycle shed. Evenings from six to ten he lived the pub life, chatting, drinking in a desultory fashion, winding down from an afternoon of work. After the pub closed came dinner, and bed, and another day.

We walked under the curlew's cry. As we passed his workshed he invited us to look inside. He worked at the front end of the tiny structure, by windows that gave him the bay and St. John's Hill. On the walls were pictures of writers he had cut from newspapers — W. H. Auden, Thomas Hardy, Walt Whitman, Marianne Moore, Edith Sitwell. The floor was a wilderness of papers, books, cigarette packages, magazines, and beer bottles.

Then we walked among the stone cottages of Laugharne, and stopped first at Brown's Hotel, a pub kept by Mrs. Ivy Williams, who was immediately introduced to "my American friends, Kirby and Don." Conversation was slow. Men and women dropped in and paused to chat. We drank our pints. To his second bitter, Dylan added a small whiskey. After an hour, we moved to Laugharne's other pub, the Cross House, where Dylan found friends already gathered and made more introductions. The circle of cronies planned a pub crawl through the Welsh countryside, Dylan not ringleader but co-conspirator. The puzzle of the night was whom to recruit as driver, whom to count on for sobriety. A platoon of names produced nobody reliable. Conversation was otherwise general, the American strangers included. I drank my pint slowly. Caitlin joined us carrying a can of milk, on the theory that whiskey mixed with milk would cure her cold. She was as easy as Dylan in this company. After another hour we went back to Brown's Hotel, which had filled, the patrons different and the same. Before closing time, we paid one more visit to the Cross House, and Dylan and I filled our pockets with bottles of beer for the return to the Boat House.

Caitlin's risotto was thick with onions and tomatoes. Dylan ate four enormous helpings. Now we talked about poetry again, especially such matters as the fees paid by magazines. I remember Caitlin telling Kirby how she relied on Dylan to keep her warm at night; he was like a bloody gas fire, she said. Then she went off to bed, tired, and Kirby followed her, Caitlin making

Dylan promise to come upstairs soon, or she would freeze to death. That night they would sleep on a sofa, giving us their bed; if we argued with them, it was without passion: We were twice their size.

Dylan opened the bottles we had brought back from the pub, and we sat at the table talking. Feeling tender and grateful, I told him that he was a great poet. I meant it, and I had been saving it to tell him. He shook his head; he said that he was not: At best he was a minor poet. There were three good poems, he said; the rest was trash. He was not being flippant; he was melancholy. He forgave me for being stupid — he expected no more — but he would not agree with my stupidity. I asked him which three. He told me "Poem in October," "Poem on His Birthday," and "This Bread I Break." I didn't remember the last one. "Oh," he said, "it's an early, Hardy-ish piece of mine."

Unwilling to hear him disparage himself, I tried to argue with him about his poems; I suppose my own self-esteem was under attack. I told him that his villanelle, "Do Not Go Gentle," was a favorite of mine. He shook his head again. "Why don't you like it?" I said.

"Because I didn't write it," he said.

When he said it, I understood him. "You mean Yeats," I said. I remembered Robert Frost asking, "Who wrote this poem?" at Bread Loaf. Dylan nodded his head: The language came from Yeats, he said. I told him I liked the newest poem of his I had seen, "Lament." He said that it began all right but ended badly; he had become bored, he said, and hurried the end. Then I saw: He disparaged his work in the service of standards that demanded great poetry or nothing. This was the boy who would show Keats his heels. When I argued he took none of my comfort. When I put forward the notion that writing with his intensity must be painful, he waved the idea away. Writing poetry was easy, he said; not exactly *easy* — it was slow — but the poetry was always there, always available. Poetry was a dark river flowing down there somewhere; he could send the bucket down anytime he wanted, and come up with poetry. Two lines a day. But anyway — he shrugged the subject away — he wouldn't write poetry much, the rest of his life.

I asked why.

There was more money in prose.

All night at the pubs, and in our walking back and forth, Dylan had talked about money. He didn't want to do another American tour, he said, and Caitlin surely didn't want him to, but he needed the money. He didn't want to go up to London this week, to read for a BBC schools program — he wanted to work on his play instead — but he needed the money. And when he talked about writing prose for money, it is melancholy to realize that he was talking about earning fifty dollars for a short story instead of twenty-five dollars for a poem. He could have done as well ferrying people across Carmarthen Bay. In a few minutes several complacent securities, fixed in my head like stars in the old astrology, crashed forever. Even if, when you grew up, you turned out to be Dylan Thomas, life could be neither simple nor easy nor happy.

Then I heard a voice bellowing "Dylan!" — Caitlin's fierce voice — "For *Christ's* sake come up here!" He finished what he was saying. "Dylan! Dylan!" He stood and emptied his bottle and climbed the stairs to sleep beside his cold wife.

When we walked down to the kitchen the next morning, Caitlin was making porridge. Her daughter Aeronwy, nine years old, was asking Caitlin to comb her hair. Three-year-old Colm wandered about underfoot, a small Dylan with piled golden curls, rumpled and angelic with an expression at once innocent and mad — like the romantic Dylan painted by Augustus John. The real Dylan remained upstairs. I made conversation to which Caitlin grunted replies. Looking at the two children present, I thought to ask about the absent one. Stupidly, I asked if Llewelyn liked poetry. "No," said Caitlin, with scorn that was not directed toward her son. "Not at all." What *does* he like? I asked, stuck in a conversational cul-de-sac that I had created. "Nothing," said Caitlin. "Nothing at all. Nothing for him to do except be a fairy." Even as I heard her speak, I knew that her sentence had nothing to do with Llewelyn or the Public School Problem; it had to do with my fatuousness and Caitlin's universal anger.

She was still combing Aeronwy's hair, and turning to stir the porridge one-handed, when Dylan's voice — mellifluous as ever — called downstairs, "Caitlin, where is my tie?"

"I don't know, Dylan," she called back.

After thirty seconds' pause — Colm was dragging on Caitlin's skirt — Dylan's voice called with a greater urgency, "Caitlin, *where is my tie?*"

She shouted back instantly, "Dylan, I cannot help you now."

He repeated his question a third time in his lowest register: "CAITLIN, WHERE IS MY TIE?"

She was as quick, shrieking, "Dylan, I *cannot* help you now. I'm making breakfast and combing Aeron's hair! Find it yourself!"

After ten seconds, the great instrument upstairs pumped out a sentence that filled the pink-washed Boat House with its somber melody: "Fuck you, then, you cruel bitch!" The commas around "then" were visible, printed on the shuddering air; in the word "cruel," Dylan rolled the *r* and prolonged the *l*. It was beautiful. Kirby and I tried to look as if we had not noticed. Caitlin, Aeronwy, and Colm hadn't.

SHERRY AT OXFORD

We started for Oxford at nine-thirty, which was a good thing, because the reading was at half past eight that night. We stopped in Laugharne while Dylan, ever the dutiful son, said goodbye to his mother and father. We stopped for petrol, and people at the pumps were making noises I could not decode; Dylan confirmed that it was Welsh, and that he couldn't understand a word. For the first hour we drove steadily, but at ten-thirty the pubs opened, and during the next four hours I suppose we spent about forty-five minutes driving. At one pub Dylan challenged me to a game of darts; he let me *almost* win, then swept me off the board with his delicate, practiced wrist. In another pub we played shove ha'penny: same thing. The publicans greeted Dylan fondly for the first hour or two while we drank within pub-crawling distance of Laugharne; reminiscence flowed like Bass. At noon Dylan led us to a shiny pub in a city we drove through — I can't remember the city — and we ate sausages and Scotch eggs and potato salad with half-raw potatoes.

At two-thirty we were able to drive again. Most of the afternoon in the car we improvised on the American game that awards points for hitting pedestrians, high scores for degree of difficulty — like zapping a pole-vaulter carrying his pole — or degree of cruelty. Dylan had never before encountered this *jeu*. He loved to develop jokes, carrying them on for hours. His ultimate invention he scored for twenty points, as I remember; it was "a crippled nine-year-old blind orphan nun leading a three-legged tom kitten on a string." After a moment of silence he added, "Three more points if she's pregnant."

It was a near thing, getting to Oxford. At about four-thirty, Dylan led us out of our way to park beside a closed pub where he knew the landlord *well* and was *certain* that the doors would open for us. It never occurred to me to argue with Dylan or to disobey him; he gave no orders, but his charm was so engaging, his apparent friendship so overwhelming, that you did what he asked. We knocked and knocked. Fortunately the landlord never came to the door.

We arrived in Oxford at six-fifteen and drove directly to New College, where the sherry party began at six. When Dylan heard where we were taking him, he told us that he hated sherry, and hated sherry parties worse than sherry. Was there a pub we could go to? There was a tiny local near New College called The Turf, which you could find only by assiduous search. We drank beer again, in the minuscule public bar where a coal fire burned in October. Meanwhile, back at the sherry party, forty-seven major Oxford poets were convinced that we would never arrive. The three of us showed up precisely at seven, time to go to Oxford's Café de Paris for supper. The Café de Paris — onomastic fraud — was a chips-with-everything 1951-English greasy spoon.

Afterwards, Dylan and I mounted steps to the small stage of the Rhodes House auditorium, and Dylan walked past me to sit down as I assumed the podium for my nervous introduction. The hall was packed with students who had bought memberships at three-and-six to hear the fabled Welshman. (Dylan put our finances in order for the term; we acquired a fortune to invest in South African sherry for our pre-reading parties.) As I prepared to open my mouth with the unnecessary information that our reader was Dylan Thomas, I heard a buzz and a titter from the audience, the kind of thing that convinces a nervous OUPS president that his fly is open. Afterwards I learned the provenance of the whisper. My ancestry is partly Welsh; my hair was curly, my cheeks ruddy, my belly protrusive, and my chin recessive. Apparently we made amusing bookends, although I rose a head higher than Dylan. "Little Dylan and big Dylan," people were saying.

After his superb reading, we took Dylan back to our flat on Banbury Road and brought along half a dozen Oxford poets. I had laid in a supply of beer, and Dylan sat in a corner chair drinking Tolly and talking quietly. He took a fancy to one young woman, but he did not give her the *Advocate* treatment; she was flattered more than she was embarrassed, and his fancy though passing was genuine enough. When people made motions as if to leave, Dylan felt called upon to provide a curtain. From his chair in the corner he told an anecdote that (it was clear) he made up as he went along. He spoke slowly, mimicking, telling about a keeper in the London Zoo who fell in love with a warthog. I'm not sure that Dylan knew what a warthog looked like, but he knew warts and he knew hogs and warthog was good enough for him. The keeper Dylan invented — he

knew him from a pub, he said, when he lived near the zoo —
had a wife but preferred the warthog and grumbled in bed at
night at his bad luck in sleeping arrangements. Then the
warthog took sick, and Dylan made stories out of the keeper's
anxiety, his increasing resentment of his healthy wife, and his
devices for curing the ailing beast. At the end of the story the
keeper bought a large fish and artfully rotted it in his warm
kitchen at home until it reached a level of putrefaction that
revived and restored the exhilarated warthog of the London
Zoo.

Oxford poets took off on their bicycles, and Dylan and I
drank the last bottle of Tollemach Ale. I was complaining about
some Sunday-paper critic who used phrases like "death-wish."
Out of brutal innocence I added, "What a dumb idea anyway.
Who wants to die?"

Dylan looked up at me. "Oh, I do," he said.

"Why?" I said. I thought of what I had heard in Laugharne
the night before.

"Just for the change," he said.

In the morning he looked rested, bright-cheeked, with an
orange-red shirt and a blue bow tie with white polka dots. He
wore gloves as usual like Mickey Mouse, or like Michael Jackson only two-handed; he wore a tweed jacket with no topcoat
although the day was chilly. We set off after breakfast for the
depot, arrived early, and drank horrid British Railways coffee.
Then he touched me for two pounds and went off to London —
to the BBC, the Mandrake, somebody's bed, Caitlin's rescue, a
five-day hangover, and death in a year's time.

PUBLIC SUICIDE

In a year's time I was living in California. The one connection
between Oxford and Stanford should have been Dylan Thomas,
who planned to fly west for poetry readings after doing *Under*

Milk Wood in New York. Then one noon Richard Wilbur's postcard told us that Dylan lay dying in New York. The afternoon paper reported his death. Little as we knew him, like many casual acquaintances we were fond of him; he had been kind and funny — and he had written beautiful poems. Appalled, we lived with private grief. But all year we met the public grief; gradually public grieving, which was mythic and impersonal, took private grief away. At Stanford that year, and in San Francisco, I met people who talked in familiar terms of Dye-lan and Kate-lin,* and told outrageous stories. A graduate student from Berkeley, who visited Stanford, made much of the fact that she had "had an affair" with Dylan when he had visited her college two years earlier. When she had written Dylan in Wales, Caitlin wrote wrathfully back; she showed people Caitlin's letter.

Everywhere were stories, the Merry Tales of Master Dylan: how drunk Dylan grabbed matronly breasts; how drunk Dylan, in charge of infant Llewelyn, mislaid him in the long grass in his portable crib, where he slept the night through; how drunk Dylan, at an *Advocate* party in 1950, rode a Radcliffe girl to the floor and copulated in public. Which was a lie. The Merry Tales was a book of lies — some of them Dylan's lies — which began in Wales, moved to London, came to America with his readings, increased with his popularity before his death, and multiplied after his death, growing like a corpse's hair in the grave. The anecdotes accounted for much of Dylan's popularity. Of course many people admired his readings, and some people admired his poems, but the Merry Tales made him notorious and sold his *Collected Poems*. In November of 1953 there was only one more thing he could have done to increase his popularity, and he did it. Celebrities, asked to name their favorite poet, spoke of a dead Welshman they had never read. Producers commissioned a crude, exploitative play called *Dylan*. *Under Milk Wood*, written for BBC radio and a few pounds, played to

---

* Because of the folksinger, people now pronounce Dylan as Dillon, but Kate-lin remains among us. Dylan's Caitlin pronounced it Cat-lin, an Irish form of Kathleen.

standing-room crowds in New York. In Hibbing, Minnesota, Bob Zimmerman rejected his last name for the name of a dead poet martyred for his art. Kenneth Rexroth — sometimes a great poet, sometimes foolish — wrote an elegy accusing "you" of killing Dylan Thomas. "You killed him! You killed him. / In your God damned Brooks Brothers suit, / You son of a bitch." Everywhere, people told us what he died for and who killed him, politicizing a dead drunk.

Because the "dead" derived from the "drunk," Dylan's death was a slow, twenty-four-year suicide. When you persist in anything likely to kill you, you are on your way to being a suicide — drugs and cigarettes and drink as much as crazy driving. Suicide always has camp followers, but there are moments in history when it acquires general chic. Goethe's *Sorrows of Young Werther* made suicide fashionable in Europe for a decade. More recently, in England and America, literary suicide has sponsored a popular program. After Dylan's death Sylvia Plath's suicide created a female Young Werther. Anne Sexton's suicide a decade after Plath's was as predictable as Halley's Comet, but not so rare. When A. Alvarez attempted suicide and failed, he wrote a popular book about it; he called his book *The Savage God*.

The suicides of the two women were different enough: Sexton's suicide was public, Plath's private — though Plath had imagined a public for it. I suggest that there is something called public suicide, whether the coroner's report indicates self-murder or not; Dylan Thomas, like Jack Kerouac and Brendan Behan, was a public suicide in his alcoholism. John Berryman and Ernest Hemingway were public suicides in their drinking, who accomplished the coup de grace by more violent means.

Sylvia Plath's favorite poet for a time in college was Dylan Thomas. She wrote poems that recounted her early suicide attempt, and threatened another. "Like the cat," she wrote with melancholy inaccuracy, "I have nine times to die." Perhaps that assertion is public enough, but she did not experience in her lifetime fans who stood below the building where she perched on a ledge and cheered her on to jump. She only imagined that a crowd watched her performance of death and resurrection:

> What a million filaments.
> The peanut-crunching crowd
> Shoves in to see
>
> Them unwrap me hand and foot —
> The big striptease.
> Gentlemen, ladies,
>
> These are my hands,
> My knees
> . . .
> Dying
> Is an art, like everything else.
> I do it exceptionally well.

Her irony, and the bitterness of her sarcasm at her own expense, amount to self-criticism; they are efforts she directed at herself to dissuade the self-destructive impulse. But many posthumous admirers show no such restraint; they applaud her suicide, find her a martyr to male chauvinism, romanticize her murder of the poet she was — and of the greater poet she might have become. We mustn't deny the suffering, horrible and vivid in her last poems, which she snuffed out with gas from the oven, but we must abhor the glorification of her death. Despite *The Savage God*, suicide is neither primitive nor divine.

Anne Sexton's flirtation with death was public and chronic, encouraged by poetry-groupies and death-groupies across the country. Her booking agent once guaranteed a lecture committee that Sexton would weep on the platform. Barkers at the sideshow of literature, consumers of suffering — teachers and students, would-be poets, critics, morbid observers — applauded her tears and goaded her to surpass herself, to call her own bluff. Death collectors, they too found in themselves an urge to destroy themselves, but they muted it; they evaded or avoided confrontation with their own darkness by encouraging Sexton to greater and greater confrontation with her own. The peanut-crunching fans paid Anne Sexton a lecture fee to wail their miseries for them.

Denise Levertov refuses the striptease that killed Sexton and Plath. After Sexton's suicide, Levertov wrote:

> My own sadness at the death of a fellow poet is compounded by the sense of how likely it is that Anne Sexton's tragedy will not be without influence in the tragedies of other lives.
>
> She herself was, obviously, too intensely troubled to be fully aware of her influence or to take on its responsibility. Therefore it seems to me that we who are alive must make clear, as she could not, the distinction between creativity and self-destruction. The tendency to confuse the two has claimed too many victims. . . .
>
> Innumerable young poets have drunk themselves into stupidity and cirrhosis because they admired John Berryman or Dylan Thomas . . .

In Lewis Hyde's analysis of alcoholism in Berryman's poetry, he writes about a *Life* article that glorified Berryman's drunkenness:

> . . . there are the typical photographs of the poet with the wind in his beard and a glass in his hand. . . . Like Hemingway, they got him to play the fool and the salesman the last ten years of his life.
>
> I am not saying that the critics could have cured Berryman of his disease. But . . . in the future it would be nice if it were a little harder for the poet to come to town drunk and have everyone think that it's great fun.

Let the final sentence be engraved over the desks of lecture agents, program chairmen, and poets. The poet who survives is the poet to celebrate; the human being who confronts darkness and defeats it is the one to admire. For all his vanity, Robert

Frost is admirable: He looked into his desert places, confronted his desire to enter the oblivion of the snowy woods, and drove on.

TWENTY-FOUR YEARS

The year Dylan died, I studied microfilm of his worksheets for "Ballad of the Long-Legged Bait." It was clear that he wrote the way he said he wrote, scratching out hundreds of alternatives until he got his line right, then adding it whole and finished to the ongoing draft of the poem. When he told me he wrote this way, I was astonished; it seemed to imply that his mind commanded the poem before the poem started. I could not write that way. As with many poets, a poem starts vague in my mind, clarified only by pen on paper, by revision and rearrangement draft after whole draft. As I pondered his worksheets and reread his other poems, I understood gradually how I was mistaken. No more than I did Dylan work out a notion of the poem in advance. He was not writing *poems,* he was writing *poetry.* He started with a general scene or idea that supplied minimal coherence — rural place or pantheistic vision — and then improvised his poem as he improvised an American movie or a joke about a warthog, only more slowly and more grandly. Out of the sounds of words, out of amusement, out of love for spectacle and bombast, out of *talent,* he made up his poems — two lines a day.

Dylan was the word-maddest of word-mad young poets. All poets start from love of words, and of wordplay. Then they learn to love poetry as well, or the Muse herself, and make poems from this love of poetry — hoping to add new stars to the heavens. But the great poets as they turn older look past the Muse — who is objectified taste, composed of all great poems of the past — to pursue vision, to discover motions of spirit and of human consciousness, which it is art's task to enlarge. Sometimes a poet developed past the love of words will lose poetry altogether, will disavow language in favor of vision, and write endless boring sonnets like Wordsworth's. Often the best poems happen when lines cross; when poets write in pursuit of the spirit while their words still roar with years of obsession and love. The luckiest poet is like Yeats; from the time he could say that he sought "an image not a book," he kept words and vision together.

Poetry, Dylan said, was a dark river flowing inside him, to which he could lower the bucket daily. The river had beautiful words in it, but free of the river their structure remained watery. Of the three poems he was willing to acknowledge, that night at the Boat House, the earliest is most a whole single poem, written like so many early Thomas poems with repetitive syntax in a riddling diction.

> This bread I break was once the oat,
> This wine upon a foreign tree
> Plunged in its fruit;
> Man in the day or wind at night
> Laid the crops low, broke the grape's joy.
>
> Once in this wind the summer blood
> Knocked in the flesh that decked the vine,
> Once in this bread
> The oat was merry in the wind;
> Man broke the sun, pulled the wind down.
>
> This flesh you break, this blood you let
> Make desolation in the vein,
> Were oat and grape
> Born of the sensual root and sap;
> My wine you drink, my bread you snap.

"An early Hardy-ish piece," he called it. "This Bread I Break" especially resembles a Thomas Hardy poem called "Transformations":

> Portion of this yew
> Is a man my grandsire knew,

Bosomed here at its foot:
This branch may be his wife,
A ruddy human life
Now turned to a green shoot.

These grasses must be made
Of her who often prayed,
Last century, for repose;
And the fair girl long ago
Whom I often tried to know
May be entering this rose.

So, they are not underground,
But as nerves and veins abound
In the growths of upper air,
And they feel the sun and rain,
And the energy again
That made them what they were!

The Hardy is less dazzling but I think it is a better poem. There is nothing in Dylan's poem so touching as "May be entering this rose," where human particles walk as if through the door of a house or between the portals of a church. The voice of an old man speaks in Hardy's poem; it is located, and we absorb the old man's feeling about impending death and molecular survival; his emotions illuminate something beyond the poem or its words. In Dylan's handsome stanzas, the words watch themselves in the mirror and the words love what they see.

"Poem in October" and "Poem on His Birthday" are not poems but poetry, each of them a long and gorgeous rendition of weather and landscape, bird and water. They are determinedly joyful and optimistic, as only a doomed man would make them. But

Pale rain over the dwindling harbour
And over the sea wet church the size of a snail
With its horns through mist and the castle

from "Poem in October" could replace

> I hear the bouncing hills
> Grow larked and greener at berry brown
> Fall and the dew larks sing

from "Poem on His Birthday" — and except for the form and shape and a change in the weather, no one would be wiser. Throughout the *Collected Poems,* we find poems with interchangeable lines. Form and shape and honey-in-the-mouth make the poems small monuments of English literature. They are wonderful, but they are small exactly because form and shape do not alone make great poems. When Thomas refuses to mourn the death by fire of the child in London, we do not experience the child's death; we hear noble words arranged by rumors of pantheism. When we cut through the glorious vegetation of "Fern Hill," we see that the soil and rock underneath are commonplace: It is pleasant for a city child to come to the country on a summer vacation; but then we grow up.

Dylan never put his poetry in service to anything but poetry. He served the Muse; he wrote pure poetry. But what is pure poetry *pure* of? It is pure of thought and pure of feeling, pure of vision; its largest emotion is love for itself.

The alcoholic, Lewis Hyde says, cannot go outside himself, lacks compassion and empathy, loses spirit by drowning under spirits. But why does a man choose this death? Maybe his culture applauded his dying, but he undertook to die before his culture knew he existed. Why in particular was it necessary or inevitable for Dylan Thomas to take on himself the suffering and death of alcoholism? Not that drinking is suffering in itself; drink begins as gregarious pleasure, even euphoria, and it relieves immediate pain. At Brown's Hotel and the Cross House in Laugharne, four hours at night after four hours of writing, Dylan's friendly pleasure was only the smallest death. But he was not a stupid man, and he knew that present pleasure created future pain; nothing in Dylan found power to overcome the craving for alcohol and death. Laugharne pubs led to London, New York, the *Advocate,* and the ten thousand bars — hangovers, vomiting, blackouts, the horrible visions of delirium tremens.

The craving was for death, and not only "for the change." It has been suggested that Dylan chose his suffering as punishment for the sin of writing poems. Such a notion sounds as romantic as suicide worship, but the notion that poetry is sinful has classic sources. Plato found poets heretics to the church of reason. Ideas of poetic sinfulness take outward form in stereotypes that associate poetry with forbidden sexuality, with absinthe and orgies, with romantic alienation. Dylan's behavior (at the *Advocate* party, for instance) danced to the tune of these stereotypes; beneath them, maybe we find the provenance of self-destruction. To make poems is to add metaphors of the forbidden child to ideas of the rational adult, making a third thing that enlarges human consciousness. Plato called the irrational insane and prohibited poets from his Republic. To make poems is to violate Platonic standards of civilization; because poets grow up in civilization, subject to its prohibitions, a Plato inside them censors the internal Orpheus or Dionysus.

Thomas was brought up by his mother in a Welsh church of sin and the Devil. When he became a poet he joined the Devil's party, and to poetry added other wickednesses available to a young man of his day: He smoked cigarettes, he talked lewdly about women, and he drank. Throughout his life Dylan praised wickedness and laughed at piety or respectability — and throughout his life he was frightened of Satan, of vampires, of black magic and goblins. When Dylan saw Aleister Crowley in London — Satanist black magician who called himself the Great Beast — Dylan was terrified and would not remain in the same room. Dylan knew that he was damned. He was damned because he agreed to be damned, early in life, as if he had sold his soul to the Devil.

Through much of his life, he spoke of his days as numbered, finite, his early death already determined. In London during his last year he spoke of his death as imminent. In his last week in New York he told people around him that he would soon die. He told John Brinnin that in his alcoholic visions he had already seen the gates of Hell. That October he was thirty-nine, and he had been a poet for twenty-four years. At fifteen he wrote lines and fragments of poetry as brilliant as he would ever write. Precocious, he progressed rapidly and wrote prolifically. *Eighteen Poems* appeared when he was twenty, and by that age he had drafted at least half the work in his *Collected Poems*. From then on, the dying took over. In the last wretched decade of his life, he made about a poem a year. In the despair that overtook him, he no longer even read poetry unless it was pushed on him; he had given up on poetry in his anguish, and the poems that remained to him were poems he had loved when he was young.

He lived twenty-four years after he began to be a poet; the Devil is known to sell his services for various terms, and one of the traditional figures in a Satanic contract is twenty-four years. For his twenty-fourth birthday, Dylan wrote the poem:

Twenty-four years remind the tears of my eyes.
(Bury the dead for fear that they walk to the grave in labour.)
In the groin of the natural doorway I crouched like a tailor
Sewing a shroud for a journey
By the light of the meat-eating sun.
Dressed to die, the sensual strut begun,
With my red veins full of money,
In the final direction of the elementary town
I advance for as long as forever is.

In his last weeks, when he was not raving or vomiting, he strove to revise *Under Milk Wood*. He wrote near the edge of oblivion that would close his living eyes. In old stories about the Devil, he gives us what we ask for and it is our ruin. Dylan wanted poetry, and he got it, but he asked for nothing more.

Notes on
T. S. Eliot

❧

DATED LETTERS

"Mr. Hall," began the letter, which I received as a junior in college, "I wish that you would date your letters." It was my first communication from T. S. Eliot, and I have dated every letter, note, and postcard I have written since. It is hard to credit the authority Eliot's name commanded in 1949, much less his signature. Had his words begun, "Mr. Hall, I wish you to commit arson upon the person of an elderly gentleman residing in your vicinity," I would have set out to burn down a nearby old man. No one since has embodied, or seemed to embody, such authority — not Robert Lowell, not Allen Ginsberg, not Elizabeth Bishop, not Robert Penn Warren. Perhaps none of them would wish the power that Eliot possessed or seemed to possess. It doesn't matter; no one can assume the center of that stage as Eliot did: There is no longer such a stage.

In retrospect I suspect that the appearance of authority was Eliot's joke played on pomposity: on literary journalists in England, on professors in the United States. Doubtless when he was young and ambitious his authoritative manner intimidated some London literary sorts; doubtless the same manner served as carapace for the reticent foreigner. But Eliot's deadpan hidden (Old Possum) humor smiled at the center of his behavior. Although he was eminently serious, and serious about his role as man of letters, for him the role's solemnity carried its comedy. This comedy was lost on almost everyone; it was essential to the comedy that it be lost.

The Harvard Advocate is the Harvard literary magazine. Poets the *Advocate* published as undergraduates include T. S. Eliot, Wallace Stevens, and E. E. Cummings. In my day — class of '51 — The *Advocate* published Adrienne Rich, Robert Bly, Kenneth Koch, Frank O'Hara, L. E. Sissman, and John Ashbery. Several of us were editors.

Back in 1938, the *Advocate* printed a special T. S. Eliot issue, gathering essays and memoirs about the *Advocate*'s most famous alumnus and reprinting his undergraduate poems. The issue was successful, and doubtless pulled the magazine out of one of its financial crises. Ten years later, in the fall of 1948, we trembled on the perennial lip of crisis, and again seemed ready to succumb. Once or twice a week, all year, we received letters from people wanting to buy a copy of the 1938 Eliot issue, which had gone out of print ten years past. From time to time, we would entertain the idea of another Eliot issue, to raise money. The suggestion went no further, until one night, as we gathered to paste up the magazine, we discovered that we were six pages short. This fecklessness was not without precedent. The people who ran the magazine were literary types, far beyond efficiency or other narrow concerns. We worked hard, but we worked hard to keep standards high, which is to say that we worked hard at rejecting things. When there was an argument, the negative could be counted on to win.

The *Advocate* of Eliot's day, in his memory, was as nasty as the *Advocate* of mine. "Everyone threw his poems into a basket," he remembered later in life, "and then they held a round robin to see who could say the most sarcastic things about the other man's work." In between, one American poet had bad luck with the *Advocate*. When Robert Lowell was a freshman at Harvard, he tried out for the editorial board, which twice a year held competitions for new members. As he remembered it, the *Advocate* encouraged him to show up and tack the carpet (we accomplished our redecorating by means of these competitions; I painted woodwork in February of 1948) and then told him not to bother to return. Lowell transferred to Kenyon College, studied with John Crowe Ransom, roomed with Peter Taylor, befriended Randall Jarrell, and with *Lord Weary's Castle* in 1946 turned out to be the best of the young poets — a sequence of events not lost on subsequent *Advocate* editors.

We discovered in October or November of 1948 that negative judgment had cooperated with bad arithmetic to leave us with six blank pages. The issue was scheduled, and our printer wanted no more antic chaos. If we delayed the issue we would lose sales, which were already small. For a while we considered leaving the pages blank, as testimonial to high standards. This proposal had its charm, but perhaps would not have pleased the trustees, brokers, and lawyers and other hard-headed sorts to whom we would soon perforce appeal. The literary editor of the moment — he carried the title "Pegasus" — came up with a suggestion that carried the day: We should reprint Eliot's poems, and thus make sure that we sold the issue out; we could even pay off a few debts. It seemed like a good idea. Because these were the days before Xerox, we had to type the poems out, to deliver copy to the printer in the morning. No one could find the old Eliot issue, but we kept bound volumes from the first decade of the century, where Eliot's fragile young poems lay in columns.

The refrigerator was full of beer that night. Pegasus picked two of the drunker editors to type up Eliot's poems while the rest of us finished pasting galleys. We discovered that a blank page remained, even after we reprinted Eliot's poems. Someone suggested that we dedicate the issue to Mr. Eliot himself, in honor of his sixtieth birthday, which had been the subject of celebrations and publications earlier in the year. The typists delivered the copy, we fabricated a dedicatory note for a blank page at the start, and next morning delivered a sloppy bundle to the printer. When we picked up a thousand copies a week or two later, we were initially pleased; the Eliot Supplement looked almost deliberate. Then we read over the dedication to Eliot on the first page. Our printer, though a pleasant and tolerant man, had the drawback of Emersonian self-reliance. When he read in our typescript that we were dedicating the issue to T. S. Eliot in honor of his sixtieth birthday, he decided that we had made a simple error in typing. After all, no Harvard undergraduate was likely to be sixty years old; we discovered that we were congratulating T. S. Eliot on turning sixteen.

The issue sold out quickly. Within weeks, we began to receive requests from academics and librarians eager to acquire T. S. Eliot's undergraduate poems. Soon we had collected a hundred letters, many of them including checks. One of us knew a pamphlet printer who volunteered to print up a thousand copies of the Eliot poems as a booklet which we could sell at a profit. It seemed sound business. Within a week or two we found ourselves wallowing in boxes of T. S. Eliot's juvenilia.

None of us at any point considered consulting Mr. Eliot. None of us, I think, had read over the pages that we published. This was not so strange as it may seem. Eliot was so dominant a figure, so central to everyone concerned with modern literature, that we had read and studied his undergraduate poems long before. Doubtless all of us on the *Advocate* read Eliot's poems in our first week as editors, reading them *in the original* from the antique bound volumes shelved against a wall. Our teachers had read them in the old Eliot issue, and for years had handed them around like John Donne in manuscript. If we had bothered to look at the new issue, we would have discovered our misspellings, omitted words, transposed stanzas, and general thorough incompetence.

Not having noticed it, nor considered Mr. Eliot's rights or feelings, we cheerfully sold the pamphlet for a dollar, distributing it in local bookstores and by mail order. Bags of mail orders arrived at our offices. We cashed checks, paid off outstanding debts, and spent long hours addressing envelopes. I remember the day a polite letter arrived from a librarian at Yale, ordering six copies and enclosing a check for six dollars. Letters came from all over the country, from England, from Germany. We set about editing another issue of the *Advocate,* defending high standards as ever, secure in the annuity supplied by reprinting our earlier editor.

One day my tutor Harry Levin handed me a copy of our Eliot pamphlet and suggested that I take a look at it. It was annotated in pencil, in a small and precise hand that took relentless note of misspellings, omitted words, transposed stanzas, and general thorough incompetence. A prominent artistic Harvard alumnus — I think it was Lincoln Kirstein — had sent Levin the annotated pamphlet with a note suggesting that perhaps the boys ought to be advised about their errors and about the use to which these errors were being put. For Lincoln Kirstein and other artistic alumni received this annotated pamphlet from the Yale University librarian to whom I had mailed six copies a few weeks before. I believe that this fellow concerned himself with acquiring manuscripts.

One of the alumni gifted with our botched and pirated pamphlet was Mr. Eliot himself. His letter dropped down on us like a wolf on the fold. Among other styles, Mr. Eliot had mastered the invective of English wrath; he was able to express rage with a steely, syntactic magnificence that surpassed our limited American experience. We were withered by the letter, as fig trees are withered by messiahs; therefore, we admired the letter greatly, treasured it — someone stole it, I think — and we tucked the crippled pamphlets away in a closet, whence they disappeared like confiscated wine from Italian government warehouses, as each editor departed with seven or ten souvenirs.

Eliot's anger was entirely appropriate. We had perpetrated enormities: reprinting poems without asking permission, not considering his rights or privileges, and in addition botching every poem we stole. But Eliot threatened no lawsuits, no vengeance. With something as amorphous and changeable as a college magazine, mind you, it is difficult to take action or to seek revenge: By the time you discover the committed outrage, the editors responsible have left college. When Eliot's letter arrived at our building, our old Pegasus was living in an eight-dollar-a-week room in Manhattan, writing Shakespearean sonnets and working as a scab housepainter. I was the new Pegasus, and to me it fell to answer Mr. Eliot's letter: to explain, apologize, and pass the buck.

As it happened, I needed also to bring up another, related subject. I would have been writing Mr. Eliot anyway, if a Yale librarian had not supplied him with reason for writing first. A publisher had asked me to edit an anthology from the bound volumes of the *Advocate*, collecting the juvenilia of famous men. Besides Stevens, Cummings, and Eliot, Harvard undergraduates who had appeared in our pages included Theodore Roosevelt, Franklin Roosevelt, Leonard Bernstein, John Reed, Malcolm Cowley, John Dos Passos, Norman Mailer, Howard Nemerov, Conrad Aiken, Robert Benchley, Van Wyck Brooks, John Wheelock, Edwin Arlington Robinson, and Arthur Schlesinger, Jr. One name in particular, the publisher assumed, would sell more copies than the rest of the names put together. If we did not have permission to include Eliot's poems, we could pack it in; there would be no book, there would be no contract, without Eliot's poems.

When Eliot's missive arrived at the *Advocate*, I needed to answer him with a letter in two parts. Part one apologized for piracy and dismemberment of his poems. Part two asked permission to reprint the same poems in *The Harvard Advocate Anthology*. In effect, I asked him to support the magazine that had just stolen and disfigured his work. Part one, written with some disingenuousness, expressed melancholic outrage over the activities of earlier editors. Part two put it to him: As the new Pegasus, I had been invited to edit . . . et cetera; in order for the anthology to succeed, we needed . . . et cetera; the magazine was in financial distress . . . et cetera. I wrote in a style as supple as President Harding's; I probably signed myself with a middle initial; I did not date the letter.

Eliot's answer was gentle, with only a touch of asperity. I cannot find the letter, but I believe that I remember what he said: He gave us permission to reprint his poems; he moderated his earlier justifiable anger, supposing that an undergraduate magazine existed as a place where young editors learned by making mistakes. In giving permission to reprint his poems, he made one shrewd reservation: We were to print any of his undergraduate poems that we wished, except that we were to omit one of them — not one poem in particular, *any* of them. He did not say, but we understood: At some future time, Eliot could himself reprint his undergraduate poems, claiming correctly that these poems were collected together in accurate and authorized versions for the first time. *Poems Written in Early Youth* (1967) refers to an earlier pamphlet issued "without permission, and with many misprints."

In months to come, Eliot and I corresponded a little. I sent him proofs for *The Harvard Advocate Anthology*, so that he might assure himself of accuracy. The book was published in December 1950, just after I met him for the first time. I took him to an *Advocate* party that fall, on one of his visits to Cambridge. I borrowed a car to pick him up, though our building was no farther than five hundred yards from the guest house where he stayed. I remember little of that party, but I remember picking him up. Two young women sat inconspicuous in the back seat of the convertible, one of them my date, the other a literary person from Bennington engaged to the roommate from whom I borrowed the car. As Mr. Eliot bent to enter the seat beside the driver, I realized that he had not observed the occupants of the back seat. I hastened toward protocol, waving urgently in the direction of the back seat and shouting, "Mr. Eliot, I'd like you to meet . . ." He twisted and jumped, seeing the women, reaching for his hat and rising at the same moment, so that with an abrupt jerk upward he hit his head on the doorframe of the car and knocked his hat off.

We settled down and traveled to the *Advocate,* where a hundred undergraduates and teachers crashed the party to observe the lion, and martini drinkers staggered shoulder to shoulder. When I had delivered Eliot I retired to a corner. From time to time I staggered forth, to bar or bathroom, and on one of these occasions I bumped into Mr. Eliot, sober and preparing to leave. He looked at me with a pleasant smile and said that he understood that I would be attending Oxford next year. Actually, it was only a hope; I had not yet won the fellowship I looked for. I told him that I *might* be attending Oxford next year. Ignoring the conditional, he asked me to look him up when I got to London; perhaps I would drop in on him at Faber and Faber, and perhaps at that time I would let him see some of my poems.

LONG UNDERWEAR

In London in September of 1951 I found a cheap hotel off Upper Shaftsbury Avenue, not far from the British Museum. It was only a few blocks from Russell Square, which was the address of Faber and Faber, and Mr. Eliot's business address. I had found the hotel on a tip from friends, and its proximity was fortuitous. As soon as I had taken the suitcase to my room, my first day at the hotel, I walked out to find Russell Square and number 24. All summer I had carried suitcase and typewriter through Italy and France and Scotland, working from time to time on my old poems, occasionally beginning a new one. I didn't do much work; I felt a little separate from my poems, and typing up a manuscript for Eliot began to bring me back to them. I left the poems, together with a note reminding Mr. Eliot of my identity — dated, the return address highly legible — with a uniformed porter at 24 Russell Square. Less than a week later, a small blue envelope with the Faber imprint turned up on the mail table in the lobby. Mr. Eliot asked the pleasure of my company at three in the afternoon on Thursday, October 4.

He had been inviting young poets to call on him for more than twenty years. The memoirs of English poets tell how each of them, at some point or other, received an invitation to meet Mr. Eliot. As publisher, he kept his eyes open for young writers; as older poet, he was generous and kind; as critic and editor, he made over tea the estimate of young poets that conversation adds to the printed page. When the English poets received their blue envelopes, they knew that Eliot had been reading their poems in the columns of the English weeklies. The letter was perhaps a sign of approval, at least of interest. In my case, I had no such assurance. His invitation was sheer generosity, perhaps coupled with old school feeling toward Harvard and the *Advocate.*

On the appointed day, I walked around Russell Square for an hour or so rehearsing paragraphs of literary banter, until three, and precisely at that hour I presented myself to the uniform in the foyer of Faber and Faber. I was shown to a small waiting room, and almost immediately summoned to the lift that would take me to Mr. Eliot's floor. I must have seemed nervous, because the elevator man (also in uniform) reassured me that Mr. Eliot was an extremely *pleasant* gentleman, and did I *know,* he was actually an *American* gentleman? but really he was like *one of us.* In my terror I must have spoken no more than a monosyllable or I would have revealed my nationality.

Reassured, I was led down a rickety corridor to a small office and to Mr. Eliot. He stood and smiled and shook my hand. The office was neat and compact, manuscript in tidy piles, books. I sat in a chair beside his wooden desk, no room for other chairs. On the wall in front of him, where he sat, hung several photographs; I recognized Virginia Woolf. But I looked little at his photographs of others. I looked at the world's greatest living poet.

Eliot had turned sixty-three only a week before, that autumn of 1951, but looked at least seventy-five. I don't think I noticed this anomaly then, because I did not take seriously the difference between sixty-three and seventy-five. The man who saw himself as an aged eagle when scarcely forty had endured subsequent aging accordingly. His face was pale as baker's bread. He stooped as he sat at his desk, and when he stood he slouched like the witch with the gingerbread house. His head shook slightly, from time to time, almost as if he nodded toward sleep. He smoked, and between inhalations he hacked a dry, deathly smoker's hack. His precise speech was slow to move, as if he stood behind the boulder of each word, pushing it into view. Eliot was cadaverous in 1951.

I wish I could say that when we spoke panic drained from my marrow bones, that I relaxed and enjoyed conversation with the world's greatest living poet. It's not true; I enjoyed my visit as one might enjoy having climbed to the top of Marble Arch, or having walked a tightrope across the Crystal Palace, but afterwards I was exhausted and drained and triumphant, rather than enlightened or charmed — as I might have been had I not insisted on regarding my companion as monument more than as man. But it was I who *acted* like marble. I remember little from the meeting, but I know that I was solemn; I was so aware of the historical significance of this moment — "I shall be telling this ages hence" — that I weighed every word as if my great-grandchildren were listening in, and I feared to let them down by speaking idiomatically, or by seeing the humor in anything.

Mr. Eliot went through my poems. He had written little notes in pencil in the margins and these notes cued him to small remarks: "Good line, there"; "I think you can trim this one down a bit." I don't suppose that Eliot told me anything about my poems that I didn't know. They were, I think, not good enough for him to help me with them.

We talked a good bit about American poetry, as of 1951, a subject about which we both knew something. I praised Theodore Roethke, of whom he said little. I praised the Robert Lowell of *Lord Weary's Castle;* Faber was printing Lowell's first English collection. I praised Richard Wilbur, whom Eliot also admired, and whom he expected Faber to publish (the book came out six years later). Wilbur was someone, Eliot said, whom they had been keeping an eye on. There were others; they had kept an eye on Wallace Stevens, for instance, and now they would publish his selected poems. Eliot's phrasing seemed to suggest that Wallace Stevens was a young or otherwise new poet.

Now Stevens was nine years older than Eliot; *Harmonium*, Stevens's first book, appeared in 1923, one year after "The Waste Land." When I sat in Eliot's office that day, I thought he was showing ignorance about Wallace Stevens, mistaking him for younger than he was. Now I know better. He was not being ignorant; he was being grudging. He had never been quite certain about Stevens, perhaps because Stevens's gorgeousness could seem self-indulgent to Eliot, or the aestheticism provincial. The ignorance that Eliot affected was a mild put-down in the classic English manner. When Churchill pronounced "Marseilles" as "Mar-sales," we heard not mispronunciation but condescension. There was a tone to Eliot's remarks about Stevens that I failed to pick up because I had not studied English manners. If I had picked it up, I might have recalled something Stevens had said about Eliot a year before; now the one remark recalls the other — two aged lions displaying claws for each other, each in characteristic form. When I asked Stevens, on a Saturday, if he could stay over in Cambridge until Monday and attend an *Advocate* party for Eliot, he refused, saying that it would have been nice, really, because he had never met Eliot; but he had to get back to the office. Actually, he went on, he had never read Mr. Eliot much; he was afraid it would influence his work.

My leg was pulled. I believed him. I never considered that there was war on Olympus, or even harsh words. Instead, I allowed myself to consider that the great were weird.

There were reasons enough for breaches between Eliot and Stevens — breaches that Eliot, by planning a Faber edition of Stevens, began in 1951 to close. There is always strain between the people who stay home and the people who go away. Our attention centered so much on American writers who lived abroad in the first third of the twentieth century — Henry James remaining in England and taking citizenship; also in England Pound, Eliot, for a time Robert Frost; Gertrude Stein in Paris, Archibald MacLeish, Malcolm Cowley, and for five years Pound; Hemingway, Fitzgerald, and H.D. all over Europe; Pound working out middle age in Italy's Rapallo — that we ignored the many writers who stayed home. Writers gathered in New Orleans and Chicago, on the West Coast, in Boston, and most copiously around New York. Some figures prominent in New York have become obscure — Mina Loy, Alfred Kreymborg, Waldo Frank, Gorham Munson, Matthew Josephson — but others have entered the pantheon, like Marianne Moore, William Carlos Williams, E. E. Cummings, Hart Crane, and Wallace Stevens. (All of these poets except Stevens visited Europe; none settled there.) A persistent myth about Wallace Stevens, like the notion that Ezra Pound grew up in Idaho, understands that his poetry arose *in vacuo* from an insurance office and a Hartford suburb. To be sure, Stevens lived in Hartford during his later years and worked as vice president at Hartford Accident and Indemnity. But he spent years crucial to his life as a poet in New York, from 1900 to 1916, among the poets of Greenwich Village and other company not associated with the insurance industry. He was thirty-six when he moved to Hartford. In the years before the Great War — the Armory Show took place in 1913 — on into the 1920s, there were picnics at Alfred Kreymborg's in the country, with William Carlos Williams motoring over from Rutherford and poet-hordes descending from Greenwich Village including Marianne Moore with bright red braids piled on her head. There were parties, arguments, affiliations, and disaffections. The friendship (and rivalry) between William Carlos Williams and Wallace Stevens was central to American poetry — like so many friendships: Pound and Eliot; Eliot and Aiken; Pound and Williams and H.D.; Ransom and Tate and Jarrell and Lowell.

William Carlos Williams made his hatred of "The Waste

Land" well known; it set his own work back, he said, by twenty years. Eliot never concealed his distaste for Williams. All the homebodies, I think, resented the exiles, and when the exiles returned — not only Malcolm Cowley but Archibald MacLeish and others — they returned with guilt which turned into reproof toward the writers who remained abroad. The distaste for Henry James, displayed by Americanist critics in the thirties and forties, was evidence of this battle.

But back to 24 Russell Square, October of 1951.

We talked, as he put it, about "our literary generations." We talked a little about England, of which I knew nothing, and of Oxford and Cambridge. We talked prosody, which was my obsession. (At Oxford, I would write a two-hundred-page paper for my B.Litt. degree: "Eighteenth Century Prosodists, with Especial Attention to Edward Bysshe and Joshua Steele.") We talked about poetic drama. I was writing a three-act play in blank verse; Eliot's plays, and his essays about dramatic poetry, had informed my ambition.

Soon it was four o'clock, or nearly, time for Eliot to conclude our interview and take tea with his colleagues. He stood up, slowly enough to give me time to rise before he did, granting me the face of knowing when to leave. When this tall, pale, dark-suited figure struggled successfully to its feet, and I had leapt to mine, we lingered a moment in the doorway while I spluttered ponderous thanks and he nodded smiling to acknowledge them. Then Eliot appeared to search for the right phrase with which to send me off. He looked me in the eye and set off into slow, meandering speech. "Let me see," said T. S. Eliot, "forty years ago I went from Harvard to Oxford. Now you are going from Harvard to Oxford. What advice may I give you?" He paused delicately, shrewdly, while I waited with greed for the words that I would repeat for the rest of my life, the advice from elder to younger setting me on the road of emulation. When he had ticked off the comedian's exact milliseconds of pause, he said, "Have you any long underwear?"

I told him that I had not, and paused to buy some on my

dazzled walk back to the hotel. I suppose it was six months before I started laughing.

LLHUDE SING POSSUM

That year at Oxford I won the Newdigate, broadcast a poem on the BBC, sold poems to the *World Review,* and published two pamphlets with the Fantasy Press. When the *TLS* reviewed the pamphlets, with a generous condescension, Eliot wrote me a congratulatory note on prize and publication. He suggested that I drop by for another visit, on a future trip to London. Thus in the autumn of 1952 I called on him again at Faber and Faber, as I would several times in the future. Now the visits begin to blur into one another, and my memory is less distinct. The second time I was perhaps not quite so overwhelmed, not quite so humorless.

In the spring of 1953 I saw him again, at an evening devoted to Ezra Pound held at the Institute of Contemporary Arts in London. Pound was still under guard, indicted for treason but judged mentally unfit for trial, at St. Elizabeths in Washington. The ICA meeting — a rally supporting the notion that Pound should be set free — was chaired by Eliot and included short talks by Herbert Read and J. Isaacs, and readings of Pound by Peter Russell and me. Peter Russell read Pound because he was a leading English Poundian; I read Pound because I was a poet with an American accent. R. P. Blackmur sat in the front row near Eliot's friend John Hayward. The occasion was invigorating and without issue. Eliot was kindly and passionate, but said nothing exceptional. There was nothing exceptional about the meeting, barring one incident. In the course of his talk, J. Isaacs commended F. R. Leavis. Mildly. Whatever else you thought of Leavis, said Isaacs, you had to give him credit for his praise of "Mauberley." But this faint encomium precipitated a small riot. On the platform we heard shouts of "Shame!" from the back of the hall, then some scuffling and more shouts. Two people were ejected from the premises of the ICA, on Dover Street in the West End. Later we discovered that they were John Davenport — Dylan Thomas's friend — and Graham Greene. It was suggested later that they had overprepared for their visit to the ICA. After the meeting, Peter Russell and I composed a cable for sending to St. Elizabeths: "Ezra is icummen in. Llhude sing Possum."

From 1954 to 1957, I was back at Harvard as a Junior Fellow in the Society of Fellows; Junior Fellows, who may come from any discipline, spend three years doing what they please. The Society consists of ten Senior Fellows — professors largely, from various fields, whose duties include the election of new Junior Fellows — and about twenty-four Junior Fellows, of whom perhaps three quarters are in residence at any time. The Junior Fellows are often impressive. Monday nights, we had dinner together. At my first dinner I sat next to a young man and asked him what he did. "Mathematical linguistics," he said, to my bewilderment; I had met Noam Chomsky.

We started with sherry in the front room of our quarters in Eliot House, a tall brown paneled room with the stiffness of a common room. Then we repaired to the adjacent dining room, where we sat at a long table shaped like a flattened U, and ate good food. Guests were essential to these dinners. It was an unwritten rule that they be eminent. At the age of twenty-five, I once found myself introducing two Nobel laureates to each other. Edmund Wilson turned up twice a year. I spent an evening talking with Vladimir Nabokov when *Lolita* was still unpublished in the United States, restricted to its two-volume green paper Olympia Press edition. Mr. Eliot visited Cambridge once a year, and while he was there he would take dinner with us. Once, someone asked a Junior Fellow if he had sat next to Eliot at dinner the night before.

"I couldn't," said he. "John Hollander was sitting on both sides of him."

It was only coincidence that the stunt was not attributed to me. It must have been the year when I hardly spoke to Eliot, except for a greeting over sherry. One Monday morning — when I knew that Eliot was coming to dinner that night — I came to Harvard Square early, to spend a lazy day wandering among book stores and drinking coffee. I hovered near the Harvard Book Store when I was greeted by the anthologist Oscar Williams, who was visiting Cambridge from New York. I knew him only slightly, and had found him friendly but insinuating. I knew it would be foolish to mention Eliot's presence in town. Someone had told me that Eliot despised Williams for his self-promotion; Eliot made a rule that none of his poems were to be reprinted in paperback anthologies, in order to avoid appearing in books edited by Williams. The anthologies were good ones, as anthologies go, somewhat disfigured by the editor's predilection to print quantities of his own work. (Randall Jarrell once praised Williams's gall in a review, remarking that it was really *something* to call yourself five times the poet Thomas Hardy was.) Williams's anthologies printed photographs or etchings of poets — I think the first to perform that service — and readers became familiar with cameo fringes of great poets' faces, perhaps showing in sequence Emily Dickinson, William Shakespeare, Oscar Williams, Walt Whitman, and John Milton.

This morning Williams suggested coffee, so we sat together at a counter on Massachusetts Avenue and talked poetry. He presented me with a signed copy of his latest paperback, and after half an hour we drifted apart. When I arrived at the Society of Fellows that night, the first person I saw drinking sherry was Oscar Williams. In a book store later in the day he had met an astrophysicist Junior Fellow who, realizing that Williams was a poet and anthologist, felt that it was only polite to invite him to dinner with Eliot. The astrophysicist, however, had never met Eliot and felt uncomfortable. He hurled Oscar Williams in my direction and fled.

Eliot was chatting with Arthur Darby Nock at the table that held the sherry. It became obvious that I must perform an introduction. Eliot turned slightly at my approach, recognized me, smiled pleasantly, and said something like, "Ah, yes. How pleasant to see you again."

I said, "Mr. Eliot, I would like you to meet Oscar Williams" — a barefaced lie.

Eliot put out his hand, smiling, and did a double take. The smile withered, like the speeded-up film of a flower touched by frost. The hand withdrew a little, and then returned to be embraced and pumped by Oscar Williams's hand. The voice — more English, I thought, than I had ever heard it, with an *a* in the last syllable as broad as the Mississippi — laid out a sentence as if mounting a butterfly on a piece of velvet: "Ah, yes," said T. S. Eliot to Oscar Williams, "I recognize you from your photographs."

Eliot's sentence would, I thought, have extracted the backbones from an army of Gaul, but Williams was nothing daunted. With a friendly grin he acknowledged Mr. Eliot's equality. Egalitarian, he said, "Yes, I recognize you from yours, too."

The conversation had extended as far as it could go. But Eliot was prepared for one further move before he returned to Professor Nock, who was standing at the periphery of this circle, benign and uncomprehending. "It is a distressing fact," said Eliot, "of growing older" — I had the momentary sense that he searched for an end to his sentence, a conclusion that would give a spin to his heel as he swiveled away from his new acquaintance — "that one comes to resemble one's photographs." As Williams rushed to agree, Eliot nodded lightly in my direction and turned back to Professor Nock, who resumed a conversation interrupted midsentence.

INTERVIEW WITH TAPE TECHNICIANS

The third year of my fellowship Eliot missed his annual visit; he got married instead.

When I left Cambridge to teach at the University of Michigan,

I quickly found occasion to write him. The Department of English wanted Eliot to read his poems, and I knew that he liked to pay for his annual American visit by doing a poetry reading or two. I wrote him and asked if he would come to Ann Arbor. In the course of the letter, I said that I regretted not seeing him the year before. When his refusal arrived, Eliot made characteristic humor out of his inability to take last year's transatlantic trip. An alteration of domestic arrangements, he told me, necessitated a relocation of his residence — or words to a similar Latinate music.

Looking back over the letters that Eliot wrote me, I see other refusals to read in Ann Arbor. Forty years after the fact, I sense that I made a social error: I never mentioned payment when I asked him to Ann Arbor; I suppose I feared that mention of money might sound vulgar. (It was my vulgarity to fear that I might sound vulgar.) When Eliot refused, always with circumstantial detail and friendly noises, he gave a variety of reasons. Maybe he avoided asking "How much?" because he would have felt awkward to say that the fee was too little. Or maybe my letters, in their mistaken reticence, sounded as if I expected him to read for nothing, like a poet invited to Oxford.

In 1959 we met in New York, and I interviewed him for the *Paris Review*. For some time that magazine had been interviewing novelists, beginning with the first issue's interrogation of E. M. Forster. The *Paris Review* invented the contemporary literary interview, printed in dialogue form, which has become a standard item in literary quarterlies. Running low on major novelists, the magazine in 1959 was ready for poets, and asked me (I was poetry editor) to begin the series by interviewing Eliot. In the spring, Eliot visited the United States with his bride, and we arranged to conduct the interview at Mrs. Louis Henry Cohn's apartment. Mrs. Cohn and her late husband, dealers in rare books and manuscripts, had been friends of Eliot for some years, and the Eliots stayed with her when they visited New York.

The day before, I came to New York to visit Robert and Carol

Bly; the night before the interview, Louis and Dorothy Simpson came to dinner. Neither Simpson nor Bly had met Eliot; both admired him; both wanted to make his acquaintance. Thus I arrived at Mrs. Cohn's apartment, the next morning, equipped not only with a deck of questions on three-by-five cards, not only with a cumbersome reel-to-reel tape recorder, but with two tape technicians. As introductions were made and the interview started, Bly and Simpson affected working-class invisibility, and checked such technical details as electric plugs with studious professionalism. As the morning wore on they dropped their guards. When Mrs. Cohn brought out the Scotch — and Eliot lectured us, briefly, never to destroy Scotch whiskey by contact with ice cubes — they sat on the sofa and drank their drinks and laughed and joined in the conviviality.

My card file served me well. When Eliot's answers provoked further questions, I followed the lead of his talk. Then when his answers slowed down, or when we refreshed our drinks, I flipped ahead in my cards, weeding out the questions already answered or bypassed, and organizing the ones that remained. Eliot answered my questions, as one might have predicted, in paragraphs — as if he had known the questions, as if he had prepared the answers. Nowadays writers are used to questions, from audiences after poetry readings as well as from journalists with tape recorders, but Eliot belonged to an earlier era: If you had something to say about poetry you wrote an essay. So his fluency in speech, responding to my interrogation, came neither from the lecture platform nor from the experience of being interviewed; it came instead from years of excellent talk. Of the several interviews I have conducted, the one with Eliot required the least revision.

I saved until last the question I wanted most to ask, but feared to. I shouldn't have hesitated.

Thirty years old, I had recently published my second book of poetry. When I was adolescent I conceived of growing up as climbing a mountainside; implicit in the notion of my mountain was a plateau. One would reach this plateau at some point in one's twenties; one would be *a poet* — and then one would walk along this plateau until one died. I suspect most adolescents hold some such misconception, which derives from the values placed on age by our elders: "You'll understand when you grow up." It also derives from the wish to relax, to stop struggling, to give up the struggle. When I was twenty, I thought that when I published poems in a good magazine, I would know that I was a poet — which meant, really, a *good* poet. When I was twenty-five, and my things had appeared in the *Hudson Review* and *The New Yorker,* I still didn't know. When I had a book, I hoped, *then* I would know. From the age of fourteen I had been trying to be a good poet. When did you get to find out whether you were any good or not? Finally now, approaching the margin of thirty, I thought I knew the answer. Reading Eliot's essays had helped. Here is the last exchange in the interview:

INTERVIEWER: One last thing. Seventeen years ago you said, "No honest poet can ever feel quite sure of the permanent value of what he has written. He may have wasted his time and messed up his life for nothing." Do you feel the same way now, at seventy?

ELIOT: There may be honest poets who do feel sure. I don't.

In editing the interview for publication, I omitted a couple of phrases. When I first asked him if he now felt sure of his work, he answered quickly, "Heavens, no! Do *you?*" I hastened to assure him that I didn't.

When we arrived at the apartment that day, and I laid eyes on Eliot for the first time in two years, I was shocked. When I first talked with him at Faber he had been an old sixty-three, pale and stooped with a hacking cough. Now, at seventy — but with a new young wife — he looked like George Sanders; now he looked debonair, sophisticated, lean, and handsome, with a deep tan just acquired in the Caribbean. During the interview he threw his head back to laugh a vigorous laugh. Gone were the cigarettes and the cough, gone the appearance of old age.

Instead, he was a fond husband. Mrs. Eliot wasn't with us when we started the interview but joined us in progress — an almost matronly young woman, fleshy and warm. As soon as she arrived, Eliot became more animated. When his answers were especially well phrased, he glanced in her direction as if to measure her response to his wit. When we interrupted the questioning for a drink, Eliot moved to the sofa to sit beside his wife. They held hands, and continued to hold hands for the rest of the morning. A friend of theirs later told me that he had seen Eliot at a dinner party eating his soup left-handed, with some difficulty, because he was seated on his wife's left and his right hand was engaged with her left, under the table.

THE REENACTMENT OF THINGS

Writing about Eliot, I want mostly to tell what he was like as I saw him, to provide notes on the man I encountered. But for a moment I will speculate, to suggest some biographical or psychological notions about the man and the poet. The 1988 publication of the first volume of his letters provided some context for this private or reticent man; and we have access to new biographical information, especially Lyndall Gordon's scholarship.

Eliot's first marriage was painful for husband *and* wife. It nearly ruined Eliot's life, and whether or not the marriage was responsible, Vivien Eliot's life was ruinous. If I must suggest that this bad marriage was crucial to Eliot's poetry, it is not to suggest that the miseries were worthwhile; there are no scales on which to balance the wretchedness of human beings against the accomplishment of works of art. Art's triumph endures in a world separate from the old mire and fury. It is true that works of art conceived in personal wretchedness may console millions of human beings, remote from the artist and the artist's family;

but, as the observation of a cause never justifies (or invalidates) a result, so the success or failure of a result never invalidates (or justifies) a cause.

In 1915, Eliot did not consider himself a poet. Having written "Prufrock," he was considered a poet of the first order by Ezra Pound and by his old Harvard friend Conrad Aiken, but he was uncommitted to the art. He was a Ph.D. candidate in philosophy at Harvard, and it was obvious to people he met — in 1915 in England — that his interests were academic and philosophical, that he would take his degree and become an eminent professor of philosophy in an American university. Like many talented young people, he seemed to grow away from poetry as he grew older. Then suddenly he met Vivien Haigh, married her abruptly and almost surreptitiously in a registry office, decided to remain in England, and abandoned his doctorate and with it his American academic career. Instead, he took what work he could find to support himself, and he wrote poems. This combination of events identifies Vivien, England, and the life of poetry.

My summary omits the *miglior fabbro* — or maybe the Pandar — of this marriage. Ezra Pound in 1915 thrived at the height of his generous, energetic, brilliant advocacy of poetry and poets. He wanted Eliot to marry poetry (not the Department of Philosophy), and if Vivien or any other young woman would help his project, Pound would leap to accept the help. Pound's generosity to other writers promoted or encouraged their work; the private life was of interest only in relation to the work. Consider that when Pound discovered Eliot and "Prufrock," he must have felt like Emerson reading Whitman; he asked for this poet and this poet arrived. Consider that Pound then discovered that his providential poet intended to settle for a Cambridge lectern and the respectability of Brattle Street.

Pound manipulating Eliot discovered the bohemian concealed inside the rolled-umbrella body. In 1915 the languid Eliot felt Pound's inferior in energy and decision. In time Eliot would prove as languid as granite and just as volatile, while Ezra Pound with his hit-or-miss judgment flitted like a drunken but-

terfly from flower to flower of evil. But, briefly in 1915, Eliot
surrendered to Pound as the chicken coop surrenders to the
flooded river. This surrender included his impulsive marriage to
an attractive, vivacious, intuitive, volatile, erotic young woman:
the awful daring of a moment's surrender. Imagine the heady
amative excitement of Eliot's initial encounter with Vivien. They
met through Scofield Thayer of *The Dial,* a literary meeting.
Pound assumed that Vivien and Thayer were lovers; Pound's
judgments are unreliable, but at any rate Vivien's erotic experience surely exceeded Eliot's. We know a little of an earlier affair
of Vivien's. After the marriage we know that Vivien took a
tumble with Bertrand Russell; in some letters we find hints of
other encounters. On the other hand, we know from Eliot's
poems and letters how much his own sexuality frightened or
appalled him. We know something of his times and circumstances, his background and his education; he was victim of his
own history, which included misogyny or gynophobia intact
from Leviticus through Saint Paul to his Puritan ancestry. Imagine the release of sexual feeling, and imagine the guilt and disappointment. Imagine, then, eighteen consequent years of in-
compatibility and suffering.

Vivien became mad. It is presumptuous to assume that Eliot
drove her mad; her history of mental trouble began before they
met. When people fall in love they are on their best behavior
and believe that they have turned a new leaf. At first, Vivien was
stable enough; maybe Eliot was briefly a sexual creature. But
any cures were momentary, and gradually each lover returned
to the old pattern — with disappointment, blame, and guilt. The
marriage of "Tom and Viv" — the title of an exploitative play
of 1984 — was dreadful to observe. Virginia Woolf wrote in
her diary about Vivien: ". . . was there ever such a torture since
life began! — to bear her on one's shoulders, biting, wriggling,
raving, scratching, unwholesome, powdered, insane, yet sane to
the point of insanity." Once Edith Sitwell addressed Vivien by
name, meeting her in London, and Vivien answered: "No, no:
you don't know me. You have mistaken me *again* for the *terrible*

woman who is so like me." Among other eccentricities, she joined the Fascist party. When Conrad Aiken visited them, Eliot remarked, "There's no such thing as pure intellect," and Vivien laughed at him. "Why what do you mean? . . . You know perfectly well that *every* night you tell me that there *is* such a thing: and what's more that *you* have it, and that nobody *else* has it." Glumly Eliot said, ". . . you don't know what you are saying."

Vivien's instability and illness ended in madness and commitment to hospitals; Eliot appeared cold and withdrawn as he overworked to pay Vivien's medical expenses.

Although the marriage was bad, it was not only or always bad. The literary intelligence that Eliot found in Vivien remained intermittent; she was a writer of ability without discipline. She hovers over "The Waste Land," enabling and cursing, powerful and pathetic. Vivien was insightful, clever, witty, vivacious, depressed, nervous, and mad. Eliot was — as we say in the demotic tongue — crazy about her. It is traditional to understand that writing poetry is dangerous, that poets may well be punished like Prometheus for an impious gift. Some people court their own punishment by falling in love with it or by marrying it. Typical of the marriages of artists is the intensely creative woman who loves the neurotic, possibly psychotic man; she cannot live or work without him. He is her secret Muse, bringing her poetry and at the same time tearing her life apart. Roles reverse when the artist is male; and the same murderous beneficent relationship may occur when artists are homosexual.

Eliot married poetry knowing that poetry was unstable. Because the form of poetry connects it to the crib, poetry is often the mother, and Eliot's mother Charlotte was a poet. Vivien was as much unlike Eliot's mother as could be, yet she was poetry. To marry the mother is at the same time wholly forbidden and wholly desirable. It is clear from Eliot's poems that impotence, or at least sexual incompetence and coldness, obsessed him during his marriage to Vivien. Maybe Eliot married Vivien in order to be impotent, to suffer, and to write poems. When he separated from her, he chose a monastic grief, out of which he wrote his best work in *Four Quartets*. Fifteen years after the legal separation, Vivien died in 1947 in a mental hospital in London. It was ten years before Eliot could rise from the grave to marry again.

The marriage, the religious conversion, the separation, dour years of devotion and self-denial, and the remarriage all parallel events in Eliot's poems and plays. I do not suggest that the life explains the poems. But Eliot's doctrine of impersonality was camouflage, whether he was aware of subterfuge or not. His poems before Vivien are young, literary, clever, without psychic depth or intellectual profundity. "The Love Song of J. Alfred Prufrock" is the best, combining a young man's self-mockery with his reading of French symbolists and Henry James. Maybe Prufrock's fear of the body points toward the Fisher King, but mostly it is Prufrock's style that matters in this poem, from his opening gesture toward realism — "Like a patient etherised upon a table" — to his final Tennysonian mellifluousness. (One can take this conclusion straight as beautiful poetry or crooked as self-criticism by pastiche; it is better crooked.) With the poems written after his marriage, Eliot approaches emotions outside literature. Although the exoskeleton of "The Waste Land" is anthropological, although much of its material derives from reading, the poem is as personal as confessional poetry. "The Waste Land" is the twentieth century's monument to the nervous breakdown:

> On Margate Sands.
> I can connect
> Nothing with nothing.

Although we have known for decades that Eliot went to Margate to recover from nerves, as we said then, for many years we refused to read the poem he wrote. The monument to breakdown is not generalized; it is the breakdown of a man who had read widely, certain lines sticking in his brain and accruing personal and nonhistorical significance; it is a breakdown associated with forbidden sexuality. Breakdowns provide opportunities for artists. One never knows what new structure the shattered life may assume, if the life bears itself into reconstitution. For one artist the exposed conflict may result in grateful monogamy, for another in satyriasis or promiscuity, for another in homosexuality, for another in impotence or frigidity. The barrenness of "The Waste Land," and the Fisher King's dilemma, suggest an inability to conceive offspring if nothing else. And the fantasies — in which the poem anticipates not so much confessional poetry as surrealism — make a nightmare of babies and of death-kissing sexuality:

> A woman drew her long black hair out tight
> And fiddled whisper music on those strings
> And bats with baby faces in the violet light
> Whistled, and beat their wings
> And crawled head downward down a blackened wall

An earlier version of this scene is the typist's weary sexual encounter with the clerk, which is how — with sordidity and squalor, without pleasure — we imagine the adult sexuality of our parents.

> What is that sound high in the air
> Murmur of maternal lamentation

Eliot's conversion took place before the separation from Vivien; conversion made the separation morally possible. In the poems that record his soul's travel, we watch Eliot in all genuineness give up hope for any kind of regeneration, be it sexual or spiritual. The track of this abnegation is "Ash Wednesday," a superb poem, more beautiful than "The Waste Land" though not so engrossing. In the shorter "Journey of the Magi," he gives us in objective story a personal, retrospective account of the difficulties of conversion — but it is "Ash Wednesday"'s loss of hope that allows hope to be born, that dramatically displays the motion of the soul and names the locus of the conversion. After conversion, the *Four Quartets,* which explore the spiritualized emotions of a Christian, contain further autobiography, but the literary source is largely Dante.

It is in the last of the *Four Quartets* that Eliot experiences his Dantesque encounter with a ghost, the terza-rima portion of "Little Gidding," maybe the greatest moment of modernist verse in English. The meeting is dreamlike, occurring in the early morning, but this dream resembles an encounter that could have taken place as Eliot walked the streets of London while an air raid ended. Silly arguments have tried to identify the ghost whom Eliot meets, speaking of Yeats, of Pound (not dead yet), of Irving Babbitt. But the poet made himself clear: "Both one and many . . . a familiar compound ghost / Both intimate and unidentifiable." He describes the mechanism of dream: "I assumed a double part, and cried / And heard another's voice cry." Eliot holds dialogue with himself, using a composite dream figure, so that he may accuse himself of his own moral failure. No one condemns Eliot more vehemently than he condemns himself.

> In the uncertain hour before the morning
>> Near the ending of interminable night
>> At the recurrent end of the unending
> After the dark dove with the flickering tongue
>> Had passed below the horizon of his homing
>> While the dead leaves still rattled on like tin
> Over the asphalt where no other sound was
>> Between three districts whence the smoke arose
>> I met one walking, loitering and hurried
> As if blown towards me like the metal leaves
>> Before the urban dawn wind unresisting.
>> And as I fixed upon the down-turned face
> That pointed scrutiny with which we challenge
>> The first-met stranger in the waning dusk
>> I caught the sudden look of some dead master
> Whom I had known, forgotten, half recalled

Both one and many; in the brown baked features
The eyes of a familiar compound ghost
Both intimate and unidentifiable.
So I assumed a double part, and cried
And heard another's voice cry: 'What! are *you* here?'
Although we were not. I was still the same,
Knowing myself yet being someone other —
And he a face still forming; yet the words sufficed
To compel the recognition they preceded.
And so, compliant to the common wind,
Too strange to each other for misunderstanding,
In concord at this intersection time
Of meeting nowhere, no before and after,
We trod the pavement in a dead patrol.
I said: 'The wonder that I feel is easy,
Yet ease is cause of wonder. Therefore speak:
I may not comprehend, may not remember.'
And he: 'I am not eager to rehearse
My thought and theory which you have forgotten.
These things have served their purpose: let them be.
So with your own, and pray they be forgiven
By others, as I pray you to forgive
Both bad and good. Last season's fruit is eaten
And the fullfed beast shall kick the empty pail.
For last year's words belong to last year's language
And next year's words await another voice.
But, as the passage now presents no hindrance
To the spirit unappeased and peregrine
Between two worlds become much like each other,
So I find words I never thought to speak
In streets I never thought I should revisit
When I left my body on a distant shore.
Since our concern was speech, and speech impelled us
To purify the dialect of the tribe
And urge the mind to aftersight and foresight,
Let me disclose the gifts reserved for age

To set a crown upon your lifetime's effort.
First, the cold friction of expiring sense
Without enchantment, offering no promise
But bitter tastelessness of shadow fruit
As body and soul begin to fall asunder.
Second, the conscious impotence of rage
At human folly, and the laceration
Of laughter at what ceases to amuse.
And last, the rending pain of re-enactment
Of all that you have done, and been; the shame
Of motives late revealed, and the awareness
Of things ill done and done to others' harm
Which once you took for exercise of virtue.
Then fools' approval stings, and honour stains.
From wrong to wrong the exasperated spirit
Proceeds, unless restored by that refining fire
Where you must move in measure, like a dancer.'
The day was breaking. In the disfigured street
He left me, with a kind of valediction,
And faded on the blowing of the horn.

Some impersonal poet. Another modernist promulgator of the artist's remove is James Joyce, the most autobiographical novelist in the history of the art. By this point we know enough of Eliot's life to be able to understand things he might allude to when he speaks of "the rending pain of re-enactment / Of all that you have done . . . the shame / Of motives late revealed, and the awareness / Of things ill-done and done to others' harm / Which once you took for exercise of virtue." This last twist causes the most biting remorse: the wicked thing done with conviction of nobility.

Domesticity precedes ideology, for all men and women. The feelings between parents and children, siblings, men and women as lovers or as spouses — these relationships penetrate the life of genius as much as they penetrate the lives of the rest of humanity. To insist on the primacy of the family affair is neither to denigrate nor to reduce the poem or the idea: That Marx entertained notions about his father, which informed the structure of Marx's thought, says nothing about the validity of Marxism; but who writes about Marx, and ignores family relationships, ignores the man. Indeed, Eliot wanted us to "ignore the man" — and from his wish arises the New Critics' dogma indexing the biographical heresy.

THE CODGER

Working over the interview with Eliot was easy. On April 6, I sent him a typescript of the interview, with new questions suggested by the text, and with eighteen queries. When I changed my question to fit his answer, I asked his indulgence; when I found a word awkward or ambiguous, I suggested another word or asked him to fix it; when I didn't understand a reference, I asked for explanation. His reply of four pages, dated 16 April, accompanied a text of the interview on which he had made corrections. Because he spoke prose, he needed make only small revisions. Speaking about Conrad Aiken to the tape recorder, he had called him "a kind creature," and the phrase looked condescending in type; it had not sounded so in speech, and Eliot revised "creature" into "friend" for print. When at the end of the interview he told me that he was still unsure of the value of his work, he went on to say that "no intelligent writer knows if he is any good." The sentence sounded arrogant or dogmatic; he cut it out. He answered my eighteen queries mostly by revising the text. He corrected my spelling of Omar Khayyam. He changed prepositions, removed a passage that he claimed no longer to understand, and made substitutions for single words. One paragraph, about formal verse as counter-revolution, he wholly recast. He answered my six new questions so that five of them entered the text — two questions about his old theories of poetic drama, another about revising other people's poems, another about the poet and nuclear annihilation, and another about meeting Yeats. The sixth exchange I decided not to add to the interview; I had asked him, on the insistence of a *Paris Review* editor, if he had ever given thought to writing fiction. His answer: "Never."

The interview appeared in our twenty-first issue, later the same year, together with poems by Geoffrey Hill, Ted Hughes, and both tape technicians.

During the interview I asked Eliot whatever happened to the manuscript of "The Waste Land," and he told me the familiar story of how it had disappeared after John Quinn's death. (In 1968, Eliot dead three years, the manuscript turned up — and has been published in facsimile, elegantly edited by Mrs. Eliot, complete with Pound's cuts and comments — discovered after all in John Quinn's papers, which had been deposited at the New York Public Library and never thoroughly examined.) In 1959 we assumed that Quinn's papers had been searched, and that the manuscript was irretrievably lost. Shortly after doing the interview, I heard a rumor: Someone was offering the manuscript to the Morgan Library for $200,000! Thinking that I needed to footnote the text, I wrote Eliot to ask if it was true. It was the first he had heard of it, and it did not please him. He asked me to investigate. There followed a comic series of letters. The Morgan Library denied that it had been offered the text; instead, they had heard that Yale was dickering for it. When I wrote Yale, Yale denied all knowledge, but had in fact recently heard that the Morgan was negotiating for it; perhaps if I wrote them again . . . ? Then another letter arrived from Yale, and the information was startling. The manuscript had been found, and it was being offered to a large university in the West. I kept Eliot apprised. It depressed him — these enormous sums offered for his scrap, sums he would never see. When the price in the rumor dropped to $100,000, he professed to have lost interest, the sum was so small.

When the rumors petered out, he decided again that the manuscript was lost forever; he died, I suspect, satisfied that his drafts would never turn up.

.   .   .

In the autumn of 1959 I went to England with my family, and lived in the village of Thaxted until the summer of 1960. Eliot wrote in October, pleased with the interview which had just appeared; he asked me to visit him in the spring; just now, the Eliots were off to the United States. But when spring came we drove to Italy for the interview with Ezra Pound, and I did not see Eliot that year. Back in Ann Arbor, I had a letter from Charles Monteith, Eliot's colleague at Faber and Faber, asking me to revise Michael Roberts's *Faber Book of Modern Verse* and add some new poets to it. Michael Roberts brought modern poetry to England with his Faber collection in 1936. I had met dozens of poetical Englishmen who had discovered modern poetry through Roberts's anthology. After the war, as new poets emerged and published, the collection fell out of date. Roberts died in 1948, leaving behind notes toward a new edition, which Anne Ridler used when she made a second edition (without American poets) in 1951. By 1963 Faber wanted a third edition, American poets included. Monteith asked me to do the edition for a flat fee, which is contrary to writerly economics, and the fee was minuscule: one hundred pounds. When I wrote back to accept the task, I asked for more money. I did not get it. I suppose that I would have done it for nothing if Faber had asked me to do it; I suppose Faber understood.

But I bring up the subject not just to say the obvious — my edition appeared in 1968 — but to add a further note on T. S. Eliot.

In a letter that began by telling me again that he could not come to Ann Arbor for a reading, Eliot said he was pleased that I would do a new edition of Roberts. Then he added that of course he and his colleagues wanted my own work to be represented in the anthology. Perhaps, however, it would be best for me not to make the final selection of my poems, but to leave space for them, and forward to Faber an appropriate selection of my poems larger than the space saved; then Faber could choose among them, and print a note at the front of the anthology advising the reader that the editor's poems were included at the insistence of the publisher, who had done the selection. This procedure, he suggested at the end of a paragraph, might allow me to avoid the criticism that had been directed at a certain contemporary anthologist.

You do not become the leading literary figure of the English-speaking world without shrewdness. Possibly Eliot considered that I might choose my worst poems, and wanted therefore to reserve judgment on which poems to print. I doubt it. He suggested the procedure solely to allow the note for the front of the book. I wrote him immediately to say that, although I was grateful for the suggestion, I would not print my own poems in this edition of *The Faber Book of Modern Verse*. Eliot answered to say that he approved my decision. I doubt that he expected me to accept his scheme; I think he enjoyed the scheming.

In 1963 I returned to England for a year, and saw Eliot for the last time. When I arrived in Thaxted that summer Eliot wrote that he was "still a hobbling convalescent," but that he spent three afternoons a week at the office. He suggested that I come up to town and have a cup of tea with him. I saw him on August 28, 1963. He looked frail, sickly, and happy. He met me at the door of his office, smiling and making a pleasant noise, possibly a chortle; Old Possum had turned into Old Codger. His motions were deliberate and his head shook, but this was not the old man of sixty-three whom I had met in this office twelve years before. This age was genuine, and not an effect of self-denial. He was affectionate, calling me "Donald" as he had not done before (in his scheming letter I had remained "Mr. Hall"), and telling me that our *Paris Review* interview was the best that had ever been done with him. Talk of his interview led us to talk of my conversation with Pound, and then to Pound himself. Eliot spoke of his old friend with sadness, with evident affection, and with an objectivity that seemed almost medical. He said that of course Pound was megalomaniac. The doctor at St. Elizabeths had pronounced on Pound's megalomania, Eliot told me, and diagnosed him well. Pound's new self-denigration was merely the other side of megalomania. Then Eliot slipped a little to the side of what he had been saying, remembering, I think, past annoyances over Pound's judgment — annoyed but not angry, still affectionate as one remains affectionate toward a brother who always gets into trouble. Pound was always an extremely poor judge of people, Eliot told me; extremely poor.

Then he rambled on about an English poet, flatterer of Pound's, whom I will call Peter Beckwith because it does not resemble his name. (I will change another name and circumstance in a moment. That afternoon, Eliot expressed numerous suspicions of people and their motives.) He was afraid now, he told me, that Peter Beckwith was trying to exploit Pound, and he explained what he thought Beckwith was up to. He feared that Professor Buttermarch, at a prominent American university, was conspiring with a dead poet's surviving son-in-law to snatch manuscripts from the poet's widow. He said fierce things about Buttermarch, who was an opportunist — Eliot's voice turned tense with anger — and a dangerous man who made a career of duping widow executors of literary husbands. There was anxiety in his voice, as he looked toward his own death and imagined the birds gathering around the corpse, and around his young widow.

We talked about his plans for this winter. He needed for his lungs' sake to leave wet London. They would go to Nassau. No, they would not visit Cambridge again, he said sadly, in answer to my question, because his sister had died the winter before. With the death of his sister Ada he lost his last remaining close tie to Cambridge. No, they would go only to Nassau, and they didn't like it much, but they knew what to expect. They had tried Barbados once, two years before, but they had suffered an unpleasant experience. The manager at the hotel had become angry at them, and ruined their visit, because they refused to be exploited. The manager had wanted to have a huge party for them, and introduce them to everyone he knew, but the Eliots wanted to rest, not to meet a hundred strangers. Eliot told the manager that they would be perfectly happy to visit him and his wife at their house, but please not to have a large party where they would have to meet all sorts of people. The manager, he told me again, had wanted to *exploit* them.

He brought up the subject of the illness that had almost killed him in London the winter before. One evening an ambulance had rushed him to the best hospital in London for bronchial troubles, he told me, where he had a private room without charge. The old Tory praised National Health; they treat one so marvelously, he said. But it was Valerie who had saved his life. His eyes filled with an old man's sentimental tears as he told me that his wife had saved his life.

Again, I noticed the pictures on the office walls. Looking with me, he mentioned Marianne Moore with affection and levity, praising her as a performer: No one, he said, could drop papers on a platform with more skill than she could. There was the same photograph of Virginia Woolf I had noticed in 1951. There were drawings of Goethe and Blake, in which Eliot fancied a resemblance around the eyes. There was a new large photograph signed with a flourish by Groucho Marx. Eliot told me that he and Groucho had never met but that they had exchanged photographs, and that they ought to be meeting soon, since Groucho said that he would be coming through London. He asked me if I would like to meet Groucho Marx. I regret to say that I will not be telling *that* story; I heard no more of it.

In response to his suggested invitation, I asked Eliot if he could come out to Thaxted. Perhaps by spring he would feel strong enough; certainly, he said, we must see a great deal of each other. I told Eliot that my wife was singing in the choir at Thaxted Church; my young son was enlisted to wear a white robe and walk in procession; I was learning to ring bells. He laughed. I must beware, he said, of becoming a church warden, since once you become a church warden it is very hard to stop being one. "I was a church warden for twenty-five years before I could get out of it." Then he talked about ritual and doctrine again, about Tractarians and Dr. Pusey. But ritual without doctrine, he added, was nothing. I changed the subject.

Later I asked him if he was writing anything, and he said with some wistfulness that he was not: He had been too ill to write anything; he hoped he would be able to write something that winter. He would like to write another play, but first he had to write an introduction to the paperback edition of *The Use of Poetry and the Use of Criticism,* the book made from his Charles Eliot Norton Lectures at Harvard in 1932. He had re-read the book just recently, and discovered with pleased surprise that it was a good book. I said that in the past he had deprecated it; he corrected me, saying he had been *modest.* He mentioned that he had hurried to finish writing *The Use of Poetry and the Use of Criticism,* because he had been about to give another series of lectures at Virginia. He did not mention the title of *After Strange Gods,* but shook his head and said that the Virginia lectures had turned into a bad book, a bad book, a bad book.

The hour of four o'clock approached, as it had done before. I rose, and Eliot remained sitting. Benign and fragile, he smiled and said goodbye, and said again that we would certainly see a great deal of each other that year. Almost thirty years afterward, I can still see him there.

A year and a half later, in January of 1965, I read in the paper that he was dead. I heard from friends about the service in Westminster Abbey which Pound appropriately attended. The end of Eliot's life was generally appropriate: He suffered in early and middle life, turned Christian, lived through a hard coming to Christianity and through a painful middle age; but in old age he found honor, joy in a second marriage, and died full of years and glory.

Rocks and Whirlpools:
Archibald MacLeish and
Yvor Winters

THE FACES

Two of my teachers were Archibald MacLeish and Yvor Winters. From the 1930s into the 1960s, MacLeish's poetic reputation flourished, but by the time he died in his ninetieth year in 1982, the literary stock market had devalued him. On the other hand, Yvor Winters's poems were never popular. His eccentric and belligerent criticism drew attention away from his poems, which were sparse, spare, and sometimes beautiful. The two men were unlike in a thousand ways. MacLeish's face was handsome, benign, and horsey with a long upper lip; its expression was welcoming, friendly, confident, joshing. Winters's face denied itself expression, looked cold and impassive, which is just how Winters wished to look; he admired words like "cold" and "impassive."

It should surprise no one that these appearances concealed their own opposites. Private, loyal, combative, and passionate, Winters's rock-hardness formed the carapace of an anxious psyche; MacLeish's engulfing gregarious heartiness concealed a diffident spirit. Maybe everyone is rock, everyone is whirlpool. Although these men neither sank ships nor drowned sailors, each could be dangerous; at least, each embodied a danger. In memory's gallery I hang their faces — one sober, glaring, shaky with certainty, the other laughing and sturdy with self-doubt.

THE BOYLSTON PROFESSOR

One afternoon, I had a conference with Archibald MacLeish scheduled for two o'clock. It was his first term as a teacher, and we scarcely knew each other. I knocked on the great oak door of Widener W five minutes late — I am never late; it must have been deliberate — and, as I crossed the office to sit beside him, I heard him make loud boyish noises of regret. He told me, laughing, that I must *never* be late again. Just at two o'clock there'd been a knock on the door, and he had called out, "Come on in, Don, you old son of a bitch," only it hadn't been me, but a stranger from the *Harvard Law Review!* He pretended to wipe sweat from his forehead, as if he were a high school student and the assistant principal had caught him smoking.

Two years before he became Boylston Professor, MacLeish visited Harvard to read his poems in December of 1947. We took a close look at him. He resembled a college president with his stony good looks and high forehead. We knew his face not from anthologies of poetry — celebrity photographs had not reached Parnassus — but from newspapers and magazines. We knew the story: After Hotchkiss, Yale, and service in World War I, he entered Harvard Law School, then practiced with a prestigious Boston firm. But he broke the pattern: The young Bostonian professional, slated to make partner, chucked it all and moved to Paris in 1923 to join the Lost Generation and undertake the lives of a poet. When he returned to the United States in 1928 he was famous (as poets were famous in 1928) or notorious for "Ars Poetica" (1926): "A poem should not mean / but be" was quoted whenever journalists deplored (or praised) modern poetry. Two years later, *New Found Land* contained the best work he would ever do, including the sonorities of "You, Andrew Marvell":

> And here face down beneath the sun
> And here upon earth's noonward height
> To feel the always coming on
> The always rising of the night:

In 1933 *Conquistador* won him his first Pulitzer Prize. When Cleanth Brooks published *Modern Poetry and the Tradition* in 1939, one chapter gathered "Frost, MacLeish, and Auden." It seems now like a sandwich with a strange filling — but taste, fifty years back, *always* seems bizarre. Frost-MacLeish-Auden balanced one chapter devoted to Yeats and another to Eliot. Where were the other American poets of the moment? Wallace Stevens turned up in the introduction among "others" with "claim to inclusion," for instance Ezra Pound and Donald Davidson. William Carlos Williams and Marianne Moore went unlisted.

Eight years later, when he read at Harvard, MacLeish had long since detached from his fellows of the Lost Generation. During early Depression years, he worked for Henry Luce's *Fortune* — rather, say, than writing for *The Nation*. After a year directing the Nieman Foundation at Harvard, he went to Washington in 1939 as Librarian of Congress, a Roosevelt appointment rewarding the poet gone public, Paris aesthete turned political. The next year MacLeish wrote *The Irresponsibles*, an essay in which he attacked modern writers for insufficient awareness of the dangers to democracy. He contributed to speeches for the President, and was appointed assistant secretary of state under Edward R. Stettinius in 1944. At the Senate hearings on his confirmation, he was ridiculed for his poetry, some of which sounded to conservatives not only obscure but leftish; the day was saved — as MacLeish told the story — when a senatorial supporter revealed that he had played football for Yale.

When Roosevelt died Truman appointed James Byrnes as secretary of state and MacLeish left office. He had published little poetry during his Washington years, only *America Was Promises* (1939), which served the patriotic cause. When he read at Harvard in 1947, beginning his return to poetry, he addressed a skeptical audience reacting against the pious solidarity of the war years. But if we were cynical, we were also fascinated; if we looked askance at the smooth-faced, friendly figure that solemnly said its poems, we were also impressed by his eminence.

We were MacLeish's potential students when it was announced, a year or so later, that he had accepted the Boylston Professorship of Rhetoric and Oratory at Harvard. This chair goes back to a time when public speaking loomed large on campus. With MacLeish's appointment the position was confirmed as a precinct of creative writing. (Incumbent is Seamus Heaney, who followed Robert Fitzgerald; Robert Lowell and Elizabeth Bishop taught at Harvard from time to time alongside MacLeish and Fitzgerald.) Earlier, institutional Harvard showed little interest in hiring writers in permanent positions. When Vladimir Nabokov was put up for a professorship in Slavic, the linguist Roman Jacobson suggested appointing an elephant to teach zoology. But in the late 1940s Harvard Square pulsed with artistic energy. Especially the theater thrived; some veterans broke loose from the Harvard Dramatic Club, took over the Brattle Theater, and put on a series of excellent, mainly Shakespearean productions. There were poets in the neighborhood, and MacLeish's appointment suggested that Harvard might remember when Longfellow and another Lowell taught there.

The neighborhood: Undergraduates during my four years included Robert Bly, Adrienne Rich (Harvard and Radcliffe took classes together), John Ashbery, Kenneth Koch, Peter Davison, L. E. Sissman, and Frank O'Hara. The novelists John Hawkes and Harold Brodkey were students; John Updike arrived as a freshman in my senior year. Robert Creeley quit Harvard in 1947 to raise chickens in Littleton, New Hampshire — and we met when he came south, a long conversation at Gordon Cairnie's Grolier Book Shop. If one sat on Gordon's sofa long enough, one sat haunch to haunch with the poets of the Western world. I met Richard Eberhart there, Conrad Aiken, Allen Curnow from New Zealand. When he came to town, T. S. Eliot dropped by. At the Grolier one encountered graduate students and spouses: Richard Wilbur, Ruth and Walter Stone, Alison Lurie. Outside Harvard, Cambridge and Boston filled with poets: Robert Frost lived beside the Square fall and spring; John Holmes, teaching at Tufts, lived nearby; so did Samuel French Morse and John Malcolm Brinnin. Dudley Fitts lived in Andover to the north; in the western suburbs, Anne Sexton and Maxine Kumin began writing. W. S. Merwin spent a year in the area, like Ted Hughes and Sylvia Plath. When we started the Poets' Theatre in 1950, John Ashbery and Frank O'Hara and Robert Bly gathered in the Cambridge living room of Dick and Betty Eberhart. A catalyst to the Poets' Theatre was Archibald MacLeish, who had written verse for radio and theater.

With MacLeish's appointment we learned that he would teach a writing course the next autumn. Bly and I took it; so did George Plimpton. At our first meeting, we sat around an oval table at the top of Widener. I remember encountering the famous face, as MacLeish strode into class carrying books and papers, open-countenanced and friendly. How anxious he must have been, beginning a new life at the age of fifty-seven. He talked about the life of writing, and in his nervousness he spoke not of Hemingway, Fitzgerald, or Dos Passos but of Ernest, Scott, and Dos. Despite his celebrity, he needed our admiration; therefore we withheld it. At our first meeting, a naval veteran characterized something MacLeish said as "middle class." Sensing in that vulnerable face his injury, twenty-one-year-old sharks tasted blood. Someone else took the offensive at the second class; at the third meeting of the class, it was I who led the assault. My pretext was small enough: Talking about modern writers, MacLeish used a hackneyed figure, as we all do in speech, talking about "Joyce's world," "Faulkner's world," and "Yeats's world." I attacked the usage as solipsistic; there was only one world, I explained. MacLeish was taken aback, probably by an acerbic tone more than by force of logic; he stumbled trying to answer. When I skipped class next week, Bly told me that MacLeish was disappointed because he had prepared a refutation of my argument, bringing in Aristotle for support. After another week or two, MacLeish stopped class meetings and met us only in conference.

Or there was one more group meeting during our year-long class, a Christmas party at the MacLeishes' rented house in Louisburg Square on Beacon Hill. We met Ada MacLeish for the first time. The occasion was generous, and pleasant enough; I remember one negative moment. MacLeish suggested that each poet recite a poem. Bly recited "The Puritan on His Honeymoon." Someone asked me to say "The Poet as Social Worker." It was not a poem I would have chosen, tetrameter couplets that satirized preachy political poets, written not about MacLeish but in general reaction to popular-front pieties. When I said it at Louisburg Square I remember MacLeish — author of *The Irresponsibles,* author of *America Was Promises* — staring at the floor with his mouth a straight line. "An interesting social document," he said.

It was remarkable, and typical of the man, that he remained kind to me. I spent hours in conference with him, manuscripts spread over his desk. He concentrated on *ear,* which was fine with me because it was sound that wedded me to poetry in the first place. To all of us he emphasized ways of working. In class meeting, he had praised the habit of writing every day on a schedule. It didn't matter at what hour you worked; what mattered was working every day. I tried out his advice. Every day after lunch I carried my typewriter to a cubicle in Lamont Library and worked two hours on my verses. The next year I began rising at six, walking to the Square with paper and pencil to occupy a booth at an all-night cafeteria called Albiani's, writing for two hours while drinking black coffee from plastic mugs. Then I walked back to Eliot House and breakfast.

In the culture I was born to, "work" is a golden syllable. My Connecticut grandfather, who stopped school at ten and labored a fourteen-hour day, sang the virtues of woik-woik-woik — as the southern New Englander said it; in New Hampshire, it was wuk-wuk-wuk that the old farmers praised. I grew up knowing that we work for the night is coming when we work no more. Then one day in conference, MacLeish remarked that I was lazy. Oh, my indignation! I assaulted him with testimony of hours bent over the typewriter, I numbered pages piled and drafts redrafted. But he had discovered a vulnerable place, which amused him, and he continued to probe it. Although it became a joke, his accusation never lost its potency. In later years, whenever I saw him, I overwhelmed him with figures of labor; he would hear me out, as I listed prodigies, until he laughed at my need to justify myself.

On the other hand, he was right; at least, he was right when I was young. Once Henry Moore told about sculptors who tap-tap-tap'd at stone day and night, twelve hours a day if you like, and were still lazy. They put in their hours and withheld their spirits. When I was young, I tricked myself by a busy laziness, as with my project for MacLeish. Beginning the course, he assigned us all a major project. We could write whatever we liked — poems, stories — and he would read what we showed him; but we were each to undertake one long enterprise which we were to name in the autumn and complete in the spring. After all, MacLeish was a poet of large undertakings. The novelists each wrote a novel, but in 1949 poets wrote rhymed lyrics, so that we needed to go afield for our projects. Robert Bly wrote a long narrative in blank verse. My project was a rhymed play called *The Minstrel's Progress,* adapted without permission from a children's book by Eleanor Farjeon, *Martin Pippin in the Apple Orchard.* Most speeches were octosyllabic couplets; there were love songs in varied rhymed stanzas; one character ranted in Skeltonics; I invented a wizard who spoke nonsense that parodied Hart Crane. It played one night in the spring of my senior year, with Harry Levin, Richard Eberhart, Richard Wilbur, and Archibald MacLeish sitting in the front row. Popular acclaim has never brought it back. *The Minstrel's Progress* contained many lines, many rhymes, and many meters — but it was lazy.

His notions of professionalism and seriousness, writing on a schedule every day, were useful to me, trying to grow up as a writer. I'm sure they were useful to others. The young writer may glory in his amateur status, improvising out of wit and love for poetry, not to mention self-love, but if we will grow up as writers, we must learn to settle into daily labor. MacLeish was helpful, and continually kind. Then why did I withhold devotion or even gratitude? I was intolerant of him — impatient, quick to find fault — and I was not alone. Other students and colleagues mocked him, and among literary people who did not know him, the index of contempt ran high. When Dylan Thomas in a London pub recollected his visit to Harvard, he said he had liked everybody except MacLeish, because MacLeish had been in government. Robert Pinsky's *The Situation of Poetry,* forthright in praise and blame, refers to the "bland, even smug attitude" of MacLeish's "Ars Poetica," disliking the poem as we dislike a complacent acquaintance. Annoyance with this agreeable fellow turns up everywhere. Looking at traces of correspondence between MacLeish and Ezra Pound, we find Pound abusive. Robert Frost missed no opportunity to put him down or show him up. Edmund Wilson showed contempt on many occasions, devastatingly when he published "The Omelet of A. MacLeish" in *The New Yorker,* a parody that included critical grounds for contempt. It begins, using the marginal notes (out of Coleridge) that MacLeish was known for:

And the mist: and the rain in the west: and the wind steady:
There were elms in that place: and graven inflexible laws:
Men of Yale: and the shudder of Tap Day: the need for a man
    to make headway

MacLeish breaks an egg for his omelet.

Winning a way through the door in the windowless walls:
And the poems that came easy and sweet with a blurring of Masefield

(The same that I later denied): a young man smooth but raw

Eliot alarmed me at first: but my later abasement:

And the clean sun of France: and the freakish but beautiful
   fashion:

Striped bathhouses bright on the sand: Anabase and The Waste
   Land:

*He puts plovers'
eggs and truffles
into his omelet.*

These and the Cantos of Pound: O how they
   came pat!

Nimble at other men's arts how I picked up
   the trick of it:

The *New Yorker*'s editor Harold Ross ran into MacLeish at the Algonquin just after Wilson's parody appeared. Embarrassed, he could only mutter, "That must have hurt. That must have hurt."

The parody does not mimic *The Hamlet of A. MacLeish* (1928) but the cadences and manners of *Conquistador* (1932), with its ur-style that derives from the French *Anabase* of St. John Perse. MacLeish was a derivative poet, and his imitativeness partly accounts both for his unpopularity and for his popularity. When we like a poet, we want *more,* and other poets are always ready to produce the *more* we want. MacLeish's *The Pot of Earth* (1925), three years after "The Waste Land," supplies an epigraph from *The Golden Bough* and uses part titles: "The Sowing of the Dead Corn" and "The Carrion Spring."

> We are having a late spring, we are having
> The snow in April, the grass heaving
> Under the wet snow, the grass
> Burdened and nothing blossoms, grows
> In the fields nothing and the garden fallow;
> And now the wild birds follow
> The wild birds and the thrush is tame.
> Well, there is time still, there is time.

This tenth-carbon Eliot comes from MacLeish's third book.

On the other hand, his best work made its own noises, and we must judge poets by their best work. Anger against an artist seldom reflects disinterested judgment. MacLeish's success offended people for a number of reasons other than his imitativeness: Prolificness is always subject to innuendo (as Joyce Carol Oates can testify), and MacLeish published books in 1924, 1925, 1926, 1928, 1929, 1930, 1932 — and two in 1933. Then, his success seemed in excess of deserts, which angers everybody, as he won Pulitzers in 1933, 1952, and 1958 — the first two for poetry, the third for *J.B.* Then also, he appeared to be comfortable, never a patrician but accepted in American-patrician circles, with his friend Dean Acheson as exhibit number one. We prefer our artists poor; we resented his ability to pull out of law and live in Paris without employment; we resented the house at Conway with its servants and the winters in Antigua. Edmund Wilson's "Omelet," for all the justice of its complaint, sneers like the Harvard undergraduate's "middle class." We were intolerant because he was famous, derivative, rich, popular, lucky, prolific, and diffident. Sometimes he seemed to write too easily, in a thin language — small matter spread lightly over pages of pleasant diction. As I make this complaint, I notice that I accuse him of a busy laziness, of putting in hours and withholding spirit. Maybe he discovered in me a fault he condemned in himself: It would not be the first such occasion in history.

Sometimes MacLeish wrote beautifully. Setting aside the derivative work, we can take pleasure in the sound and feeling of:

> And over Sicily the air
> Still flashing with the landward gulls
> And loom and slowly disappear
> The sails above the shadowy hulls
>
> And Spain go under and the shore
> Of Africa the gilded sand
> And evening vanish and no more
> The low pale light across that land
>
> Nor now the long light on the sea:

And here face downward in the sun
To feel how swift how secretly
The shadow of the night comes on

We can admire the one-sentence sonnet "The End of the World":

Quite unexpectedly as Vasserot
The armless ambidextrian was lighting
A match between his great and second toe
And Ralph the lion was engaged in biting
The neck of Madame Sossman while the drum
Pointed, and Teeny was about to cough
In waltz-time swinging Jocko by the thumb —
Quite unexpectedly the top blew off:

And there, there overhead, there, there, hung over
Those thousands of white faces, those dazed eyes,
There in the starless dark the poise, the hover,
There with vast wings across the canceled skies,
There in the sudden blackness the black pall
Of nothing, nothing, nothing — nothing at all.

This poem provides pleasures of skill, like watching a juggler in the circus described; but the vision of emptiness goes beyond mere skill, and if Madame Sossman requires us to remember Madam Sosostris, MacLeish's ventriloquism is harmless. Or we can remember lines of elegy:

Between the mutinous brave burning of the leaves
And winter's covering of our hearts with his deep snow
We are alone: there are no evening birds: we know
The naked moon: the tame stars circle at our eaves.

It is the human season. On this sterile air
Do words outcarry breath; the sound goes on and on.
I hear a dead man's cry from autumn long since gone.

I cry to you beyond upon this bitter air.

Dead brother Kenneth, airman in the Great War, foreshadowed MacLeish's dead son Kenneth fifty years further on. The poet's best work is elegiac, with a special rage for emptiness, for blank faces at the edge of the void. While we fear or dread annihilation, these lines make their music. From time to time in his later work he reached this note again, and made poems less noticed but equal to his best. W. J. Bate read "Winter Is Another Country" at the Harvard memorial service in 1982.

> If the autumn would
> End! If the sweet season,
> The late light in the tall trees would
> End! If the fragrance, the odor of
> Fallen apples, dust on the road,
> Water somewhere near, the scent of
> Water touching me; if this would end
> I could endure the absence in the night,
> The hands beyond the reach of hands, the name
> Called out and never answered with my name:
> The image seen but never seen with sight.
> I could endure this all
> If autumn ended and the cold light came.

WINTERS IN CALIFORNIA

When I arrived in Palo Alto, September of 1953, to begin a year's fellowship at Stanford, I was to call Yvor Winters. On the telephone I met the unanticipated man. The deep voice inquired, "Do you have enough money?" I told him we were all right. "Come over tonight," he said, "and I'll cook a big steak." I was surprised, after the severity of his figure in his criticism, to engage an affable provider who invited us for a California cookout. We followed directions to Portola Drive in Los Altos. When he met us at the door, I recognized the face by moments of the prose style: fixed and somber, without volatility of expression, like his voice that seldom varied pitch but retained its blue timbre. I also met the unaffable side: "You come from Harvard," said Winters when we stepped inside, "where they think I'm lower than the carpet." A moment later he added, "Do you realize that you will be ridiculed, the rest of your life, for having studied a year with me?"

At Oxford I had met a poet from Stanford, student of Yvor Winters, who told me about the Stanford Fellowships in Creative Writing. I applied, sending poems as required, and forgot about it. In April or May came the letter inviting me to spend the next year at Stanford on the *dolce* stipend of $2,000. Therefore I put graduate school off for a year and looked toward study with Yvor Winters, of whom I had been aware for as long as a decade. When I spent my allowance on poetry books in my early teens, James Laughlin helped the budget by providing a pamphlet every month for a dollar hardback, fifty cents paper. I first came upon Yvor Winters when he was a Poet of the Year with *The Giant Weapon* in 1943. New Directions was my provider then, publishing Ezra Pound and William Carlos Williams; with the help of Laughlin's annuals and pamphlets I discovered Gertrude Stein, Robert Duncan, the prose poem, Kenneth Rexroth, Henry Miller, surrealism — and Yvor Winters, conservative dogmatist of logic, Saint Thomas, and metrics.

As an undergraduate I read Winters's criticism when he collected his first three books into an omnibus volume called *In Defense of Reason*. Although he was first and always a poet, in the forties and fifties he was more famous as a critic, because of his belligerence, intransigence, and eccentricity; his learning and intelligence were largely overloooked in favor of these more colorful qualities. I had been reading New Critics: Eliot the forerunner, I. A. Richards, Allen Tate, John Crowe Ransom, and R. P. Blackmur, who provided the model for my undergraduate essays. Ransom in *The New Criticism* applied the label to Winters, but surely Winters stood to the side of all canons of accepted taste and behavior. As he acknowledged when we met in 1953, people ridiculed him.

When we find a critic who prefers Robert Bridges to Gerard

Manley Hopkins, we treat the discovery as a gift to our amour propre. It became standard in the forties and fifties to allude to Winters as the man who called T. Sturge Moore a greater poet than William Butler Yeats — although the alluders by and large knew nothing of T. Sturge Moore. Winters had read everybody, and Winters had distinct and unorthodox opinions. His first critical books appeared in 1937 and 1938, but essays or reviews had appeared from the early twenties on — many in *Poetry*, later in *The Kenyon Review* and especially in *Hound and Horn*. *Primitivism and Decadence* (1937) told in its subtitle what it attacked: "A Study of American Experimental Poetry." *Maule's Curse* (1938), "Seven Studies in the History of American Obscurantism," took care of the predecessors: Hawthorne, Cooper, Melville, Poe, Very and Emerson, Dickinson, and Henry James. In 1943 came *The Anatomy of Nonsense*, where chapters carried double titles like "T. S. Eliot, or the Illusion of Reaction." By this time, readers understood who provided the reality of reaction.

There were great critical quarrels when I was too young to follow them. In that "Age of Criticism," doubtless some critics merely enjoyed argument, but for Winters his convictions carried the weight of life and death, or at least sanity and madness. Some critics would stop short of facing a firing squad rather than recant an opinion, but Winters was never so lily-livered. Once he and Allen Tate quarreled bitterly over editorial policy at *Hound and Horn;* Winters enjoyed claiming that Tate boarded a train in Nashville with a ticket for California, packing only a brace of dueling pistols and two bottles of bourbon. Winters told how the bourbon ran out in Texas and Tate turned back to Tennessee.

The summer after Oxford, my wife and I spent a month in the eastern United States. I found my old copy of *In Defense of Reason* and read it through — with a dry mouth. It was one thing to read Winters, taking pleasure in his intelligence and condescending to his judgments; it was another to imagine him face to face. In the environs of Cambridge I asked people about him. Most of them knew him only by his essays — and wished me luck. Richard Wilbur had met him; I asked what Winters was like. "Well," said Dick carefully, "I asked him why he raised Airedales. He said, 'Because they can kill any other dog.' " In hot September, my pregnant wife and I drove from Connecticut to California, arriving early one afternoon, exhausted, and found the rooms in Menlo Park that we had engaged from Oxford. From that first night with Winters I remember not only his generosity and aggression; I remember how he introduced his Airedales — the great Black Jack above all — and the flora of the West; he loved dwelling on the abundance of vine and flower. He showed me a pomegranate, then split the fruit and demonstrated how to eat it; the New Englander took lessons in California.

Winters was friendly, warm, and fatherly; Winters was pugnacious and nuts.

That night we also talked about the year ahead. For the fellowship, I was required to enroll as a graduate student, but the only course I needed to take for credit was Winters's workshop. I would take no other courses, but would write poems and read *ad libitum.* Also I would hear Winters lecture, for he required fellows to audit one of his courses each term. Why had he spent his life erecting this edifice if he didn't want others to inhabit it? I planned to take temporary rooms there; doubtless, I daydreamed that I would argue him out of his unreasonable prejudice against William Butler Yeats.

In eight months, I learned more about poetry from Winters than I learned from any other teacher. Mostly I learned practical or writerly things, finally rejecting his theology but taking him as model for parish work. Winters revised my notions of prosody, overturning the structure I had worked up from the age of seventeen, and which I had recently applied in an Oxford thesis. From Winters I learned notions of diction that forbade hack metaphors of common speech — monosyllabic verbs like *dart, cup, churn, shield,* and *etch;* disyllables like *harbor, mirror, cradle, echo* — quasitropes that weaken the language even of good poets on a bad day. Winters had an Airedale's nose for language. In our writing class, if one of us committed a cliché, he would lean back in his chair, gaze toward the ceiling with a soulful expression, and intone with plush sonority, "The pine tree, like a lonely sentinel, stood etched against the sky."

In winter quarter, he taught the English short poem; we studied Thomas Wyatt, Ben Jonson, Fulke Greville, Barnabe Googe, George Herbert. We concentrated on sixteenth- and seventeenth-century lyrics, then dwindled through romanticism toward Robert Bridges, T. Sturge Moore, and Thomas Hardy. We studied the poems that were the fixed stars of Winters's astronomy, and the classes were dense with his knowledge and passion, his intelligence and authority. One day a graduate student spoke up in favor of George Gordon, Lord Byron; the young man never spoke again. I suppose the English lyric was Winters's best course, but it was the autumn course from which I learned most, because it was the first and because I resisted it the most. He called it "The Theory and the Practice of the Criticism of Poetry" — Winters was master of the light touch — but he might have named it "The Systematic Destruction of the Collected Poems of Gerard Manley Hopkins and William Butler Yeats." When he assaulted Hopkins first, I held back — out of ignorance, diffidence, and to save myself for the next poet. When it came to Yeats, each day Winters would go through several poems, beautifully reading each aloud, then shredding it into excelsior; my defense followed.

Digression: Winters was a wonderful reader, and when I describe the way he read aloud, I will touch on a paradox at Winters's center, maybe the same Heraclitean reversal, or appointment in Samarra, that lives at the center of any passionate advocate: *He did the opposite of what he claimed to do.* Reading poetry, his voice was deep, furry, rich, and intense. He kept a level pitch, refusing (as he thought) dramatic or musical enhancement. He read this way on principle: The words themselves should do the work, and not anybody's performance. Yet when Winters read aloud, reading Yeats or Jonson or Hart Crane or even a student, his voice was thrilling. It was *magic,* to use a metaphor that would have made him vomit; Winters's dark hairy timbre was solemn, bottomless, convincing, *romantic;* he was a performer as compelling as Dylan Thomas, whom he despised for performing.

Everyone writing about Winters encounters such contradictions, dazzling not because they are unusual for humankind but because Winters exemplified them to an extreme degree. These contradictions imply no hypocrisy; they speak of conflict that makes energy. Winters's internal contradictions account for his power; within him one fierce brother raged against the force of the other's protest and decision. Both brothers were adamant, indefatigable, unconquerable, wrong, and right.

When Winters finished reading a poem by Yeats he delivered a brief, incisive, destructive line-by-line analysis of its bad thinking, bad writing, and bad morals along with sentimental, dishonest, corrupt feeling. Sitting amid the splintered wreckage of a poem I had long admired, Winters would turn with a restrained leer and ask, "What does Mr. Hall have to say?"

Certainly my presence — my continual defeat — was pedagogically useful. Every now and then, Mr. Hall had nothing to say; mostly I tried reassembling the poem's pieces. I knew the poems well and enjoyed argument. Winters never interrupted me, but puffed on his curved pipe and looked downward until I had finished. Then he would destroy my argument — quickly, item by item — as he had originally destroyed the poem. He was the best arguer I ever argued with, shameless perhaps, but rigorous and devastating. The case rested and the jury never deliberated. I cannot quote from our confrontations. I recall that he skipped over "The Gyres" — in one quarter he couldn't destroy everything — and I brought him back. Not one of Yeats's best poems, "The Gyres" contains lines I chant to myself walking or driving alone:

> For beauty dies of beauty, worth of worth,
> And ancient lineaments are blotted out.
> Irrational streams of blood are staining earth;
> Empedocles has thrown all things about;
> Hector is dead and there's a light in Troy;
> We that look on but dance in tragic joy.

His comment (not angrily but smugly; he *had* me) was simply, "Ancient Pistol." I agreed: I *like* Ancient Pistol, as he thunders out Shakespeare's pastiche of Marlowe's Tamberlaine bombast; I like Marlowe.

And I like Yeats. Defeated in argument, day after day, I never lost my love for Yeats's poems. Of course Winters reached and modified me: I discriminated more, found Yeats sometimes a liar, sometimes practitioner of a bardic tone that disguised a sentimental or formulaic resolution. When Winters disliked a poet, he was accurate in naming the faults, but I think he often exaggerated the effect or extent of the faults, as in his essay on Robert Frost. My experience with Winters left my romantic standards and tastes largely unshaken. He persuaded me of the excellence of some poets I had not known — Greville, for instance — but he never dislodged Keats. I think of a story about taste in literature, an anecdote that MacLeish told. When Richard Burton and Elizabeth Taylor made *Who's Afraid of Virginia Woolf?* at Smith College, they visited the MacLeishes' Uphill Farm for a weekend; Burton's brother, whose name was Jenkins, accompanied them, and the two Welshmen recited poems they knew by heart. Learning that MacLeish was unaware of the poems of R. S. Thomas, the brothers outdid each other reciting lyrics by the contemporary Welsh parson. Then Burton and Jenkins quarreled over Coleridge's "Kubla Khan." Jenkins said it was a bad poem: disgusting, awful. Burton praised it: magnificent, superb. Jenkins repeated that it was nothing at all, whereupon Burton commanded silence and spoke the whole poem, perfect from first syllable to last. MacLeish told me that Burton's recitation was a great performance, and when he ended, drawing the last syllable out, the still air shook with the memory and mystery of his speaking. Then, into the silence, brother Jenkins spoke his word of critical reason: *"See?"*

Winters's writing class, that year, was two women and two men. At the beginning of each class Winters asked for manuscripts of our poems. For a few minutes we sat in silence as Winters read, his eyes expressionless as he scanned our lines. When he was done, he read each poem aloud and passed the manuscripts for silent reading. He asked our opinions, then delivered his own compact, small essay on each poem. Our errors allowed him to touch on everything: metrics, rhythm, rhyme, grammar, diction — and of course bad thinking or avoidance of thought in the name of emotion. He was a quick study and he left nothing out; there was no ambiguity in his judgment nor doubt about its provenance. At first I brought in some old poems from a collected works accumulated piecemeal over the years. Old poems fared poorly. What was the point of my presence if I were not to be made over? I learned about my sentimentalities; I became aware of slack thinking, corrupt figures, and prosodic licentiousness. I started bringing only new poems to class.

Like many writing teachers, he did not wish to teach out of our endeavors only. He brought into class some poems that he loved, that did not fit his other courses. He went through Valéry's "Ébauche d'un Serpent" and "Le Cimetière Marin," as well as poems by Baudelaire and Rimbaud. He said them aloud, with an accent that sounded just fine to me; he would paraphrase, giving alternatives, almost like Stanley Burnshaw's *The Poem Itself*. Under his influence, I translated a Corbière for his class. Also, he praised a few contemporary Americans. He praised and recited Louise Bogan and Adelaide Crapsey. From Winters I first heard of Stanley Kunitz. Berryman's "Homage to Mistress Bradstreet" came out in *Partisan Review* while I was at Stanford, and Winters dismissed it out of hand. There were contemporaries whom I admired, whom I praised to Winters; I got nowhere advocating Wilbur and Lowell. I liked Theodore

Roethke, whom Winters had praised for his first book, *Open House* (1941) — well-made poems in narrow quatrains like Louise Bogan's. When *The Lost Son* (1948) moved into surrealism or nonsense in its title poem, Winters hurled Roethke headlong. Because he had praised early Roethke, his contempt for the fallen angel was devastating.

That December I was Christmas shopping when Roethke telephoned out of the blue; he talked with my wife for an hour. He had seen a poem of mine in the *Hudson Review* and liked it — which gratified him because I had praised him in an article I had written in England. Over the telephone he was talkative and expansive, suggesting that he might bring me to the University of Washington for a poetry reading. A month or two later I had a note from him saying that the department's budget had run out, and he couldn't afford to pay for it himself; the Aga Khan phase was over for this year, he said. I found out later the blood chemistry of his enthusiasm: The telephone call had come from a hospital where he underwent treatment for mania.

In the spring I went to hear Roethke read his poems in San Francisco at the opening of the Poetry Center. I loved the reading. He was funny, outsized, performing in ways that would have confirmed Winters's worst notions. He did routines and gags, a shy man's way of showing off. At one point he said, "I understand there are spies here from Police Commissioner Winters," and I jumped in my seat.

Winters preferred my new poems to my old ones; I became a brief Wintersian. Twice a week I arrived early for writing class in order to talk with him. Mostly when I knocked he was sitting at his desk reading poetry. His low loud voice told me to come in, and when he saw me he put a bookmark in his book. He turned in his dilapidated morris chair to face me, and I tried things out on him, enjoying the forthright starch of his opinions. When I expressed some doubt about Robert Penn Warren's "Ballad of Billy Potts," I heard, "Red Warren can't write." We also joked. I liked seeing him laugh; his considerable belly jiggled. We worked a running gag about New England and California. One day he puffed at his pipe, deadpan, and wandered into a little speech: "Yes, that New England countryside, I know it well . . . Flat, with a few rivers meandering through it . . . I spent a whole summer in Gambier, Ohio." He laughed like a four-year-old at my outrage.

When Winters changed his literary opinions over his adult life, the changes went in one direction: He became more Wintersian. I wish he had entertained the notion that he might be wrong, but it was not his nature. On occasion I watched him tilt a little, and was grateful. Once as I entered his office, I asked him what he was reading. "Hart Crane," he said, and grumbled forcefully again about Crane's romantic pantheism. "Then why do you read him?" I asked. He answered shortly, "Because he's so beautiful."

About everything he cared for, he developed distinct ideas verging on absolute dogmas. He smoked a tobacco in his omnipresent pipe which he declared the best tobacco there was — and he *proved* it by the authority of his assertion. His characteristic force (voice, determined eye looking into your eye, plain speech invoking absolute knowledge) compelled assent. Alas, it was this tobacco he died of in 1968, tongue cancer with its gradual destruction of speech — this man of voice and mouth. Even when he was not smoking, he dangled the pipe from his lips, tarry stem rubbing against his tongue. After his first operation, he feared that he would lose speech. Janet Lewis remembered, "They took a part of the tongue and then they brought some skin from the side of the mouth to give him a new tip." She remembered him saying, "If I can't read it, I can't teach — poetry."

He talked with love and authority of his Airedales. He never told me what he told Wilbur, but he believed in the uprightness of Black Jack, and he used dogs in argument. Once I defended a late Yeats poem that ends, "Man has invented death," by saying that only humans were conscious of death. Winters ended the discussion: "Dogs fear death."

From time to time Winters invited students to his house to watch boxing on his television set. He had boxed in his youth, and enjoyed talking about pugilistic technique. It was entertaining to hear lectures about counterpunching from the voice that mostly spoke of caesuras and the absolute. I knew nothing about boxing and believed whatever he said. Philip Levine, who was a later fellow, had boxed himself — and watching fights with Winters mostly won the weekly bet; he felt that Winters never quite grasped the sport. Another old student remembers Winters's prediction that Sonny Liston would make short work of young Cassius Clay; later Winters commented that all the experts were wrong. And he was an expert.

He was combative, this admirer of Black Jack and Bobo Olson; sometimes he spoke as if he glimpsed the world from a periscope. Once as I entered his house I saw a copy of *Critics and Criticism,* the collection of essays edited by R. S. Crane to assemble the Chicago Aristotelians. "Are you reading this?" He nodded and smiled with satisfaction; he'd read enough of each essay, he said, to be sure that he *had* them. He was combative, but Yvor Winters was not a potential subscriber to *Soldier of Fortune.* Casual readers of Winters assume that his conservatism extended from literature to politics. In his time he was a liberal Democrat, fierce in opposition to McCarthy and other demagogues of the right. Philip Levine called him "profoundly egalitarian in the way that only men and women of enormous self-confidence can afford to be." In terms of American domestic politics, he was an academic liberal. On the other hand, if we use political labels seriously, not as in American party politics but as indices of intellect and spirit, Winters was high Tory, with a Tory's respect for personal liberty and reverence for precedent and durability.

In my time, graduate students in English at Stanford were either for Winters or against him. For a few poets, it was possible to work with Winters for a year or so, learn something, and leave Stanford without becoming beholden: Thom Gunn, Philip Levine, Donald Justice. Still other poets attended Stanford and stayed out of Winters's way: Wendell Berry, Robert Hass. Others were profoundly his students but retained or regained their own egos and went their own ways: J. V. Cunningham, Edgar Bowers, Alan Stephens, Robert Pinsky, James Mc-Michael, and doubtless others. But some surrendered; some gave themselves over into vassalage. Certain strong teachers and writers develop not students but disciples. Everyone compares Leavis at Cambridge to Winters at Stanford, teachers and critics largely incomparable except in their relationship to students. Charles Olson was another. Intelligent leaders with power of character attract men and women who have a vocation for following, whose ecstasy is obedience or replication, whose bliss is to lose their identities in a leader or parent. Some of Winters's followers became head-nodders, and wrote poems that mimicked Winters's manner without achieving Winters's power. It was a defect in Winters that he approved of some imitators, but of course for him it seemed that the disciples were merely sensible. One can't avoid Roy Campbell's quatrain:

> You praise the firm restraint with which they write —
>   I'm with you there, of course:
> They use the snaffle and the curb all right,
>   But where's the bloody horse?

The power or energy in Winters's best poems derives from conflict between form and reason, on the one hand, and an opposing dark chaos (demonic possession, madness) on the other; form and concept strive mightily to overcome a powerful enemy. For the imitators, the cage that they fabricate, with inch-thick reinforced steel walls, incarcerates one mouse.

When I studied with him that year, I admired his helpful intelligence, his certainty, humor, and brutal charm. But when I left in June, I knew that I would soon say or publish something he regarded as anathema, then he would write me a letter to fry my eyeballs. ("He was always much fiercer in his letters," Janet Lewis said in an interview, than "in the flesh.") I never considered staying at Stanford, but something happened late along that confirmed my necessity to bail out of this airplane. We attended a party at Winters's house late in spring. In a crush of students and faculty, Winters asked a small favor: Would I fill the ice bucket from the bag in the kitchen? Asking the favor, he addressed me as "son." When I heard the monosyllable, I went weak in the knees. *Geronimo!*

We knew a little of Winters's origins and personal history, and more has appeared in print since his death. There has been no biography, but perhaps when his letters become available someone will write his life. He was born in Chicago in 1900 but reared near Pasadena in the California that he came to love. His family moved back to Chicago when he was an adolescent, and there he first showed his precocity. In 1917, when he was still sixteen, Winters began undergraduate studies at the University of Chicago where he joined the Poetry Club that included Glenway Wescott and Elizabeth Madox Roberts. At the same time he met Harriet Monroe, founder and editor of *Poetry*, who invited him to the magazine's offices where the young Winters could consult the huge collection of modern poetry.

Shortly thereafter this idyll ceased and Winters underwent a long period of isolation. Tuberculosis required him to spend the next three years in a sanatorium near Santa Fe, largely in bed, reading and writing when he could find the energy. "The disease filled the body," Winters wrote of Adelaide Crapsey, who suffered from the same disease, "with a fatigue so heavy that it was an acute pain, pervasive and poisonous." Yet in 1919 Yvor Winters published six poems in *Poetry;* he wrote his first book of poems and most of his second while he was at the sanatorium. When he was released from the hospital in 1921 he taught public school in New Mexico, then resumed formal studies at the University of Colorado, concentrating on Latin, French, and Spanish. He had read French and Spanish poems earlier, in his isolation; he told me that some early experiments in prosody derived from misunderstanding French pronunciation of poetry.

Experimentalist he was, these years of his youth, appearing in avant-garde magazines like *Broom, Secession,* and *This Quarter.* From New Mexico he corresponded with Marianne Moore, whom he admired, who mailed him books when she worked in the library. When she edited *The Dial* Moore published his poems and one book review. The young Winters was devoted to the generation of American modernists, the fathers whom he would later dismember. He had good words for Eliot and Pound at first, then quickly found fault. It was Moore, Wallace Stevens, and above all William Carlos Williams who became his mentors. But it is difficult to remain an artist, or to develop, as the follower of a talented and accomplished parental generation. Harold Bloom has noted and detailed the engines of conflict. Possibly it is more difficult when the remarkable generation consists of elder siblings; closeness of age exacerbates forms of rivalry. Winters and his contemporaries — Hart Crane and Allen Tate, both born a year before him — were eleven to twenty years younger than the great crowded generation born mostly in the eighties of the previous century: Wallace Stevens 1879, William Carlos Williams 1883, Ezra Pound 1885, Marianne Moore 1887, T. S. Eliot 1888. Some poets of a sequent generation remained followers their whole lives, admirers of the elder brothers and sisters (MacLeish was born in 1892). Young males needed to rebel against the fathers or elder brothers if they themselves were to develop. Hart Crane, Allen Tate, and Yvor Winters — a grumpy and volatile troika, these brothers — battled with elder siblings. Thomas Parkinson has edited *Hart Crane and Yvor Winters: Their Literary Correspondence* — Tate's presence hovers over the book — and shows the young poets arguing, praising, and blaming with all the partisanship of artists in their twenties. Out of intense friendship and rivalry among poets, much poetry derives.

History, including literary history, combines with the personal or accidental. It is impossible to understand Winters without taking account of the bitter isolation that tuberculosis conferred upon him — the personal accident — but I suspect that the generational literary struggle was just as determinant. Winters became a fierce and competitive rebel assaulting the poet-armies of unalterable modernism established above him. The later, conservative Winters is *more* rebellious than the young experimentalist. That he attacked modernism in the name of reason, abstraction, archaism, and metrics is mere particularity.

When he left Colorado he took his M.A. at the University of Idaho in Moscow where he taught Romance languages. By this time he had met and married Janet Lewis, but she remained in New Mexico because she also suffered from tuberculosis. He lived outside the center of Moscow because he already raised Airedales. He thought, read, wrote his poems, and corresponded widely — especially with Crane and Tate. And in Idaho he underwent an unsettling or terrifying experience that shaped his life. Or so it appears. This experience is recorded in Winters's autobiographical short story, "The Brink of Darkness." First published in *Hound and Horn* in 1932, it was revised for republication in 1947. By taking it as autobiographical I commit various heresies (other writers do the same, notably Terry Comito, whose *In Defense of Winters* is the best book about him), but Winters wrote a story clearly consonant with known facts of his life. I suspect that he wanted or needed to leave this clue behind — a clue to the function throughout his life of what he called reason.

When Winters left Moscow for Stanford University and his Ph.D. in English, he found the short poem of the sixteenth and early seventeenth centuries, its structure often based on logic; he found meter and scholasticism, rhetoric and the plain style, Thomas Aquinas, Aristotle, and the line of poets — Googe, Greville, Jonson, Herbert — who provided him his rebellious conservatism. He found stones for the edifice he spent his life building, which was the Castle of Reason. But what did he mean by reason? He told Janet Lewis he could not teach poetry without reading aloud; is reading aloud an act of reason? When he collected his first three books of criticism as *In Defense of Rea-*

son, Winters raised eyebrows, for he is philosophically blunt, master of assertion and tirade, clear in his praise and blame — but he is more powerful than reasonable, more like Jeremiah than Aristotle. Sometimes we defend cool reason for hot reasons; we defend reason to attack madness.

In "The Brink of Darkness," the dark is insanity. The protagonist boards with an old couple in their lonely house in the country; when the old woman dies, her widower leaves the house to the young protagonist, who remains with the body for three days until the funeral. Left alone with his Airedales in this isolated place, his fear and anxiety mount. "I felt that I saw farther and farther into the events about me, that I perceived a new region of significance, even of sensation, extending a short distance behind that of which I had always been aware, suggesting the existence of far more than was even now perceptible." Details become stranger when the dogs run off and the man is alone. "One night after I had been watching the mice without moving for nearly an hour, I got up suddenly and went downstairs for a glass of water. . . . The light from the window fell on the snow outside. . . . Only, at the upper left-hand corner of the window there was darkness, a tangle of withered vines outside. . . . A slight motion caught my eye, and I glanced up at the darkened corner of the window to be fixed with horror. There, standing on the air outside the window, translucent, a few lines merely, and scarcely visible, was a face, my face, the eyes fixed upon my own."

When the dogs return, the protagonist begins to regain composure by removing porcupine quills from one of them: "my bed cover and my rugs were stained with blood." He remembers "over the past months" how he had been "disturbed, uncentered, and finally obsessed as by an insidious power. I remembered that I had read somewhere of a kind of Eastern demon who gains power over one only in proportion as one recognizes and fears him. I felt that I had been the victim of a deliberate and malevolent invasion. . . . I had begun to recover the limits of my old identity. I had begun this recovery at the time of the immersion in the brute blood of the bitch. The invading power I could not identify. I felt it near me still, but slowly receding."

"The Brink of Darkness" is affecting in its horror not because of literary invention but because of the author's intense feeling, which serves as a bloody footprint leading from the dark woods to the library stair. At the end, Winters says of his protagonist's condition: "It was as if there were darkness evenly underlying the brightness of the air, underlying everything, as if I might slip suddenly into it at any instant, and as if I held myself where I was by an act of the will from moment to moment." Forever after, in poems and in criticism, *will* is central to Winters — the will to reason that is alternative to madness. When he reprinted the story, late in his life, he added an explanation: "Winters says that this story is a study of the hypothetical possibility of a hostile supernatural world, and of the effect on the perceptions of a consideration of this possibility." The note tells us, "Once I felt captured by a hostile supernatural world." In the criticism, he alludes to demonic possession when he speaks of the Earl of Rochester; and he takes every opportunity to praise Robert Bridges's "Low Barometer," which enacts an experience of possession, terror, and self-rescue.

Winters feared madness all his life. The right ideas, combined with willpower, could keep madness off. On the other hand, ideas like Hart Crane's succumbed to madness or even engendered it. In *Forms of Discovery,* he remarks, in the eighteenth century,

a high incidence of madness among poets of more or less recognized talent: Collins, Gray, Chatterton, Smart, Blake, and others later; the same thing happens in other languages. A psychological theory which justifies the freeing of the emotions and which holds rational understanding in contempt appears to be sufficient to break the minds of a good many men with sufficient talent to take the theory seriously. Conversely, such a theory tends to equate irresponsible behavior and even madness with genius.

In *The Anatomy of Nonsense* in 1943, his chapter on Henry Adams, he speaks of his own

> belief that a balance which is artificial, or which is, in my terms, a habit formed by willed perseverance deriving from rational understanding of the need for it, and which preserves one from madness, is in its own nature a good; for madness is in its own nature and quite obviously an evil.

Winters's life and work determined to avoid this evil.

Some of Winters's early experimental poetry remains readable after many decades. There are one-line poems imitated from Native American sources:

NOON

Did you move, in the sun?

There is also muscular free verse in the studied line of William Carlos Williams, but the bulk of his *Collected Poems* is rhymed, metered, abstract, willful, and didactic.

> The poet's only bliss
> Is in cold certitude —
> Laurel, archaic, rude.

Sometimes Winters makes the mistakes he censored others for: technical laxities of forced rhyme, meter upheld by awkward word order, and dead metaphor. This is the first stanza of "Defense of Empire":

> The nervous light above my door
> Towers high with blossoms; all their scent
> Is shaken with the climbing roar
> Of planes which thread the firmament.

"Roar" makes an animal noise, but there's nothing else that belongs to an animal, not even "scent," because the odor is

florific. "Towers" is a commonplace extinct architectural metaphor, and "thread" is worse.

But we judge poets by their best work — or there are no good
poets. Let the reader forget his objections to archaism, and observe the irritable Thomist fend off Christianity:

A FRAGMENT

I cannot find my way to Nazareth.
I have had enough of this. Thy will is death,
And this unholy quiet is thy peace.
Thy will be done; and let discussion cease.

From the colloquial — "I have had enough of this" — to the
magisterial closure, from allusion to assertion, Winters loads
pages of feeling into four quick lines. To my mind his best poem
is this one:

TO THE HOLY SPIRIT

*from a deserted graveyard
in the Salinas Valley*

Immeasurable haze:
The desert valley spreads
Up golden river-beds
As if in other days.
Trees rise and thin away,
And past the trees, the hills,
Pure line and shade of dust,
Bear witness to our wills:
We see them, for we must;
Calm in deceit, they stay.

High noon returns the mind
Upon its local fact:
Dry grass and sand; we find
No vision to distract.
Low in the summer heat,
Naming old graves, are stones

Pushed here and there, the seat
Of nothing, and the bones
Beneath are similar:
Relics of lonely men,
Brutal and aimless, then,
As now, irregular.

These are thy fallen sons,
Thou whom I try to reach.
Thou whom the quick eye shuns,
Thou dost elude my speech.
Yet when I go from sense
And trace thee down in thought,
I meet thee, then, intense,
And know thee as I ought.
But thou art mind alone,
And I, alas, am bound
Pure mind to flesh and bone,
And flesh and bone to ground.

These had no thought: at most
Dark faith and blinding earth.
Where is the trammeled ghost?
Was there another birth?
Only one certainty
Beside thine unfleshed eye,
Beside the spectral tree,
Can I discern: these die.
All of this stir of age,
Though it elude my sense
Into what heritage
I know not, seems to fall,
Quiet beyond recall,
Into irrelevance.

Ignore our conventional Mosaic injunctions against "thee,"
"thou," and "thy." Hear the firm control of this trimeter line;

hear the adamant will to truth, the fierce necessity to acknowledge perceived reality however desolate; reside in Winters's resolved art.

This poem belongs to the late forties or early fifties, when Winters did his best work. By the middle of the fifties he was writing little. When I asked why, he told me — sharply; I wished I had not asked — that he would write nothing until he had something new to say. At some point I inveigled George Plimpton into assigning me a *Paris Review* interview with Winters. I was not surprised when Winters refused: If he had things to remark about poetry, he would write an essay.

My son Andrew was born in April at the Stanford Hospital. A few days later, when I picked up my mail, I found an envelope from Winters enclosing an epigram in tetrameter couplets called something like "On a Fair Infant So Fortunate as to Be Born in California." The epigram, which has been lost, continued our teasing about New England and California.

Before Andrew's birth I entertained the notion that the child arriving was my replacement, therefore implying my death. We named him after my father and me, and my morbid notion intensified. A first line entered my mind, and in two or three weeks I wrote a poem that Winters liked. This is the poem as I print it now:

> My son, my executioner,
>   I take you in my arms,
> Quiet and small and just astir
>   And whom my body warms.
>
> Sweet death, small son, our instrument
>   Of immortality,
> Your cries and hungers document
>   Our bodily decay.
>
> We twenty-five and twenty-two,
>   Who seemed to live forever,
> Observe enduring life in you
>   And start to die together.

At first, I called it "Epigenethlion," concocted Greek that I stole from an Andrew-poem written by another student. *The New Yorker* could not discover the word in the New York Public Library, and printed the poem as "First Child." In the magazine and in my first book, it concluded with a fourth stanza that Winters might have saved me from:

> I take into my arms the death
>   Maturity exacts
> And name with my imperfect breath
>   The mortal paradox.

"Maturity" is cant. An ironic eye, reading the modesty of "my imperfect breath," should cock a fierce eyebrow. The trite rhyme of "breath" with "death" seals the climax in the beeswax of platitude. (On the other hand, "exacts/paradox" is the cat's pajamas.) Blunt abstractions and cliché rhymes deviled Wintersian poems — and sometimes Winters's own.

That spring, candidates for next year's fellowship sent manuscripts to Stanford. Winters asked current fellows to read these poems and report. A close friend whom I admired submitted a blank verse narrative that I praised to Winters. Winters saw nothing in it and the subject was closed. But I had recruited another candidate. While I was at Oxford Thom Gunn emerged at Cambridge, first revealed on John Lehmann's BBC literary magazine "New Soundings." We made connection, Gunn visited Oxford, and we corresponded. When he wanted to come to the United States, I suggested that he apply for a Stanford Fellowship. Connecting Gunn with Winters was not farfetched; Gunn wrote a vigorous iambic line in praise of energy, and his poems were not afraid to think. Of course they were romantic, but Winters enjoyed the notion of tearing a poet down and building him up again.

When Winters chose Gunn as one of next year's fellows, he started to worry. He had never before brought a fellow from England, and he developed a fatherly concern for the young Englishman he had invited. Because I knew Gunn, Winters telephoned me as worries and solutions occurred to him. "Probably he can't drive. Can he drive? How will he get around? Would he ride a bike? I've got an old bike . . ."

Toward the end of our stay I asked Janet Lewis and Yvor Winters to dinner. We had been to his house many times: cookouts, parties, the Friday night fights. He was reluctant to accept. When he faced a situation requiring conventional manners, he felt alien or diffident; although he wanted to say no, his awkwardness would not let him. When they arrived, we drank bourbon, had dinner on the porch, and returned to sit in the living room. After five minutes, Winters leapt up ready to leave, a quick departure by conventional standards; conventionally I protested. Immediately Winters collapsed onto the sofa again, sighing and looking depressed. The next time he suggested departure I let him go. Years later I discovered: A friend who knew Winters better than I did told me that for years, whenever Winters ate outside his own house, he was sick to his stomach. He felt comfortable only in his own house or at his Stanford office. Never again would he attend the Kenyon School of Letters, in the New England countryside of Gambier, Ohio. In 1959 I wrote asking if he would give a paper at the 1960 meeting of the Modern Language Association. I chaired the poetics group that year; John Hollander and Paul De Man gave papers, and Winters would have completed an eldritch trio. He answered in January of 1960 and demurred characteristically by Absolute Statement: He would never, ever, travel anywhere for the rest of his life. He did, actually — to attend his daughter's wedding; rumor has it that he flew all night, both ways, to minimize his time away from home.

In June of 1954 I drove east from Palo Alto to Connecticut, my family flying ahead. I drove the Morris Minor coast to coast solo in three and a half days. Not sleeping a great deal, I went over my year, feeling loyal and affectionate, full of things I learned from him — but without illusions about a future relationship. In 1956, when I had published a book of poems and some essays, the letter arrived that excoriated me: It went on and on, with much anger and much punitive rhetoric, with accusations of literary and moral fault that were accurate enough. Although I had expected it, the letter was upsetting; on the whole it helped me, to align or realign both purpose and deportment.

Only once after leaving California did I see him — a year after his letter, at his daughter's wedding in Cambridge. At the reception we talked together, friendly enough, and joked about California and New England. A few years later I was member of a jury convened by the Yale University Library to choose the winner of the Bollingen Prize. As I recollect, Louise Bogan, Adrienne Rich, Robert Lowell, and I favored Winters, and my last connection with Yvor Winters was a telephone call from the office of the director of the Yale Library in Connecticut to Portola Road in Los Altos — home of Airedales, former goathouse. The director told Winters that the Yale Library had just awarded him the Bollingen Prize. There was a pause as Winters sorted things out: The *East* was giving him a prize — Yale University of the Ivy League, where they thought he was lower than the carpet. When the director handed me the phone, without revealing my identity, I said my name and congratulated him on the prize. I heard relief in his voice, as the mystery was solved. I heard pleasure as well — no one wholly disdains the laurel — when he said, "Oh, *you're* there, are you?"

THE NEW ENGLAND LANDSCAPE

From Menlo Park, that autumn in California, I applied to Harvard Graduate School, but my thoughts were elsewhere. Because I had known Richard Wilbur when he was a Junior Fellow, I knew that the Society of Fellows had once elected a poet, among its logicians, physicists, biologists, and scholars of Aramaic. Some literary scholars were elected from time to time, like my teacher Harry Levin, who never did graduate work; I aspired to the same nullity — no teaching, no class work. Wilbur, who was married with small children, had kept an office in Adams House where he could read and write; he wrote the poems of *Ceremony* while a Junior Fellow. When I was an undergraduate, Wilbur and I attended Suffolk Downs together for an afternoon at the races. I studied the racing form, Wilbur bet on the beautiful horses, and we came out forty cents apart. I preferred following Wilbur's example — writing poems, betting on beautiful horses — to grading papers and writing dissertations.

Archibald MacLeish, continuing his generosity, suggested my name. It was in March, not long before my son's birth, that the Society flew me from San Francisco to Boston for an interview. Before Andrew was born we heard the news. For the three years of the fellowship, back at Harvard, I saw MacLeish from time to time. Although he continued his writing course — as far as I know without insult — he taught another course that was more celebrated: a General Education course, introducing poetry to students not acquainted with it. He was the ideal proselytizer for poetry, enthusiastic, fertile in demonstrating his enthusiasm. Hundreds of students sat for his lectures, and MacLeish worked hard: Each student each week submitted a three-by-five card that responded to a poem. MacLeish read all the cards and constructed lectures out of his encounters with the poems themselves and with students' responses. I continue to meet people whose pleasure in poetry began with MacLeish's class.

For three years, Archie (as he became) and I had an occasional lunch or met at parties. During this time, Archie and Ada spent a year in Eliot House as master and mistress while the John Finleys took leave. MacLeish recruited famous friends to come visit, so that legally inclined Eliot House undergraduates found themselves chatting (after dinner, in the living room) with Learned Hand and Felix Frankfurter; Dean Acheson dropped by to talk foreign policy; English majors spent evenings with Robert Frost and John Crowe Ransom.

Then I vacated the East for the Midwest, and for the next seventeen years based myself in Ann Arbor. From time to time, over the years, we exchanged letters. When I prepared a magazine piece about creative writing in the colleges, I wrote to ask about young writers who had been students in his writing class. He listed his published students, and typically added: "I don't need to remind you that my part in all this is quite literally very small." His final sentence made a noise that sounds powerful or at least suggestive but runs on empty: "There are no answers but there are questions which create the possibility of answers." When I heard this noise I felt the old impatience, which rose further as we exchanged letters about Vietnam. With his friends in government and in the Democratic party, his position was not so easy as mine; I followed my students. Archie would have been a catch for Poets Against the Vietnam War, and I needled him to take part in protests; he wriggled when he answered: "I don't like what we are doing in North Viet Nam any better than anyone else but I have no sympathy with people who say that the alternative is to get out of Southeast Asia. It wouldn't be only Southeast Asia we would be getting out of, if you will forgive my grammar." He never deserted his Democratic friends, which was loyal of him; but I heard his excuses as equivocation.

In 1975, after my second marriage, Jane Kenyon and I left Michigan for New Hampshire. When we drove down 91 through Vermont and Massachusetts toward my mother's Connecticut house, we passed close to Uphill Farm in Conway. Sometimes we stopped to visit, and in 1978 I accepted an assignment to write an article about Archibald MacLeish for the *New York Times Book Review*. The occasion was his last book of essays; the staffers at the *Book Review* did not send it out for review; instead, out of goodwill for the man, they commissioned an interview. When I asked him if I could talk with him, for the *Times*, he had just read *Remembering Poets,* and answered me saying yes, and speaking of that book's "candor, which scares the living be-Jesus out of a projected subject as he reflects on his appearance, habits, conversation, and general inadequacy!" The message wasn't hard to hear.

We visited Archie and Ada in March of 1978, a pretty day

with snow on the ground as we drove down Vermont along the Connecticut River into Massachusetts. Turning off for Conway, we climbed the road at the end of town where a sign read "Not Passable in Winter and Spring" and found that the town plow cleared the way to Uphill Farm and no farther. We parked behind the house, and as I stood stretching, the back door of Uphill Farm bounced open and Archie strode out — tweed jacket over sweater, brown beret tilted rakishly on his head, hand extended, smiling, spritely: If you had been told that Archie was sixty-five instead of eighty-six, you would not have doubted. He was slightly deaf but his voice remained flexible and light, clear in the upper registers, with none of the crags and potholes usual to eight and a half decades.

This visit took half a day. We talked with Ada while Archie searched out aperitifs. Gradually realities intruded. Ada was anxious about the loss of short-term memory, and this subject became a theme of our visit. The two of them told about needing to leave notes for themselves all over the house: "Thursday, leave off car." Old age and its implication hung around them. They spoke of their difficulty, a year before, when the couple who had served them for a decade decided to retire. It was not easy to find a couple willing to live in Conway, out in the country, but they needed help: Ada said that she would die if she had to take care of this house by herself; Archie said that he would die if he had to live somewhere else. They said it, of course, the way we say that we will die if we don't have a pickled onion in the next thirty seconds. But two years earlier, MacLeish had published "The Old Gray Couple": "Everything they know they know together — / everything, that is, but one: . . . / Their deaths they think of in the nights alone."

The recent death of their sixty-year-old firstborn, Kenneth, crowded the house, detritus of their mourning heaped and piled wherever you looked. I asked Archie: No, he had not written about his son's death. In fact, he told me, he had been unable to write any poetry at all for some time now; he wondered if the poems had stopped forever. "What do you do?" he said. "Do you consciously accept silence? Wait? Begin all over again, as if in a new experience of life? Nothing needs understanding . . . more than that dwindling." I wondered if the pain of Kenneth's death might not occupy him so intensely that he could not write. He did not think so. He wanted to write again. "There are poems that come from terminal experience." (In fact he wrote poetry again, before he died, including a poem about Kenneth's death.)

One problem for the old poet, I thought that day, arises from loss of short-term memory. Some poets write well in their fifties, even in their sixties, but few later: Hardy, Landor, maybe Frost. (The best of Frost's last collection looks as if it were written earlier.) When you're writing a poem, you carry it with you day and night, for months or even years, often underneath the surface of waking thought; when you walk the dog or drive the car, a word for that poem may enter your consciousness when you do not know that you are thinking of it. When short-term memory fails, you lose that part of your brain that works when you don't know it's working.

Something else I thought that day, something I gradually became aware of during the hours of talk, and later on the drive south to my mother's house: By this time, I realized, I had become fond of the man, without any need to suppress irritation, without making allowances. I had known him from my early twenties into my fifties. Although he had always been kind to me, I had continued to feel impatience — with his heartiness, with his need for approval. At last I felt an easy affection, sympathy and even friendship. I was older; it was long since I required a Harvard-man superiority. But also, MacLeish's miseries of aging and loss had dissolved the manner or manners I had found irritating. He was a suffering human being.

MacLeish had always been a secular man. When his work was elegiac, death meant extinction. With the death of his firstborn, and with the onset of old age, he thought about survival. The author of "The End of the World" meditated on Rilke's obsession with predictions of the sun's death and the end of human life. Like Rilke, MacLeish thought of survival in terms of art. "Mozart has vanished," he said, "his music endures. There is a world that has been made by poets, musicians; that world *exists*. Are we to suppose this world will not survive us?" But I heard only the pun that he made without knowing it: the death of the son.

FACES IN DEATH

Archie lived five years more, Ada a little longer still. Ada's heart condition precluded travel; they were shut into Uphill Farm, and their memories dwindled further. The last years were not good — but when were the last years good? While MacLeish's poetic reputation diminished, he continued to be a name and a face; many old friends died but the survivors stuck together, and there were younger friends. When my *Times* piece appeared, he wrote me a succession of notes about telephone calls he received, and letters — from Henry Steele Commager, he told me, from André Kostelanetz. Also, it was gratifying that a college nearby in Greenfield, Massachusetts, devoted attention to him — interviewed him to make a book, collected him in its archives, and scheduled a celebration for Archie's ninetieth birthday. It turned out to be a memorial service.

Yvor Winters suffered a hard death, as cancer stripped him to nothing. He struggled at the end to finish his life's work in criticism. (He had written the poems he could write.) With Kenneth Fields he edited an anthology of the short poem in English; and he worked to collect and finish his essays on the short poem in English, printed just before he died as *Forms of Discovery*. The book is spotty, combining excellent old essays and passages that read like grumpy lecture notes. He ran out of time to do the book right.

When I met Winters he was fifty-three; when I met MacLeish he was fifty-seven — both younger than I am now. In my mind's eye I look at their faces for their contradictory examples. Inside me, elitist struggles always with populist, adamant upholder of permanent value against agreeable sloppy encourager of possibility. The elitist fears that he defends his ego's citadel by the force of hierarchical assertion; the populist fears that he asks indulgence and praise in return for indulgence and praise. Wanting to be as generous or affable as MacLeish yet wanting to be as rigorous as Winters, I totter from one example to the other, in temperament closer to MacLeish and in aspiration to Winters. In my twenties I sailed between them — to change the figure of allusion — with ears unstoppered and body tied to the mast of poetry's vessel.

Marianne Moore
Valiant and
Alien

❧

THE SOUP COURSE

Marianne Moore read her poems at Harvard in 1948, while I
was an undergraduate — the first time I gazed upon her tidy
and powerful person. I had read Moore as soon as I began to
read modern poetry, but I didn't take to the poems until I was
sixteen and working for a New Haven book store during the
Christmas rush. I spent my wages on books at a forty percent
discount, and in December of 1944 acquired *Nevertheless,* a
tiny volume in red cloth collecting six poems for $1.75. Reading
the title poem, which began, "you've seen a strawberry / that's
had a struggle," I remember feeling puzzled and intrigued by the
off-center junction of "strawberry" and "struggle," words
budged from conventional association. Half a century later she
remains the poet of struggling strawberries — commonplace
and weird, alliterated into irony, comical and dead serious.

On two occasions later I visited Moore at her apartment in
Brooklyn, each time to interview her, yet in *Remembering Poets*
I chose not to remember her. Although I admired her greatly, I
had witnessed only what others had reported; it was frustrating
that a 1957 *New Yorker* Profile described her in more detail

than I could muster. Later, I read Elizabeth Bishop's memoir, the best poet-reminiscence since William Hazlitt's, which for a while confirmed my decision not to recollect Marianne Moore. But in recent years I have been thinking about her: Her strangeness, her excellence, and the strange manner of her excellence intrigue me the way the contentious fruit did. Of all the old poets I met, she was the most puzzling. Puzzling over her for decades, I have arrived at some tentative notions about this frail, strong, enigmatic woman. Although I have little to offer in the way of new anecdote, I am ready to speculate about her.

Last of the poems in *Nevertheless* is the war poem, commissioned by *The Nation,* "In Distrust of Merits." The poem always recalls for me Moore's poetry reading in my sophomore year. I sat in the amphitheater at H. H. Richardson's Seaver Hall next to Robert Bly as F. O. Matthiessen introduced Moore with earnest admiration, especially for "In Distrust of Merits." I watched Moore as she listened to his praise, and watched her wince. At that moment, she distrusted "In Distrust of Merits." As late as 1967, when Grace Schulman referred to the poem in an interview, Moore said, "I don't consider that a poem. It's just a burst of feeling. It's emotion recorded." I too dislike the poem, which I find hackneyed; toward the end of a war, it gave people the truism they wanted:

> There never was a war that was
>   not inward; I must
> fight till I have conquered in myself what
> causes war . . .

F. O. Matthiessen was an intelligent Christian socialist, a good teacher and a useful critic who deceived himself with ringing falsehood as much as anyone. Standing up to read her poems, after the introduction, Moore was perplexed: She was too polite, after Matthiessen's praise, not to read the poem; she was too scrupulous not to question his judgment. Maybe the discord depressed her, for as she read her poems she was almost unintelligible, swallowing the vowels of poems and commentary alike. When she finished one poem and introduced another, it was difficult to tell when poem ended and commentary began. Listeners always had trouble distinguishing her poems from her talk — attesting not so much to the prosiness of her poems as to the finish of her speech — but in this reading the distinction was narrower than ever. She read three or four poems, including "In Distrust of Merits" with mumbled gratitude for Matthiessen's praise and with disparagement for the poem. Then, after perhaps twenty minutes, she concluded the reading; and the banquet ended with the soup course.

A few years later, when I was back at Harvard as a Junior Fellow, she returned for a conventional fifty-minute performance of her poems. This time Archibald MacLeish introduced her. As I walked through the Yard toward the reading, I came upon introducer and introducee walking together — Moore in her tricorne hat clutching books and a black purse, MacLeish handsome as ever, smiling and bending down to address his charge. MacLeish introduced us and we three walked together. Then Archie pointed toward a gray squirrel flitting among oaks, carrying an acorn, and I heard his enthusiastic voice make images to describe the squirrel; in Moore's presence, I heard him improvise a description of an animal — a brief lyrical excursus derivative of Marianne Moore.

A little later I met Moore again when she visited Cambridge for a conference trumped up by the Summer School. Every summer Harvard assembled eminences, and in 1956 the subject was the American literary magazine. The ex-editor of *The Dial* attended, together with Allen Tate, Philip Rahv, Robert Lowell, Hugh Kenner, and R. P. Blackmur. When I watched Moore meander among these Mount Rushmores of the literary moment, I realized: They are all afraid of her. She is five foot three and a half inches tall, weighs less than a hundred pounds, talks in a low mumble while looking at the floor, continually disparages herself while praising others — and they are all terrified of her.

A THREE-PART EGO

Marianne Moore was born in 1887 in Kirkwood, Missouri, a suburb of the St. Louis in which T. S. Eliot was born ten months later. Her parents separated before she was born, when her father suffered a nervous breakdown; she never met her father. Her mother, on the other hand, was as powerful as a dozen ordinary parents — a woman of independence, strength, and intelligence, scrupulous in language, moral thought, and conduct. Mrs. Moore's father, John Riddle Warner, was pastor of the Presbyterian Church of Kirkwood and admired the Reverend William Greenleaf Eliot of St. Louis (despite his Unitarianism), who was young Thomas's grandfather. (Moore and Eliot did not become acquainted for some decades; it is remarkable that these modernist titans were grandchildren of neighboring ecclesiastics.) In the lives of his children, Moore's father's existence is negligible; he seems a biological convenience — but of course his absence was a huge event, a precondition for the triad of Mary, Warner, and Marianne that formed the poet and her poetry.

If I appear to say that Moore's poems were the product of a committee, very well; maybe all poets are committees. Now that we have Charles Molesworth's biography, we begin to understand the intense intimacy of the family structure. The exclusiveness of Moore, her mother, and her brother — a singleness of three, created by the mother in the father's absence — drives one to hyperbole: Three heads on three bodies constructed a single ego three times stronger than an ordinary human ego. It is remarkable that the male of this troika, Warner Moore, was able to conduct a marriage, even to father children, without destroying the three-part structure. He needed to perform acts of separation. When he visited his mother and sister, or they visited him, his wife was often absent and ignorant of the meeting. Apparently he would walk from his house to his mailbox, read a letter from his sister, and destroy it without taking it inside the domestic nation. Seen from a distance, Warner Moore grew to resemble Colonel Blimp, naval chaplain become chaplain at a prep school, bluff and hearty figure of muscular Christianity, Republican who influenced his sister's politics. (Moore was singularly Nixonite among American poets.) But: Warner was a devoted son and brother in this system of loyalty, and he distributed literary opinions to his sister without diffidence. He played his strong part, and diffidence did not mark the Moore trinity. Scrupulosity marked it, moral and linguistic, a niceness not quite replacing piety: scrupulosity, kindness, ambition, reticence, relentlessness, eccentricity, modesty, and egotism. Not every noun in this series agrees with its neighbor: Conflict makes energy again.

The outline of Moore's life is well known and she remains mysterious. When John Warner died in 1894, the three Moores left Kirkwood for Carlisle, Pennsylvania. Marianne studied at the Metzger Institute to enter Bryn Mawr, where Hilda Doolittle was a fellow student, and took her B.A. in 1909. In 1911 she traveled with her mother in France and England, then for four years taught at the United States Industrial Indian School in Carlisle. In 1915 she began publishing in *The Egoist,* then in *Poetry* and *Others.* In 1916 she and her mother moved to New Jersey to keep house for her brother in his parsonage; in 1918, when Warner left his parish to join the navy as a chaplain, the two women moved to metropolitan New York where they remained.

Living at first in Greenwich Village — where she died fifty-four years later — Moore met Wallace Stevens, Alfred Kreymborg, Kenneth Burke, and William Carlos Williams; she published in *The Dial;* she worked at a branch of the New York Public Library from which she mailed books on loan to the tubercular Yvor Winters in New Mexico. In 1921, Bryher and H.D. published a collection of Moore's poems in London without — as Moore claimed — her knowledge or consent. From 1925 until it stopped publishing in 1929, she edited *The Dial,* and in 1929 moved to the Clinton Hill neighborhood of Brooklyn where she and I conversed thirty years later. *Observations* appeared in 1924, *Selected Poems* in 1935, *What Are Years?* in 1941, *Nevertheless* in 1944, and a *Collected Poems* in 1951. She received The Prizes. In 1954 she brought out her translation of La Fontaine, the next year her book of essays *Predilections*, then further books of poems and *A Marianne Moore Reader* which selected from her work and added curiosities, including the *Paris Review* interview. Late in life she traveled abroad, seeing old friends like T. S. Eliot. By 1966 it was clear that she could no longer reside on Clinton Hill and she moved to the West Village, Ninth Street, where she was often ill and even feeble. When Ezra Pound visited the United States in 1969 for the last time, the two old poets said goodbye and sat for a photograph. When she died in February of 1972 her old friend contrived a memorial service in Venice, where he died the following October, last of the heroic generation of American poets.

POETS TALKING

My *Paris Review* interview with T. S. Eliot took place in 1959, the interview with Ezra Pound in February and March of 1960. Only eight months later, November of 1960, I took a cab to 260 Cumberland Street in Brooklyn, the day before the election in which John Kennedy edged out Richard Nixon. Originally, George Plimpton asked me to interview Moore not for the *Paris Review* but for *Horizon,* which had hired George to oversee an interview series modeled on the *Review*'s. But *Horizon*'s editors disliked the product: They said it sounded like two poets talking. George was pleased to absorb the interview into the *Paris Review.*

We had prepared by letter. I wrote on 28 August 1960, and recalled our 1956 meeting, mentioning George Plimpton, the *Paris Review,* and my interviews with her old friends. Her postcard in answer was dated 30 August. "A compliment, Mr. Hall; those HOW WRITERS WRITE interviews are the best things in the REVIEW, I think." As she did so often, she misremembered something: The feature is called "Writers at Work." In the rest of her postcard she asked for preliminary questions, saying that they would not "inter-jeopardize spontaneity." She gave me her telephone number and ended, "I am beleaguered and so are you; but with a little work done beforehand, it might not take too long." I admire correspondents who use semicolons on post-cards.

On October 24, I sent her a three-page letter of preliminary questions. Apparently I sent it special delivery, for I had a note from her pleading that I might cease and desist from special delivery letters, which were delivered to Cumberland Street early in the morning, the bell rung on the ground floor while Moore still slept on the fifth. She had been ill, and when she wrote on 2 November, a few days before our meeting, her typed letter wandered over the page, with handwritten inserts and parenthetical injunctions: "(THIS LETTER, Mr. Hall, should not be reproduced in facsimile!!)" (The *Paris Review* reprinted a manuscript page with its interviews.) "Have had some back-sets but certainly can see you and should not have given an impression that S. Delivery letters are out of the question." I was to arrive at eleven on Monday morning the seventh, and we would continue the interview started by mail with my sample questions. "There is a little restaurant not far from me and I thought I could invite you to have lunch" (she typed the word three times: "luch lunnch LUNCH") "with me — noisy as it is!" She gave me clear instructions for achieving Cumberland Street by subway or by taxi.

The cabdriver crossed the Brooklyn Bridge and turned left on Myrtle Avenue, following the Elevated; before he turned right onto Cumberland Street, he locked his doors. He was incredulous when I told him that I was visiting an old woman who lived alone.

The old woman who lived alone buzzed the ground-floor latch quickly, as if she waited for me this bright morning early in November. Upstairs, she admitted me to the dark foyer of her apartment, from which a long hallway led to a living room overlooking Cumberland. Running the length of the hallway was a bookcase, and on top of the bookcase near the door lay a Nixon button. I installed the bulky reel-to-reel tape recorder between two chairs in the living room, kneeling to plug it in while Moore hovered above me. She appeared nervous or apprehensive — like Pound and not like Eliot — over the test and trial of an interview. Piles of books tottered beside chairs throughout the big light room, and the walls were covered with paintings. Perhaps one or two were Moore's own, though I never thought to ask. I noticed a Mexican landscape signed by Mabel Dodge. Others were old and tea-colored like the furniture, which was furry and tasseled. The room was gloriously cluttered, pictures on the wall scissored from magazines, figurines, unidentifiable objects apparently of a natural provenance — and many small effigies of animals. Objects addressed to Moore arrived in the mail with regularity; someone in Oregon spotted a beetle encased in clear plastic, and thought, "This looks like something Marianne Moore would write a poem about." Sometimes it was too much. "No more shells and feathers!" she announced on one occasion.

Some of the appurtenances of her apartment were mystifying. Doubtless an anecdote would explain each of them, but the pure fact was often wonderfully inexplicable. Hanging down from the door into the kitchen was something that looked like a trapeze — and I remembered a story. A young collector visited her with a pile of books for signing. As she corrected small errors in each edition, the collector looked around the apartment in wonder, each time puzzling over the trapeze-like object in the doorway; he was polite and did not wish to appear nosy, but finally he could not contain himself: "Miss Moore," he asked, "what's that up there in the doorway?" She answered without looking up. "Oh," she said, "that's my trapeze."

One could not be certain, but I think she understood that she was funny. She had her own irony. When she corrected the interview, she added a phrase to an anecdote about Hart Crane, from whom she had requested revisions in a poem for *The Dial:* "It was lawless of me to suggest changes."

That morning we spoke as the tape collected us. The interview makes a fair record of our conversation, although she had prepared answers to some questions sent by letter, and although like Pound she added material by post and revised her speech in draft. I asked questions from my deck of three-by-fives, followed new notions suggested by her answers, and generally lost myself — no longer aware that *Interviewer* interrogated *Marianne Moore* — in my fascination at her wandering consequent-inconsequent responses: the character of her mother, the *Dial* editorship, the milkman's courtship, remarks on her own work compounded by disclaimers, modesties, and ambitions. She spoke as she wrote, by the association of ideas.

We finished taping — maybe two hours — before lunch. She appeared increasingly relieved as we mosied toward the end, pleased by some of her improvised formulations. She smiled a cat's smile as we pulled ourselves together for lunch. She put on a long dark coat, for the day although bright was chilly. As we departed she picked up the Nixon button from the hall bookcase near the apartment's front door, fingered it and looked at me sideways, knowing perfectly well that like all other American poets I would vote tomorrow for John Kennedy. (We avoided political discussion, but I recall her fearing that the young senator might prove impetuous.) She tried setting the button against her coat, to wear for our expedition, but returned it to the bookcase. She decided, she told me, that its colors did not go with her hat.

We walked together up Cumberland Street, which was littered and dour, not yet a circle of Hell but redolent of poverty and disorder. Shops at the top of the block were shabby but adequate, including the little Austrian restaurant where she brought her guests. The large hostess, accented and obsequious, was aware of Moore's eminence, and some importance rubbed off on Moore's guest. It was the restaurant where the neighborhood dentist eats a chop every day, nodding to the retired mailman (meatloaf) and to the widow from Brazil (cabbage soup). It was the restaurant to which a small old woman (the famous poet) brings flustered admirers, who are never allowed to pay for lunch. It was insignificant that *Horizon* paid my expenses, not to mention a fee for the interview, and that Moore received nothing. If I were to journey all the way to Brooklyn to call on her, she would of course demand that I accept a coin or token for my return journey by subway; and as Moore's guest I would be treated to lunch. Oh, if one cherished delusions about the obdurate strength and willpower of this elderly spinster, one might try grabbing the check; but bring along a splint and a sling.

We drank tea. Miss Moore took chicken pot pie, as I recall, while I dug into Viennese goulash.

Back in Ann Arbor, I worked on the interview as letters arrived from Brooklyn 5, New York, with apologies and quotations. "After abandoning you so unceremoniously," she wrote on election day, "I consulted my dentist who happened to be in;" — for all her reticence she allowed herself to recount the daily life, even to dentures — "then on returning home I happened in my mail, on this thought in the Post (Sat. Evening) — issue of November 12 —" and typed a quote from Jacob Bronowski, which she applied to the subject of science and poetry. She told me I needn't use it; she sent it to me because she tended "to corroborate myself."

Five weeks later I sent her a draft of the interview with queries keyed to the text. I needed to say that I wasn't sure I had this sentence right, or that one, because a truck had gone by on Cumberland Street. I told her that she did not seem to complete an anecdote about Ezra Pound, suggested where she might incorporate the Bronowski quote, and called her attention to numerous small changes — in my questions or in her answers — that I inserted for the sake of clarity. I invited her to change my changes; mostly, she changed them. She altered in longhand the text of the interview, and answered queries in the margins of my letter with an effect of dialogue: When I hoped that I did not ask too many questions, her spidery hand answered, "Grateful."

She could write only in longhand because she was ill, with fever and digestive problems, in a Brooklyn hospital; "nothing malignant as cause of my collapse." Having handwritten over the text, she told me to have it retyped and send her the bill; I was disobedient. On a visit to New York, I picked out a green-leafed plant for delivery to her in Brooklyn — and received my recompense when she wrote a letter, speaking of my casual gift: "so rare a thing to examine and encourage as the green tropic plant, with its curious pale specks on its alligator pear-green foliage. The new leaves are especially fascinating — frail but spotted also!" A month later, in another letter, her thank-you continued and included apology for the inadequacies of her first note: "The plant was and is a very diverting one, getting new leaves now. In my abasement at the Hospital, I was unable to examine it minutely for some time; but it is true as one of the nurses said about flowers, 'They do something for you.' I found some leaves, plain; and some, with tiny transparent rice-bowl lemon-yellow spots. Strange to say, the new leaf has no spots (freckles); then after four or five days the freckles appear." Like her speech on many occasions, her letters resembled Marianne Moore poems:

> so rare
> a thing with its curious pale
> alligator-pear-green foliage
> pale but
> spotted also! "They do something
> for you." Some leaves plain
> and some with tiny transparent rice-
> bowl lemon-yellow
> spots that . . .

It was not her nature to permit indebtedness. My gift required such labor from a sick woman; there would be no more gifts.

THE WONDERFUL LUNCH

Over the next years there were a few letters expressive of grati-tude for the interview. When Viking prepared the *Marianne*

Moore Reader (1961), Moore and her editor Pascal Covici reprinted it. The *Reader* promoted her work, reprinting poems, essays, and translations; also it served to market the certified modern poet who wore tricorne hats and admired the Brooklyn Dodgers. Her correspondence with a Ford executive, about naming a new car that turned out to be the Edsel, was reprinted from *The New Yorker*. Why not? Her manner, discussing marketing with an automobile executive, is as careful as if she were editing *The Dial*. But maybe when we praise the poet by finding her charming, our condescension allows us to pull the teeth from her poems.

Our next encounter was an occasion for the promotion or exploitation of her charm. The fault was mine, for I was the conduit between *McCall's* and Marianne Moore. An editor telephoned me, spring of 1965, and then wrote confirming that they wanted an interview "similar in format" to the old one "but not in substance." They wanted me to "draw from Miss Moore her ideas on a variety [of] subjects of concern to women of all ages and stages." I approached Moore, who consented, again asking for questions ahead of time, and ended her letter, "You are very valiant, Mr. Hall!" It was a favorite word. She added a postscript: "We could go to the same little place to eat. Certainly you are a *guest*." We agreed on the date of April 23, Shakespeare's birthday, and I arranged with *McCall's* to borrow a tape recorder and receive last-minute instructions (doubtless they feared two poets talking) before I hazarded Cumberland Street again. My editor had suggested questions:

1. Her childhood in St. Louis, as daughter [*sic*] of a minister. What were the early influences? Did she live the life of a normal little girl and teen-ager, etc. Play with dolls, dream about being a mother, get crushes on boys?

   . . .

3. She was a teacher of commercial subjects. What were they? Was it unusual for a woman to be teaching in those days? How did she happen to drift into this kind of employ-

ment? I see a fascinating dichotomy here: a poet teaching commercial subjects.

4. Try to draw her out about her love affairs, if any. Was she ever engaged? Why didn't she marry? Was there some deep disappointment in her life? Does she wish she could have experienced motherhood? Grandmotherhood? This part of her life should be looked into rather deeply, if you can do it without embarrassing her.

5. For a time, she was part of the literary whirl in Greenwich Village. Did she know Edna St. Vincent Millay? Any impressions of Millay — anecdotes, sidelights? Did Moore "burn her candle at both ends" too? And, why, after the Greenwich Village years, did she settle in Brooklyn, almost the antithesis of the Village? Another dichotomy?

When I passed the questions on, I edited them:

How did you happen to teach commercial subjects?
Did you know Edna St. Vincent Millay in the Village?

On the taxi ride to Clinton Hill, another cabbie gave me another lecture. He told me that if he were driving in this part of Brooklyn at night, he would lock his doors and not stop at red lights. I told Moore and asked her if she thought of moving out; she said she received such advice daily. To move — late in one's seventies, from an apartment dense with the accumulation of years — seemed impossible. It was only a year later that she moved — back, as it were, after almost forty years — to Greenwich Village with the help of her nieces.

This time Moore met me with a hand over her mouth. She had broken her dentures, and her dentist would take a few days to repair them. She had not canceled the interview — which was generous; her appearance embarrassed her — but she could *not* leave the apartment. I knew better than to argue. We could not take lunch in the Austrian establishment; she begged my forgiveness for providing me instead her own meager lunch.

Her dental catastrophe distracted Moore. Normally she was hard to hear and now it was harder, with her hand in front of her mouth. But she warmed to many subjects, and she had typed answers to the questions in my letter. However, the final interview contains some oddities. When *McCall's* wanted further explorations of certain issues, an editor consulted her directly. When I read Moore's *Collected Prose* many years later, I discovered that some of her answers were almost identical to sentences that she had already committed to print. I cannot reconstruct what happened. I know that I did not copy sentences from printed sources and ascribe them to the interview; I suspect that the plagiarist (strong word) was Moore herself, when she prepared typed answers to *McCall's* follow-up questions. Having once found verbal formula A to answer question X, why should she improvise a new set of phrases? Or perhaps she let the mind's tape recorder replay sentences she had used before. (Another Moore, the sculptor Henry, recited the same answers to familiar interview questions over and over again; journalists appeared to steal phrases from other journalists.) The *McCall's* interview gives off a typed odor, not a vocal one; Moore typing left out initial pronouns: "Was too young." Moore speaking omitted nothing. Whatever its faults in conception and in execution, the *McCall's* interview contains material, even literary material, that is available nowhere else, and because it has never been reprinted, I reprint it in the appendix here.

This journalistic occasion allowed me to experience history's most extraordinary lunch. When we had finished recording, late morning on April 23, Miss Moore begged that I might excuse her as she prepared a bite. After ten or twelve minutes she emerged carrying a small tray which she handed me. When she brought herself a second, similar tray, we sat buffet-style in her living room and ate lunch together. My tray held several little paper cups, the pleated kind used for cupcakes, which she employed as receptacles. In one there were several raisins, perhaps seven, and in another a clutch of Spanish peanuts. There was a cheese glass (from Kraft processed spread) half full of tomato juice. There was a glass dish that contained one quarter of a canned peach. There were three saltines and a tinfoil-wrapped wedge of processed Swiss cheese. There was something sweet, cake-like, and stale. I knew that she liked health foods, a drinker of carrot juice, so that her fare surprised me. Because she lacked teeth, she ate even less than I did. In a moment, she left the room and returned with something to fill me up, but which she could not herself chew. From the package she poured on my tray a mound of Fritos. "I like Fritos," she croaked, covering her mouth. "They're so nutritious."

MAKING STRANGE

A few years later, before her death in 1972, I tried to see her in connection with another project but the visit never took place. I heard from time to time of her illness but I was loath to wish her well or send her a flower, because her necessary gratitude would burden a sick woman. My last communication from her was bewildering. On a postcard setting an hour for my abortive visit, she mentioned that she would probably have nothing to contribute, "except that I don't write Syllabic Verse although of course words have syllables. M. M." With her reminder that words have syllables, we ceased our correspondence.

It's almost as difficult to understand why she claimed not to write syllabic verse. She wrote it, some of the time. In syllabic verse the poet counts syllables rather than metrical feet. Maybe it doesn't make much sense, but in the work of certain poets — Moore, Auden, Gunn, Snodgrass — syllabics make their own strange music, often rhyming on the off-stress (stirs/others) and avoiding the softer-louder tune of iambic that measures most English poetry. In her syllabics, Moore often made a decorative stanza, as in "What Are Years?" Each nine-line bundle repeats lines of six, six, seven, nine, five, nine, seven, six, and six syllables.

WHAT ARE YEARS?

What is our innocence,
what is our guilt? All are
        naked, none is safe. And whence
is courage: the unanswered question,
the resolute doubt —
dumbly calling, deafly listening — that
in misfortune, even death,
        encourages others
        and in its defeat, stirs

        the soul to be strong? He
seems deep and is glad, who
        accedes to mortality
and in his imprisonment rises
upon himself as
the sea in a chasm, struggling to be
free and unable to be,
        in its surrendering
        finds its continuing.

        So he who strongly feels,
behaves. The very bird,
        grown taller as he sings, steels
his form straight up. Though he is captive,
his mighty singing
says, satisfaction is a lowly
thing, how pure a thing is joy.
        This is mortality,
        this is eternity.

(In the sixth line of the first stanza, she counts "listening" as two syllables, the way most of us pronounce it.) Why did Moore deny that she wrote syllabic verse? I don't know why she denied writing syllabics, or informed me that words have syllables, or called Fritos nutritious, or in a letter wrote "backset" for "set-back." I know that her mind was not like anyone else's: The radical strangeness of her mind sponsored the originality of her poetry.

To call her eccentric is true enough and says nothing unless we try defining the word. She lived at the periphery of the ordinary, not (I think) on purpose. In England especially, or in New England, eccentricity is sometimes worked up and worn like a costume; it can construct a carapace or aid an assault upon renown. But some eccentrics cannot help their eccentricity. They stand willy-nilly at the side of other people's habits and measures. When Marianne Moore wrote poems, from girlhood on, I think that she was original, and not merely because her scrupulosity demanded it; she could not make an ordinary noise if she tried.

Poetry requires difference by its nature. If poetry makes itself out of ordinary boring imprecise language (as much published poetry does), it is mediocre or bad poetry. Poetry to be beautiful must separate itself from the ordinary — by extravagance, by purity, by precision, by original vision or imagination. Sometimes, as in the work of Moore's friend Williams, poetry finds its beauty in looking natural; still, it must be different. Viktor Shklovsky speaks of literary language as needing to "make strange." A critic elucidates: "By tearing the object out of its habitual context, by bringing together disparate notions, the poet gives the *coup de grace* to the verbal cliché, to the stock responses attendant upon it." Defamiliarizing the ordinary comes to most poets by sudden insight and by hard labor. By inspiration the mind leaps to associate words normally incomparable (metaphors, connections between distant things) so that the poem's language embodies acts of discovery. Revision criticizes, disconnecting the ordinary. But some poets don't require the blood chemistry of inspiration. These poets never see the world — or interpret it in language — as others do; their ordinary minds do not resemble our ordinary minds. If a mind speaks so far outside our circle that we cannot interpret it, we call its language schizophrenic. But when unusual minds speak at the circle's edge, and from this vantage remark on the common life, sometimes we find poetic genius. In "Lapis Lazuli,"

Yeats had his three observers climb a mountain — away from the tragic scene — in order, beyond the circle, to witness the circle's history. Eccentricity affords strangeness to language and clarity to vision; and the spinster writes "Marriage."

Few poets are eccentric in this unwitting and unwilling way, not Dylan Thomas nor Robert Frost nor T. S. Eliot nor Yvor Winters nor Archibald MacLeish. Although these poets write no ordinary language, they inhabit the planet of discourse from which most of us agree to speak. Pound became crazy, but at an early age was eccentric only in the willful way of green billiard-table-felt trousers; his later madness was megalomaniac, paranoid, and topical. I suspect that Emily Dickinson, bipolar like most poets, was as eccentric as Marianne Moore. We may wonder at this coincidence: Our two most eccentric great American poets are both female. When the sex of "poet" is *m.*, to be a female poet (at all) is eccentric. Or: If poetry is proscribed for the gender, then only a character originally extraordinary will undertake the art and endure its penalties.

When we learn of Marianne Moore's life, from an early age, we learn facts that do not fit. Highly intelligent, she was a mediocre student, best in science. "I failed Italian twice." She was stubborn, hard-working, obdurate, and nothing conventional came easy. She read vastly and accumulated eclectic information. There's a story in Alfred Kreymborg's *Troubador,* telling how he and William Carlos Williams argued whether the young Moore knew everything about everything. This was the Marianne Moore of New York and Greenwich Village, beautiful in photographs, ethereal, with long red hair coiled on top of her head, friend to Stevens, Williams, Kreymborg, Loy, H.D. — the caryatid, Williams called her, supporting the edifice of American modernism. To discover if her learning extended to baseball, Kreymborg arranged to take her to the Polo Grounds on a Saturday afternoon when Christy Mathewson was pitching. All the way on the El she discoursed on poetry, even as they walked into the ballpark through the excited crowd. Mathewson threw warm-up pitches. When the umpire called a strike on the first batter, one Shorty Slagle, Kreymborg could hold back no longer.

"Do you happen to know the gentleman who threw that strike?" he asked. She answered, "I've never seen him before, but I take it to be Mr. Mathewson." When Kreymborg gasped "Why?" she answered: "I've read his instructive book on the art of pitching, and it's a pleasure to note how unerringly his execution supports his theories." *Pitching in a Pinch* was the book.

She talked with a strenuous polysyllabic precision. This pedantic speech can be a form of humor, an elevation of diction over circumstance, like Major Hoople or W. C. Fields. To note "how unerringly his execution supports his theories" sounds like Eliot when he wrote me that he was changing flats because he married, actually saying something to the effect that an alteration of domestic arrangements necessitated . . . Today this language may sound like the flight attendant who asks if we would care to purchase a beverage, but in the Latinate years of educated grandparents it was mildly funny. When I interviewed Moore, she made changes in the manuscript to elevate demotic improvisations. I taped her answering a question about her age by asking, "Can you figure that out?" On the manuscript she altered the phrasing: "Can you deduce my probable age?" If one misses the mild humor, one misses the tone.

The revision is also clearer or more exact. As I read through everything by Moore — poems of course, but also prose pieces, interviews, letters, even dedications in copies of her books — themes of accuracy and exactness repeat themselves; often they turn up in acknowledgment of failure, proofing errors, or her tendency to misquote. She loved exactness, detested error and exaggeration — and she struggled with inaccuracy throughout her life.

Poetry bothered her from the start on account of its tendency toward falsehood, from mistakes to outright lies. "I too dislike it," she said. At the beginning of the *McCall's* interview, she told why: At school she learned that poets were more devoted to shape, color, and sound than they were to truth. "I disliked poetry," she told me, speaking of herself as a child, "anything partly true and improbably lengthened out to *sound* true. As a child, I had no use for it. . . . I had to learn something called

'The Little Red Hen.' The hen's cackle was imitated: 'Cut-cut-cut-cudaw-cut.' That — well — had no verisimilitude for me. I thought, Anything but awkward fictitiousness." She disliked it yet spent a life writing it, or (as she scrupulously noted) writing what was called poetry because there was nothing else to call it.

Even among people who consider that they praise poetry, it's common to assume that poetry finds beauty in all things, even ugly ones — and therefore tells untruths for the sake of uplift. We refer to mundane or unpalatable facts as "more truth than poetry." Mistrust of poetry has a long history. According to Plutarch, Solon told Thespis that once we start telling lies — as in pretending to be a character on a stage — there's no telling where we'll stop. Plato barred poets from his Republic; his Socrates condescended to the rhapsode Ion. A Puritan parliamentarian in England introduced legislation to outlaw metaphor. Some vatiphobes find poetry deliberate deception; others imply not mendacity but idiocy, promoting the notion that poetry is beautiful but dumb — childishly concerned with surface, spectacular and ingratiating. Usually assuming wickedness rather than unintelligence, other poets besides Marianne Moore have questioned the morals of their art. Geoffrey Hill speaks of "the tongue's atrocities" and quotes Coleridge from his 1796 Notebook: "Poetry — excites us to artificial feelings — makes us callous to real ones."

Marianne Moore, writing what people called poetry, never intended artificial feelings or beautiful lies. Precision was her passion, definition at the forefront of duty. She constructed her poetry of terms made exact. Among the thousand apologies for poetry, a common one emphasizes its social and moral duty to refine language and protect it against abuse; precision's execution in language becomes poetry's beauty and justification. This rationale for poetry speaks to Moore's practice, or at least to her conscious practice: the apothegm as weapon of exactness.

Take a simple Moore for a simple example, and the results will not remain simple. In "Silence" she begins, "My father used to say" — and Solon would already shout her down: She never met her father. (A note records that the phrase comes from

"Miss A. M. Homans.") After quoting, Moore paraphrases; after paraphrasing, she invents; at the end of the poem, as if quoting the same father, she takes her last distinction from a remark attributed to Edmund Burke:

SILENCE

My father used to say,
"Superior people never make long visits,
have to be shown Longfellow's grave
or the glass flowers at Harvard.
Self-reliant like the cat —
that takes its prey to privacy,
the mouse's limp tail hanging like a shoelace from its mouth —
they sometimes enjoy solitude,
and can be robbed of speech
by speech which has delighted them.
The deepest feeling always shows itself in silence;
not in silence, but restraint."
Nor was he insincere in saying, "Make my house your inn."
Inns are not residences.

The subject? Reticence, silence, self-reliance, solitude, restraint . . . Or say: The subject is the correct life, how it is proper to live, and propriety is indicated by definition. The poem defines by revising itself; and silence is a sign for the more inward moral quality of restraint. If my father / Edmund Burke seems extravagant ("Make my house your inn"), in truth he is precise in his restraint, because "Inns are not residences."

Exact definition, yes — and what is that shoelace doing? The cat's place is clear enough, restraint and privacy (though the exemplary feline practices torture and assassination), but what is the shoelace doing in this poem? The shoelace is a precision of visual notation, almost comic by anomaly — yet without this accurate unexpected detail, the poem were no poem at all.

Moore's obsession with correctness pertained not only to the information in her poems, including quotations, but to proofreading. When one asked Moore to sign a book, she liked to take it overnight, to perform laborious repair of errors. When I first met her in 1956, she wrote in her Faber *Collected Poems:* "It is a pleasure to me, Mr. Hall, that you should see a reason to find room for this book" and "Donald Hall's copy of these Collected Poems   Marianne Moore   August 1, 1956." In pencil she added: "(corrected, unless I am blinded by hospitality and the excitement of Cambridge to other misprints)." Beginning with a misspelling in the table of contents, she corrected seven misprints, sometimes only a letter ("perturbability" for "perturability") but once a missing word; and in "Bowls" she had to alter "precisions" to "precisionists." Knowing her meticulousness, one smiles appreciatively; then, perhaps, one notices: There *do* seem to be an unusual number of misprints. Macmillan was notorious for mistakes, but my volume was Faber, printed in Great Britain, and her misprints continued when she moved to Viking. This precisionist was an incompetent proofreader.

On the other hand, there's Moore's necessity for correctness: One writer tells a story that resembles many others. In conversation with friends, she leapt from topic to topic, and when her incongruities were called to her attention she alluded to a classic crux: "Wasn't it Aristotle who observed that 'the ability to see a connection between apparently incongruous things is the sign of a poet'? Or was it 'mark' of a poet? I hate people who can't quote things correctly," Moore said, "and then I go and make all kinds of mistakes myself." The next morning, having done her homework, she telephoned her guests to set things straight. "The sentence actually reads" — she told one — " 'It is the mark of a poet to see a connection between apparently incongruous things.' " She added, apropos her error, "I feel as degraded as a worm at the bottom of an umbrella stand." (A worm at the bottom of an umbrella stand? The mouse's shoelace tail.)

On the other hand, she makes "all kinds of mistakes" herself. This mistress of quotation constantly misquoted and perpetrated errors of fact. In a letter, Patricia Willis (editor of the

Complete Prose; Moore scholar at Yale's Beinecke Library) tells me that Moore altered quotations *"all* the time." Willis feels that Moore did it on purpose: "Improvements, precisionings, concisions, etc. For example, I have found that about 160 of 231 lines of 'An Octopus' are quotations, some with inverted commas, some without, some of the former drastically re-worded, most altered a bit." For Willis, these alterations aid "voice, or persona, and . . . sound and rhythm." Yet altering the truth for aesthetic reasons went against Moore's expressed scruples. She didn't *want* to believe that reality might be enhanced and altered for the sound's sake. Maybe she managed not to know what she did.

Elizabeth Bishop's memoir, "Efforts of Affection," acknowledges Moore's uniqueness. "She looked like no one else" — Bishop tells us that she once flattered Marianne Moore by remarking that she resembled the young Mickey Rooney — "she talked like no one else; her poems showed a mind not much like anyone else's." Bishop recalls with astonishment that Moore was baffled by conventional English prosody. As Moore looked for metrical correctness, translating La Fontaine, "it seemed to be almost . . . physically impossible for her to do so. . . . If I'd say, 'If you leave out "and" or "the" . . . it will go umpty-umpty-um,' Marianne would exclaim, 'Elizabeth, thank you, you have saved my life.' " Bishop continues, "Why not believe that the old English meters that still seem natural to most of us . . . were not natural to her at all?" Suggestively, Bishop remarks on "the rarity of true originality, and also the sort of alienation it might involve."

Alienation makes strange. Maybe Moore's formal innovations, the rhythm of her syllabic stanzas and free verse, resulted from an incapacity ("physical," Bishop suggests — like color blindness) to hear the louds and softs of regular English iambic meter. William Empson in 1962 guessed that "Miss Marianne Moore really talks without stress, and only could be scanned by counting syllables, so that she was quite right to make her innovation." Sometimes she spoke with stress, accenting "Elizabeth" for instance, but her voice tended toward a monotony in which it was difficult to distinguish peaks and valleys. When I look in her critical prose, it becomes clear that she had trouble with meter. In "Feeling and Precision," an essay published in the *Sewanee Review* of 1944, she spoke of "Dr. Johnson's objection to rigmarole, in his takeoff on the ballad:

> I put my hat upon my head,
> And went into the Strand,
> And there I saw another man,
> With his hat in his hand."

So she quotes, or rather misquotes. For one thing, Johnson said "walk'd," not "went." Another mistake corroborates Bishop's suggestion. Johnson extemporized this quatrain, which parodied attempts at ballad simplicity, to show that meter did not make poetry. Of course Johnson made sure that the quatrain was metrically unexceptional: four lines of iambic tetrameter, di-*dum*, di-*dum*, di-*dum*, di-*dum*. Therefore he did not conclude with two natural anapests, "With his *hat* in his *hand*." He ended, "Whose *hat* was *in* his *hand*," a terrible line that makes his point — but not for Moore.

Nor for its original audience, as it happens. Johnson made up the quatrain in David Garrick's presence. When the actor repeated the verses to James Boswell, he made Moore's error in the last line. Boswell repeated the lines to Johnson, who corrected Garrick's mistake, saying, "Then he has no ear." In the matter of Moore herself, it is clear that she had a remarkable and innovative ear, but *not* an ear for English meter. She had an ear that Johnson would have recognized as belonging to prose, not to poetry. (Moore admired Johnson; in the sound of her poems some of Johnson's cadences mix with rhythms out of seventeenth-century prose and out of the long sentences of Henry James.) I notice her metrical error not to belittle her ear but to ruminate on the nature of her mind, to consider "the rarity of true originality" and "the alienation it might involve."

I suggest that ability often rises out of disability, that Moore made great art not only out of high ambitions, strong ideas, and hard work but out of involuntary alienation.

POEMS FROM THE CIRCLE'S EDGE

Moore's poetic qualities are hard to name. Often we define the poets we revere by their memorability. When we recall "the uncut hair of graves" or "How can we know the dancer from the dance?" or "I heard a fly buzz when I died," we pay practical homage to Whitman, Yeats, and Dickinson. Certainly Marianne Moore is memorable — one may weary over the constant quoting of "imaginary gardens with real toads in them" — but Moore's memorable lines are not like those of other poets: Only a few are imagistic (like the shoelaces) and fewer are dramatic. Her toads and gardens tend to be conceptual or apothegmatic. They draw distinctions and remain memorable by the performance of askew language reaching definition.

And by her strange compelling rhythms. Despite her Latinate polysyllables, despite her trouble with conventional meter, her language makes its noise out loud, not merely in print on the page. Similarly, late Henry James — dictated to a typist — reads well out loud for all its syntactic complexity. Moore makes her own spoken language, set against her page's visual grid. Looking at the page, the eye takes a message of formality before the mind decodes a phrase. I think of the way Robert Frost set New England speech against a grid not visual but metrical.

Her method of construction — the scaffolding on which she erects this language — is the association of ideas. Not for Moore the seventeenth-century syllogisms of Marvell, or Donne's sometimes scholastic logic. In Moore, one thing leads to another. This form of poetic construction has prevailed from the eighteenth century on, but in Moore the leaps of connection are particularly long. As in her conversation, it is often difficult to follow the associations. Winthrop Sargeant gathered a block

of speech that provides a sample. Moore started speaking of the
S. S. Pierce Company, and then:

Very discriminating grocers. Even if they do carry cigars and
wine and cosmetics along with their cheese, jam, cakes, soups,
and all kinds of crackers. I can't abide dilutions or mixtures,
but I like candy. If I drank whiskey, I would drink it straight.
I have a lethal grudge against people who try to make me drink
coffee. My friend Mrs. Church grinds her own coffee from
French and American beans. Her husband's grandfather was
a chemical inventor who invented a brand of bicarbonate of
soda. His wife is a Bavarian. Mrs. Church, I mean. She had a
house at Ville-d'Avray with a big cedar of Lebanon and a dog
named Tiquot. They had a gardener who also drove the car.
They wouldn't have begonias on the place. They did have a
few geraniums, though. Mr. Church was a close friend of
Wallace Stevens, who wrote "The Necessary Angel." He reprinted an anecdote about Goethe wearing black woolen
stockings on a packet boat. I like Goethe. My favorite language is German. I like the periodic structure of the sentences.
"And Shakespeare inspires me, too. He has so many good
quotations. And Dante. He has a few, too." That's from Ruth
Draper. At Monroe Wheeler's once, we played a game called
"Who would you rather be except Shakespeare?" I wouldn't
mind being La Fontaine, or Voltaire. Or Montaigne? No. I
wouldn't be Montaigne — too sombre. I have always loved
the vernacular. It spites me that I can't write fiction. And that
book of essays I wrote. I let myself loose to do my utmost, and
now they make me uneasy. The critics didn't care a great deal
for them, but their reviews weren't really vipish. Those readings of my verse I made for the phonograph — well, they're
here forever, like the wheat in the pyramids. I'm fond of Bach
and Pachelbel and Stravinsky. I'm also fond of drums and
trumpets — snare drums. If I find that a man plays the trumpet
I am immediately interested. . . .

It's not a poem (unlike her plant letter) but it's constructed like
a poem by Marianne Moore. One can follow if one concen-

trates. Some readers can follow "Marriage," which takes two hundred and eighty-nine lines to discuss that institution, most of the time in connection with something else. For example:

> Below the incandescent stars
> below the incandescent fruit,
> the strange experience of beauty;
> its existence is too much;
> it tears one to pieces
> and each fresh wave of consciousness
> is poison.
> "See her, see her in this common world,"
> the central flaw
> in that first crystal-fine experiment,
> this amalgamation which can never be more
> than an interesting impossibility,
> describing it
> as "that strange paradise
> unlike flesh, stones,
> gold or stately buildings,
> the choicest piece of my life:
> the heart rising
> in its estate of peace
> as a boat rises
> with the rising of the water";
> constrained in speaking of the serpent —
> shed snakeskin in the history of politeness
> not to be returned to again —
> that invaluable accident
> exonerating Adam.

This poem on marriage weds incongruous partners. She called it "a little anthology of terms and phrases that had entertained me," which is perhaps its best description; in another place, with more diffidence, she called the poem "Statements that took my fancy which I tried to arrange plausibly." What's plausible for the goose may puzzle the gander. Alien patches of language rub up against each other — bizarre collocations, strange encounters, unprecedented juxtapositions — and disjunction focuses our attention on language used as if for the first time.

Unlike Stevens, Williams, H.D., and most of her generation, Marianne Moore was a Christian. In her Christianity she resembled her St. Louis neighbor, Mr. Eliot — but in name and in doctrine, not in experience. In Moore's life we find no waste land from which there is ascent into purgatory toward possible paradise. In Moore's writing, unlike Eliot's, there is little that appears doctrinal; yet a great deal is Christian by implication, not only for its scrupulosity but for its charity. In Moore's life, Christianity included the Presbyterian Church every Sunday. When her mother died she found an old prayer that she adapted to read at the funeral, and the same was spoken twenty-five years later at her own:

> We thank Thee for the valiant dead who have made the distant heavens a home for us, whose truth and beauty are even now in our hearts. One by one Thou dost gather us out of Earthly light into heavenly glory, from the distractions of time to the peace of eternity. We thank Thee for the labors and joys of these mortal years. We thank Thee for the deepening sense of the mysteries that lie beyond our dust, and for the eye of faith which Thou has opened for all who believe in Thy Son, to behold through the darkness a shining future. May we live in thy faith and love, the hope implanted in us of immortality, until for us also the day shall break in glory, through the grace of Jesus Christ our Savior, Amen.

Of the poets I recollect here, Marianne Moore is the one who remains most mysterious, and — not incidentally? — looms larger in her poems every time I read her. Also she becomes more distinct in character. Removed from the distractions of time, her work grows firmer, her character more luminous, brave, exemplary, virtuous, and strange.

Fragments of
Ezra Pound

~

ROME: SUNDAY

In 1960, while I was spending a year in England, the *Paris Review* sent me to Italy to interview Ezra Pound. When I knocked on the door of the Roman apartment where Pound was staying with a friend, I was apprehensive. In awe of his poetry, aghast at his politics, I understood that he talked politics more than he talked poetry. A few years back the *Paris Review* had nearly scheduled an interview while Pound was still in Washington. (Pound spent the years from 1945 to 1958 in the United States, mostly in the insane asylum at St. Elizabeths Hospital in the District of Columbia, where he had been confined as mentally unfit to stand trial for treason; during the Second World War, he had remained in Italy and broadcast for Mussolini's Italian radio.) In 1956 he first agreed to be interviewed, then suddenly reneged, declaring that the magazine was part of the "pinko-usury fringe." Usury was the Devil in Pound's theology; the race of the Devil was mostly Semitic. In 1956 the *Paris Review*'s masthead included two Jewish names. At St. Elizabeths, friends of mine had told me, Pound had railed about "the most dangerous man in the world," whose name appeared to be "Weinstein Kirchberger"; it took me a while to translate.

When I knocked on the door, I feared what would answer my knock: madness, rebuff, cruelty, arrogance.

There was no mistaking him. His face was large and jagged, constructed in sharp triangular sections like modular architecture. This was the face that his friend Gaudier-Brzeska carved in marble in 1914, and that Wyndham Lewis painted in 1938 as if it were metal. Both sculpture and painting appeared influenced by cubism; now I saw that Pound's face looked as if *it* were influenced, as if it had learned its shape by admiring Cezanne's geometry. The beard, which was gray and came to a point, continued the angles of the face; his long hair flared to the sides and rose thickly on top: a magnificent head. But his eyes, which looked into me as we stood at the door, were watery, red, weak. "Mr. Hall," he said to me in the doorway, "you — find me — in fragments." As he spoke he separated the words into little bunches, like bursts of typing from an inexperienced typist: "You have driven — all the way — from England — to find a man — who is only fragments."

He beckoned me down a long corridor into a pleasant corner room, full of sunlight and books, where we sat opposite each other. Looking in his eyes, I saw the fatigue. Later I watched his eyes and mouth gather from time to time a tense strength as he concentrated his attention on a matter gravely important. Fragments assembled themselves in half a second, turned strong, sharp, and insistent; then dissipated quickly, sank into flaccidity, depression, and silence. In 1960 — though I could not know it then — Pound was verging on the brink of silence, that private cold inferno where he lived out the last decade of his life.

In his sunny room — heavy with tables, two sofas, and big comfortable chairs — suitcases lay under a desk in a corner. Three books spread themselves out on a lamp table next to an easy chair: a Confucius in Chinese, a copy of Pound's own *Women of Trachis*, and the new edition of Robinson's Chaucer. (Robert Frost kept the Robinson in his Vermont cabin, the last time I saw him.) Pound sat on a sofa and told me about his friend Ugo Dadone, owner of this flat on the Via Angelo Poliziano, formerly a general in an African campaign, injured and left for dead in the desert; Dadone, Pound said, was nearly as fragmented as he was. Over one of the sofas I noticed a signed photograph of Gabriele D'Annunzio in his aviator costume.

As Pound rambled, I listened to the voice more than to the word. Theatrical, flashy, he rolled his *r*'s grandly, and at the end of each sentence kept the pitch high until the final word or two, which he dropped in pitch while retaining volume. This melody lent a coda to every sentence, a coda I remembered from 16 r.p.m. records in Harvard's Poetry Room. (From time to time this melody sounded disconcertingly like W. C. Fields.) As an undergraduate I had spent hours listening to this voice, rapt inside great earphones in a blue chair at the Lamont Library. Pound made the recordings on May 17, 1939, on a brief visit to the United States undertaken in his megalomania with the hope and expectation that by talking to the right people he could prevent the Second World War.

When Pound recorded I was ten and perfectly ignorant of him. When we declared war on Italy I was thirteen and daydreamed of becoming a writer. By the time American and Italian soldiers actually shot at each other, I wanted to be a poet for the rest of my life, I loved Ezra Pound's poetry, and I reviled him as a traitor and a Fascist sympathizer.

The Second World War — which began in Europe when I was almost eleven, and ended in Japan when I was almost seventeen — was the bread of my adolescence, the milk of my growing up. When I hayed in New Hampshire in the summer months, I cocked the point of my scythe toward the hairy ditches, where I imagined that escaped Nazi prisoners of war hid by day. When I read the newspaper, I could not conceive that a peacetime paper could find enough news to fill its pages. Every night on the farm we listened to a radio shaped like a cathedral as Gabriel Heatter told us that the skies were black over Europe with young Americans bombing German cities in just vengeance. Every movie was a war movie, every radio show was performed before servicemen, every Book-of-the-Month

Club Selection was dedicated to the war effort. At high school the thermostat went down to 40 degrees at noon, even in the dead of winter. In gym we boys all learned to box, toughening ourselves for war, and the finals of the heavyweight division took place in the auditorium in front of the whole school. A large blond senior named George Taubel knocked out an awkward, strong young man, a good athlete named Bill Herbert, knocked him cold on the auditorium stage, and a year later Bill Herbert was dead in a wave of Marines invading a Pacific island.

Although I tested the possibilities of pacifism, although when I was fourteen or fifteen I shocked my friends by calling myself a socialist, I *knew* that the United States was right and that Germany, Japan, and Italy were wrong. Like almost everyone of my generation — and like no one fifteen years younger — I never doubted my country's general virtue. Perhaps the Great War had been a trade war — like Troy, like the Russo-Japanese — but *this* was a war for justice. Evil was Hitler, and Hitler was evil. I feel embarrassed to write it — after Guatemala and Chile, after Korea, after Vietnam, after Grenada, Panama, and Iraq — but the evil we apprehended was entirely *out there;* none of it was *in here.* When in Boston one day I watched a parade — I think it was Memorial Day, 1944 — and watched wiry, lean, intense young men march past who were the only survivors of the first wave that waded onto the tiny atoll of Tarawa, I wept and could not stop weeping, aware of Bill Herbert and the other dead whom I had known, aware also of my own fears. For I was sure that I would myself go into the army and fight in the same war, which I assumed would go on forever.

Therefore, when I bought T. S. Eliot's *Collected Poems,* at fourteen, for two dollars, I drew a circle around Ezra Pound's name in the dedication to "The Waste Land" — "For Ezra Pound *il miglior fabbro*" — and in the white space of the page wrote the word that signified my political judgment: "Nerts!" My politics belong to this story not because they were sensitive or unusual. They were (and are) conventional, naïve, ill in-

formed, and mercurial. Although my view of the morality of
nations has suffered some sophistication, unavoidable in the last
forty-five years, I have not rid myself of prejudices acquired in
youth. I find it difficult to behave politely to Germans; I avoid
setting foot in that country. Although I do not retain conviction
of general moral superiority, I retain suspicion; I want to *growl*
at Germans, and the hair stands up on my back, like a cat seeing
a dog.

If my politics were primitive, my poetics were not. About the
time I wrote "Nerts!" in Eliot's *Collected Poems,* I began to
read Pound. I read him in anthologies like Louis Untermeyer's,
who wrote angry introductions to Ezra Pound but printed him
nonetheless. I read his own collections published by New Directions. When the war was ending I met someone who had known
Pound a little and who supported my growing admiration. At
the same time, his anecdotes encouraged me to dismiss the politics as madness. This man had visited Rapallo in the mid-thirties
on his honeymoon. After a vigorous game of tennis, Pound
confided to him that the hills above the tennis courts were in-
habited by spies with binoculars, sent from Wall Street to keep
an eye on E. P., whose economic ideas, when they became public
knowledge, would ruin the Wall Street bankers' conspiratorial
hold on the world's wealth.

For me, poetry is first of all sounds. I discovered early that
Pound, who could do other things as well, had the grandest ear
among modern poets. For the sheer pleasure of sound — the
taste of it in the mouth — no one comes near him. Early in life
I discovered Pound's "The Return," a perfect symbolist poem,
but what I loved most was the noise it made, rubbing its syllables together as a grasshopper rubs its legs.

> See, they return; ah see the tentative
> Movements, and the slow feet,
> The trouble in the pace and the uncertain
> Wavering!

See, they return, one, and by one,
With fear, as half-awakened;
As if the snow should hesitate
And murmur in the wind,
                    and half turn back;
These were the "Wing'd-with-Awe,"
                    Inviolable.

Gods of the wingèd shoe!
With them the silver hounds,
                    sniffing the trace of air!

Haie! Haie!
          These were the swift to harry;
These the keen-scented;
These were the souls of blood.

Slow on the leash,
                    pallid the leash-men!

Maybe we say something about the symbolism of "The Return" if we mention a defeated pantheon, but a symbolist poem is not an allegorical poem — the symbol, it has been noted, is a new word — and I would as lief think of tired hunters, or Greece replaced by Rome, or Rome defeated by Goths, or Pennsylvania overwhelmed in the fourth quarter by Cornell. I print this poem here not in order to paraphrase it but to chew and suck upon it. (I embarrass the reader, who has put away childish things.) How the diphthongs and long vowels move together, a slow march down the page, dip and pause and glide. I can read it again and again, each time with vast refreshment of senses and world-love — as I can look again and again at Matisse's *The Red Studio*.

Early on, I found and enjoyed Pound's vigorous ballad about Christ, "Ballad of the Goodly Fere," and his Provençal and Renaissance monologues, like the violent "Sestina: Altaforte": "Damn it all! all this our South stinks peace." Later I discovered his energetic translation of the "Seafarer," then the quietness of the Chinese poems and imitations, and realized that Pound's ear had found yet another music: He had discovered the lyric potential of *flatness*. If he found this quality in translating from the Chinese, in Japanese poetry he found the tiny lyric as quick as a fly, like "In a Station of the Metro." He invented the free verse epigram, writing about "Les Millwins" or about sexual satisfaction as a bathtub draining. Later he constructed the quatrains of "Hugh Selwyn Mauberley," academically the most accepted of Pound's poems, with its eloquent stanzas on the Great War. At about the same time, he invented the looser line of "Homage to Sextus Propertius," where he became a sarcastic Whitman who could instantly switch tone into a lyric beauty. In his whole life as a poet, which the *Cantos* extends and replicates, Ezra Pound discovered a thousand ways to make a noise. Although he was not innovative as an iambic poet, on the whole his ear is the most inventive in modern literature. With the Propertius, Pound invented a discursive narrative noise that can fly to lyric touchstone-lines and accommodate narrative or reflective passages together. Useful to the *Cantos,* this diction accommodates and includes, can turn ironic *or* ecstatic, lyric *or* narrative, without altering itself to the point of indecorum. By the time of Propertius and Mauberley, Pound's sounds can move with swift sureness from tones at one end of the scale to the other.

The most mouth-luscious, limb-erotic of Pound's sounds derive from the weird combination of Sappho's euphony and a Viking drumbeat. To the Greek sweetness of assonance (the first line of the *Iliad* includes six variations on the *ay* diphthong) Pound adds the bang-bang of North Sea alliteration and warrior drum-pounding. From the quantitative dactyl (in our misreading of long for loud) he takes his falling-rhythm. In his percussive repetition of long vowels he brings the northern drumbeat of alliterative accents together with the southern mouth-hold of two, three, four, and even five *long* syllables together — true quantitative spondees, sometimes two in a row followed by the initial long syllable of the quantitative dactyl. North is muscle, south is mouth, and the combination is "Ear, ear, for the seasurge; murmur of old men's voices."

A moment ago I claimed that in the *Cantos* Pound invented a device for containing the modern world. At least this was his grand ambition. If he did not accomplish this ambition, he wrote in the *Cantos* thousands of lines of magnificent poetry by which he gathered and juxtaposed elements of a universal culture: Chinese history and Confucian ideology found parallels and divergences with American Adamses and Renaissance Medicis, with Elizabethan jurists and twentieth-century anthropologists, with his own economic doctrines of Social Credit, with Mussolini's fascism — and with the poet himself caged outdoors in Pisa at the end of a war, reasonably convinced that he awaited execution.

As I attended to Pound's sounds, I also began to learn other sides of this man.

The history of literature chronicles considerable generosity. Although poets are frequently as vain as tenors or sopranos, and although one sometimes encounters a poet murderous with envy, many poets help each other out. Thus poets often come in groups, and especially when they are young work tirelessly to rewrite each other's poems. They live in each other's vicinity, or if they must live apart, they revise each other's work through the mails. The collected poems of our best poets contain lines written by their friends. Vernon Watkins and Dylan Thomas could recall lines each had written for the other, which critics had singled out as typical of the man who had not written them.

Pound was a catalyst to other poets. His presence made poets out of people who might otherwise never have survived into poetry. Much as I love the poetry of William Carlos Williams, I am not sure that he would have been a poet without Ezra Pound — even if Williams is the better poet, as many readers think. Pound's energy and conviction pulled H.D. and William Carlos Williams into poetic commitment when the three students knew one another at the University of Pennsylvania. Later, when Pound met older writers already committed to the art, he bullied editors into publishing them, he reviewed them, he invented public relations devices like "imagism" in order to attract attention to them, he raised money for them, he got them out of jail — and on one occasion he sent one of them a pair of old brown shoes.

Pound discovered Eliot, through the agency of Conrad Aiken, when Eliot had written "Prufrock" but little else, and when Eliot seemed destined to become an American professor of philosophy. He argued Harriet Monroe into publishing "Prufrock" in *Poetry;* he encouraged and cajoled Eliot into further poems, and quite possibly into a disastrous marriage which sponsored poetry along with suffering. When Eliot's work at the bank burdened him, Pound set out to support him by subscription (which embarrassed Eliot, who put a stop to it); when Eliot fumbled toward "The Waste Land," Pound's strict and magnanimous critical intelligence cut that poem into shape.

Story after story illustrates the accuracy of Pound's taste and the generous energy with which he promoted the writers he admired. Nor was his taste limited to his own kind of work, when it included D. H. Lawrence and James Joyce as well as Eliot and the imagists; Ford Madox Ford, Edmund Blunden, Henry James, and William Butler Yeats among the elders; Ernest Hemingway, Louis Zukofsky, Basil Bunting among the youngers. Most astonishing of all, his taste found room for Robert Frost, whose literary predilections ought to have made him The Enemy. (If Pound's first task, as he says in a *Canto,* was to "break the pentameter," Frost wasn't helping.) Pound recognized quality even when it turned up in a sonnet, and leapt to promote Robert Frost — who disliked him and avoided him — without worrying about the politics of literary coteries. In the history of literature, no writer equals the young Pound in accuracy of taste or in energetic magnanimity.

When the *Pisan Cantos* appeared in 1947, most readers considered them the best *Cantos* since the first thirty. I found them moving, with their sudden uncertainty, their mingling of defiance and despair. Whatever the politics of the man who wrote the poems, the *Pisan Cantos* included great poetry. The *Pisan Cantos* also included anti-Semitism. When Pound was awarded the Bollingen Prize for the *Pisan Cantos,* there was a noisy scandal. Haters of modern poetry discovered how much they detested fascism and anti-Semitism. All the old arguments about art and morality marched forth, generally in stupid uniforms.

Let me say: I have never found it difficult to split poem from poet. Perhaps it is *nasty* that it is not difficult, but I do not find it difficult and often I find it essential. If a poet is great, the poem is the poet at his or her greatest, and the man or woman in daily life will never equal the intelligence or sensitivity of the poem, which is created by concentration and revision (or manic ecstasy) in solitude. Poets know that their poems are more important than they are — when they are writing the poems. Great poets may tell lies much of the time — to sexual objects, if seduction be necessary; to audiences, if public love be the demand; or to a convoy of toadies — but when they write their poems they must not lie. I have heard poets on platforms speak with outrageous hypocrisy — Robert Frost was worst — and then I have gone home and read the poems that tell the truth. Conversely, I have known dozens of would-be poets who were decent and honest people in daily life — playing poker, serving on committees, raising children, defending beleaguered friends, even judging other poets — who when they took up their ballpoints stole the voices of dead poets and the notions or manners of live friends; many men and women, commendable in their public lives, fake or lie in the privacy of their poems. Therefore it does not astonish me that the *Pisan Cantos* rarely resemble the harangues recorded from Rome radio. Neither the *Pisan Cantos* nor "The Return" nor "Homage to Sextus Propertius" appear to be works of someone who finds Wall Street representatives in the hills above his house, or believes in the Protocols of the Elders of Zion, or thinks that he could have prevented the Second World War by holding select audiences with senators.

It was verifiably an American named Ezra Pound who said on Roman radio, May 5, 1942:

The kike, and the unmitigated evil that has been centered in London since the British government got on the Red Indians to murder the American frontier settlers, has herded the Slavs, the Mongols, the Tartars openly against Germany and Poland and Finland. And secretly against all that is decent in America against the total American heritage.

The same Ezra Pound wrote, years earlier in *Canto IV:*

> Beneath it, beneath it,
> Not a ray, not a sliver, not a spare disc of sunlight
> Flaking the black, soft water;
> Bathing the body of nymphs, of nymphs, and Diana . . .

The same Ezra Pound wrote, years later, in a fragment from *Canto CXV:*

> A blown husk that is finished
> but the light sings eternal
> a pale flare over marshes
> where the salt hay whispers to tide's change . . .

How do I fit these pieces together? I do not fit these pieces together; they *are* together, in the mystery of a man's character and life. The ugliness and obscenity of the documented political opinions and talk is undeniable; on rare occasions this wretched stuff enters the poetry. Much of the time the poetry is beautiful. I claim: The ugliness does not modify the beauty nor the beauty the ugliness. If you wish to arrive at a composite judgment of the whole man, putting together these extremes and everything else you discover, *do so;* but do not tell me that this composite judgment of the man retroactively diminishes the value of, say, "The Return."

The composite remains bewildering. I will illustrate my own bewilderment by setting the paradoxes of Ezra Pound's life into a stick-figure narrative:

> a young man grows up vowing to be a poet, emigrates,
> publishes great poems, sets himself up wholly as an aesthete;

within his aesthetic commitments (to sculpture, music, and painting, as well as to poetry) he is generous to other artists almost without precedent; for many years his judgment is as strong as his generosity;

when his friends, and millions of others, die in the Great War, he detaches himself from aestheticism, looking for causes of war and outrage;

for a while his poems gain in resonant seriousness; then a new tone begins, a tone of paranoia and irascibility;

he finds causes in economics, demons in bankers and later in Jewish bankers, and an exorcism in his own economics;

his interest in poetry declines; he considers himself evolved into statesman and economist; his friends withdraw, finding him mad;

having discovered a hero in Benito Mussolini, he broadcasts from Italy, to his old country at war with Italy, speeches often murderous with hatred;

imprisoned, in fear of death, abject, he returns to poetry, the old voice ringing out the noble line — mixed with flashes of paranoia and racism;

the madness or the obsessions remain in his long imprisonment; and the poetry recurs, intermittent, sometimes trying to fly on one wing, sometimes flying on two;

and with release from prison nothing resolves itself, politics and poetry confused and unremedied;

until finally, convinced of failure and error, the old man sinks into silence, ten years of speechless despair, interrupted rarely by his own voice, like a voice that speaks from a tomb;

or like the tiny voice of the Sybil, quoted by Eliot at the start of "The Waste Land," who, centuries old, shriveled as a raisin, enduring, is asked by boys what she might desire; who answers, *I want to die.*

When I wrote my first letter to Ezra Pound that winter — writing from England, proposing that I visit him and interview him for the *Paris Review* — I addressed him at his daughter's place, the Schloss Brunnenburg, a castle in Merano of the Italian Tirol,

formerly Meran of the Austrian Tirol. He had lived in this castle
— with his daughter Mary, his wife Dorothy, and Mary's husband the Egyptologist Boris de Rachewiltz — much of the time
since his return to Italy. (Mary was Olga Rudge's daughter, not
Dorothy Pound's. In the thirties in Rapallo, Pound had divided
his attentions and his nights between his wife and his mistress.)
Merano's climate and isolation — the literal climate, not the
metaphorical one — did not appeal to Pound. ("It's fine —" he
told me, "if you can live — on mountain scenery.") At some
point, he and Dorothy rented a flat in Rapallo, striving to return
to the place where they had lived for many years before the war.
It didn't work out; they rented the flat on a Sunday, and on
Monday — he told me — discovered that the ground floor was
deafeningly occupied by a boiler factory. On another occasion,
a young woman in her twenties moved in with Dorothy and
Ezra; this experiment worked no better than the flat over the
boiler factory.

A few days after I mailed him my letter, I received a postcard
dated "2 Dec 59," which read:

> Shd/one distinguish between magazines
> that wish to print one, and those that
> only want one to be interviewed?
>   Yrs
>   E Pound

The asperity was what I feared and expected; it did not surprise
me; but the message surprised me: Did Ezra Pound really want
to publish in the *Paris Review*? Apparently he no longer considered the magazine an operation of the "pinko-usury fringe,"
but why did he want his work to appear there? I assumed that
Ezra Pound could print poems anywhere.

But he couldn't, of course. American magazines that paid
noticeable sums for poems — *The New Yorker, The Atlantic,
Harper's, Ladies' Home Journal* — would not have welcomed a
poem by Ezra Pound in 1959. *The New Yorker,* for instance,
was still disinclined to print a poem that Mr. Ross would not

have understood. Pound published his poems in the *Hudson Review* or in *Poetry,* and received for a *Canto,* I suppose, something like a hundred or two hundred dollars.

He required little money to live on; all his life he lived, as he put it, "on low overhead." But he could not make a living, selling *Cantos* at fifty cents a line. And I doubt that his royalties amounted to more than one or two thousand dollars a year. Teachers did not assign his books in American university classes; he was too hard. He received some income from anthology rights; again, I doubt that the annual accumulation was more than two thousand dollars. His politics kept him out of some anthologies, and diminished the extent of his representation in others.

He was worried in 1959 that he would not have enough money to support himself and his family. I suspect that this worry was unreasonable — Pound had generous and affluent friends — but it felt real enough to *him* as he faced old age.

In 1959 the *Paris Review* still endeavored to represent a generation. As poetry editor, I returned poems by prominent older poets in order to hold the *Paris Review* to its discovered shape. We published Robert Bly before anyone else did; we published W. D. Snodgrass, James Wright, Louis Simpson, Adrienne Rich, and James Dickey early in their careers. Because I lived in England early in the fifties, we published Geoffrey Hill and Thom Gunn. It made no sense to publish Pound, who scarcely belonged to our generation. On the other hand, the *Paris Review* sold copies not by printing Wright or Hill but by exploiting its elders: each issue carried its interview with a celebrated older writer. Maybe it would make sense, in the issue that contained the Pound interview, to print new work discussed in the interview. I wrote Pound asking what he had to offer. At the same time, I wrote George Plimpton asking if we could pay Ezra Pound to print unpublished work. Pound's answer came first, typed on both sides of a postcard, dated "i Dec." He had been going through boxes of manuscript that had survived the war in Rapallo. He wrote about things he had found:

Guy in Ind. wanting to print letters and forgotten translations of Heine, (probably for free,) but would serve as chronicle of past times and no reason for me to keep up american universities that never pay me anything

I am, frankly, looking for people who will feed the producer, whereas they mainly want me to help them . . . time and again by the dozen.

No doubt the supported think such an attitude very crass.

Pound knew nothing of me or my circumstances. I was freelancing that year. Maybe he assumed that I was supported for my year in England by a Guggenheim or a Fulbright; doubtless most American poets or academics whom he met in Italy were supported by grants.

Shd/a man of my age be able to USE even the little he gets? (news to you probably that such conditions exist).

In the letter I found what I later witnessed in his conversation: He tried out a quarrelsome tone, then apologized:

Worry IS bad for the temper.
                    cordially yours   and pas de bile
                                        E Pound

On the front of the postcard, at right angles to the address, he typed a postscript that wandered into obscurity while it announced his new diffidence:

this communication NOT very communicative, and not fit to post, but am being rushed to a train, and if I dont send it, you wd/have to wait God knows how long for even partial answer, and probably incomprehensible enquiry into matters unlikely to have been broached in yr/presence.

He was already thinking of me — as he thought of everyone — as a student to be coached in the ways of the world, and he mocked himself for his habit.

Through December and January I prepared myself for the interview. My Pound books remained in Ann Arbor; Charles Monteith at Faber and Faber sent me everything Faber had in print, and I read Pound all over again. Meantime George Plimpton turned up some money in New York, and I was able to tell Pound we could pay for a Poundian portfolio. (We could not pay for the interview itself; we had paid no one else.) By now, Pound had become anxious over what to print:

> Heaven knows where I will be, and if anything more than fragments will be available.

This was Pound's first use of the word "fragments."

> The mess made of proofs for *Thrones*,

— the latest *Cantos*, about to be published —

> Due to my incapacity to attend to 'em,

— incapacity unexplained, as it always would be —

> is not harBINGer for new composition, but we can hope. (*)

The asterisk led to the bottom of the page:

> I mean there are fragments of new Cantos. but . . . whether fit to release??

These fragments were substantially the passages later collected as *Drafts and Fragments of Cantos CX–CXVII.*

For some weeks, I lived in the landscape of Ezra Pound. I read and reread most of what had been written about him, criticism that was largely unsatisfactory; some of it was disfigured by pedantry, often pedantry curiously lacking in documentation and certainty; and much of it was marred by passions; Pound inspired loathing or he inspired discipleship. (Hugh Kenner's *The Pound Era* did not appear until 1972.) Early in February the BBC Third Programme rebroadcast three interviews with Ezra Pound done a year earlier by D. G. Bridson, who had visited Merano with his tape recorder and a television crew. Bridson was a knowledgeable and intelligent interviewer, and the radio programs were excellent. The television program showed film of Pound walking, Pound with his grandchildren, Pound with his bust by Gaudier; the sound for the television program was Pound's detached voice, abstracted from the radio interviews. I was able to see the television tape at the BBC studios, and take a look at the castle where I expected to see him.

Several times I listened to the radio program; it was encouraging. Pound made sense and spoke with vigor, only a year past. My anxieties lessened a little.

Late in January, Pound rode south from Brunnenburg to Rome, where he put up at Ugo Dadone's apartment in the Via Angelo Poliziano. He expected his visit to be brief. He didn't want to leave Rome for Brunnenburg but thought that he had to; on February 8 he wrote a postcard: "Aiming to get to Brunnenburg by 25th — what is latest date you need certitude?" In a February 14 letter, he said he had "committed the folly of reserving the sleeping car for Thursday." He expected to arrive at Brunnenburg by February 19, "and shall await you there." Then on February 17 came a cable: "Come to Rome Merano icebound Pound."

Later in the month I rented a Morris Minor, a station wagon, so that the baby Philippa could travel in the back, in the body of her pram, with its wheels strapped to the roof. Four-year-old Andrew sat in the back seat, and his parents in the front — as we crossed the Channel and drove through France and Switzerland, south to the sun of Rome.

Ezra Pound and I sat in the sunny room and talked. I had not brought my tape recorder with me that first afternoon. I feared he might object to the recorder; poets were always blaming technology for something or other, and this man was not only a poet but a paranoid. I wanted to avoid offending him, whom I expected to be ready to take offense.

We talked for an hour, and I saw no paranoia, no gibbering, no brutality, no readiness to take offense. I saw fatigue, or rather I saw energy and fatigue in constant war; fatigue continually overpowered energy, only for energy to revive itself by a fragile and courageous effort of will and fly its quick flag, only to fall back again under dour attack. The alternatives were precipitous and the fatigue seemed more than physical; it seemed abject despair, accidie, meaninglessness, abulia, waste. Pound would walk up and down the small, bright room, sit in a chair and read energetically from manuscript, alternating pairs of spectacles as if he were juggling in a circus; then suddenly his face would sag, his eyes turn glassy like a fish's, and he would collapse onto a sofa and into silence; in five minutes he would jump up and begin the cycle again, his speech newly vigorous and exact. As I learned later, Pound's sudden attacks of fatigue had begun long before, at least as early as 1945 when government psychologists examined him at Pisa. They continued when he was examined at Washington and incarcerated at St. Elizabeths. Unfriendly critics have suggested that these episodes were faked, to convince doctors that he was incapable of standing trial. He wasn't faking, in Rome in 1960.

We talked for an hour and a half that Sunday afternoon. I had expected to see him for a few minutes, to make an appointment to interview him the next day. I had expected him to be busy and arrogant, perhaps setting aside two hours for me tomorrow, like a dictator posing for his bust. I had expected him to impose the rules by which we would play the game. Instead, I found him worried about the interview, the way students worry about final examinations. He worried about the questions I would ask; he was afraid I would ask hard ones, afraid he could not answer them thoroughly, with wit, with full recollection.

At first I was surprised at the seriousness with which he took the interview. Most writers take interviews lightly, as gossipy interludes between bouts of composition and revelry. When writers are interviewed, they have answered two thirds of the questions before, and much of the time play a prerecorded tape for answer. But Pound undertook the interview with seriousness and anxiety, for two reasons that I became aware of: In the past, even the recent past, interviews had caused him trouble when he was misquoted or selectively quoted, or when he had been tactless or stupid. On his release from St. Elizabeths two years before, reporters had asked him what he thought of Robert Frost's part in the negotiations, and Pound reportedly answered that, well, it had taken Frost long enough. I suppose he made a flippant, mock-arrogant answer to a provocative question — he was grateful to Frost — but, as newspapermen reported it, he showed his nastiness again.

The other reason for Pound's worry was harsher: He was not sure that he made sense.

He was still obsessed about what the *Paris Review* might print in its portfolio of Ezra Pound. He told me again that the *Cantos,* newer than *Thrones,* were unfinished and therefore unprintable; and he had not written a line since July; he had been in no shape to write since last July. He spoke about blood pressure, and about pills that kept him alive; I formed the notion that he had suffered a small stroke in July of 1959, though neither of us mentioned the word.

Lacking new *Cantos* for the *Paris Review* — as he thought — he had assembled for my reading a miscellany of uncollected writing: letters to Louis Untermeyer, especially "An Autobiographical Outline," which he wrote in Rapallo in 1932, addressed to the Untermeyer who assembled biographical headnotes for anthologies, "in order to put the facts straight"; some old translations from Latin: Horace, Rutilius; translations from Heine; and his recent *Versi Prosaici,* which collected gists and piths from the *Cantos,* to abstract Pound's most central references into dense, elliptical prose.

Then there was another packet, he told me, perhaps unsuitable for publication in the *Paris Review* but vital for me to read. His eye seized on me, peering, interrogating, almost pleading; he pleaded that I listen, read, pay attention, and take seriously what he had to tell me. After a lifetime of influencing, or trying to influence — first in literary causes and then in economic and political ones — he continued to look for disciples or converts. But in Rome in 1960, he was not trying to convince me of the efficacy of Social Credit or of the intelligence of Benito Mussolini. He had been waiting for me all day. At some hour before I arrived, he had taken a walk, and had left a note in case I showed up while he was gone. Now he handed it to me:

> I will be back by 4.30 or sooner — you can go up and glance at Versi Prosaici (unpublished)
> Bunting letters
> Letters to Untermeyer
> incredibly stupid of me not to have sent you phone number.
> Can you if at your convenience wait at Dadone's if anywhere near 4.30 at any rate leave yr. phone number
> of course we shd. talk before I turn you loose on the disordered fragments
> but the chairs are comfortable
> only extracts possible for use and abusive expressions shd. be cancelled — I made peace with G.K.C. for example
> at any rate the Bunting is worth reading i.e. for D.H.
> yrs E. P.

> use of violent language DEPLORABLE but I got something done. by or in spite of it. Bunt's scribbles have educational value for D. H. however rash it may be to turn you loose on 'em in absentia.

When I left him to return to the hotel, I carried the note with me, together with the bundle of manuscript, and found the insults for G. K. Chesterton embedded in the Untermeyer letter. In the Bunting letters I found the education Pound intended for me — and it was an education I was not prepared for: Bunting's letters to Pound, in the 1930s, told him that Mussolini was no good, that Pound's thinking was cockeyed.

Pound had begun to educate me in the errors of Ezra Pound. As he handed me the bundle, he said cryptically that Bunting knew a bit more in the thirties than E. P. did. In this light self-accusation, his tone was jaunty: He tried out the notion that a man could admit his errors and even survive them. But he could not sustain the jauntiness; nothing sustained itself, during our first meeting or later encounters. Fatigue came over him like a sudden shower, and he lay back in his big chair with his eyes closed, his leonine head leaning back, in the position he held for the Wyndham Lewis portrait of 1938, with the sculptural lines turning his face to stone. That afternoon, his quick fatigue reminded me of my resolve not to waste his time or outstay my welcome. I stood up and said I had to go. He opened his old eyes, which stared straight into me with immediate energy, and he said quickly, "*Must* you go?" The voice amazed me, the tone of it; he seemed cast down or even sorrowful because I was leaving him.

But I rejected this interpretation. I told him I had to get back to my family; I would not tell him that I was leaving because he seemed exhausted. He walked me to the elevator, and we agreed that I would arrive the next morning at nine o'clock with my tape recorder. I felt anxiety build in him again. When the elevator arrived he held the door open for a moment. "You needn't think you're taking any of my time, you know," he said. "I'm at your service. I'm here to be interviewed."

Walking back to the hotel, I let the realities of the hour crash against my preconceptions. I told my wife, "I think he's lonely." She had known my fears, my expectation of arrogance or even dismissal. I told her what I had seen and felt. We agreed that, if I still sensed his loneliness the next day, I would ask him to have dinner with us.

ROME: MONDAY

The next morning I woke early, my family still asleep, and consulted the stack of three-by-fives I had collected for the interview. Next to them was my copy of the Faber edition of *Thrones,* which I was to review for the *New Statesman,* and which I was reading for a second time, taking notes in the margin. I found *Thrones,* like most of the *Cantos,* hard to read, obscure — not in thought or metaphor, not in its English diction, but in reference, full of names I did not know or recognized only vaguely from earlier *Cantos;* and obscure in its Chinese, Greek, Latin:

OU THELEI EAEAN EIS KOSMOU
     they want to burst out of the universe
amnis herbidas ripas
                  Antoninus;
                  Julian
                    would not be worshipped
"So thick the dead could not fall"
                    Marcellinus
"dead chap ahead of me with his head split
                    could not fall."
                    XXIII, 6, and there also
Assyrios fines ingressus, . . .

Without reference books, forgetting languages I had studied, I fluttered like a butterfly from flower to flower of comprehension. When I found a passage I could follow straight through, I marked it for possible quoting.

At eight o'clock I put down my copy of *Thrones* and departed the hotel room carrying my tape recorder and my stack of three-by-fives. I walked quickly to the Via Angelo Poliziano and ordered coffee and rolls in a café across from Ugo Dadone's flat, running through my questions again, looking at my watch every five minutes.

Pound answered the door dressed in pajamas, an old bath-robe tied loosely around them. His voice was quicker this morning, his gestures nervous and abrupt. He glanced at the tape recorder and groaned. It was a small Grundig machine, primitive and inefficient, that I had rented in London. To Pound it was an instrument for torture; it put him on the block of his own, exact words. As I set it up and tested it, in the sunny room, he paced up and down. He made sure again that I would print *nothing* without showing it to him first — something I had promised in my first letter. "What are you going to ask me?" he kept saying as I fussed ineptly with the recorder. For him, the interview was a contest at which he would succeed or fail. I don't think he was in the ring with anyone else. He had read my interview with Eliot, and approved of it, but I never felt that he was competing with Eliot. He competed with a notion of himself; he put demands on himself that he was afraid he might not live up to. He feared not being witty enough, not being sharp and epigrammatic and right. He feared not making sense.

He lay down on the sofa when I started to ask questions.

Before I talk further about Monday, let me say a few things about the interview. Or let me say that there were two interviews. One occupied three days in a Roman room, early in March of 1960, an interview of roller-coaster alternations for Ezra Pound, triumph and despair, an interview composed of incomplete sentences, gaps, leaps over chasms, and great Icarian plunges from sun to ocean. I will talk about that interview in these pages. The other interview can be found at the back of this book: the printed dialogue that appeared in the *Paris Review* two years later, neat and witty and energetic, with complete sentences and coherent paragraphs.

Almost any interview, which looks coherent in print, has found much coherence in editing and revision. On an hour's tape, a single topic will surface three times at widely different places; with scissors and paste, the interviewer usually assembles one topic into one sequence. Interviewing Eliot or Pound or

Marianne Moore, I would bring my stack of three-by-fives, and I would have my cards arranged in reasonable order. But when the interview began, the cards became mere comfort blankets for the interviewer. Largely. I might ask only one or two questions from the cards in a two-hour session; one question would start Pound or Moore or Eliot off, and he or she would begin to answer half a dozen other questions typed on other cards. Then the answer would give rise to another, related question, in the natural way of conversation. Eventually all my questions were answered, most without being asked.

In any interview, the natural way of conversation leads to doubling and redoubling of steps, and requires editing, joining like to like, eliminating repetition, and solving apparent contradiction. Pound understood what I would do, and as the interview continued he came to rely on my editing, the hours of scissors and paste. In all the three days, Pound seldom finished a thought at first go; frequently he could not finish a sentence. He would begin a long sentence, pause, stumble — and become aware of the rasp of the tape recorder. "No, no, no, no," he would say, and "Turn that damned thing off." (The quality of the tape was poor, but I managed to pull the words from it; when I made a copy the quality diminished, and now all you can hear is, "Turn that damned thing off.") When I turned it off and took notes instead, the change didn't help much. Instead of answering my questions he talked about his difficulties in answering them. Trying to answer a question, he would go back in time — to supply information required as a preliminary — then decide that he needed a qualification or a preliminary to his preliminary — then qualify the qualification . . . Finally he would forget where he had started. He was beset, he told me, by the Jamesian parenthesis. He decided that the Jamesian parenthesis was a quality (or defect) of the American mind.

Sometimes an hour later he would return to an old, failed answer, and pick up where he had left off. A few questions from Monday he finished on Wednesday. Each morning when I returned to him, he had made notes to complete paragraphs abandoned the day before; he worked on the interview all night, among fits of sleep. He worked on the interview after I had returned to England, and finished some of his best paragraphs or sentences in letters mailed from Italy to Thaxted.

Failure was painful for him, but he never suggested that we stop, that we cancel the interview "due to ill health." He was determined to succeed, even when he seemed hopeless. He was determined to succeed for his own sake, surely, but also for reasons that I can only call generous. "I have brought you — all the way from England," he said in a despairing moment, "and I cannot — give you an interview." It was the old man's pride that seized me by the throat. It must have been on Tuesday or Wednesday that he spoke to me, out of one of his longer silences, when it had become apparent to both of us that he would never recover a steady eloquence, that the fragmentation was irreversible; he looked deeply into me for a moment and said, "Don't — let me sound — so tired."

So I didn't. The interview contains no words that Pound did not speak (or write) and no ideas or implications that he did not, I'm sure, intend; neither does it correctly represent, for any stretch longer than two inches of text, the dialogue that took place on the Via Angelo Poliziano. Not all his pauses were failure and forgetting. Sometimes he paused for the right word and it came to him. When he assembled a sharp or clever phrase, he smiled and looked at me for approval or confirmation. Sometimes a question raised in him recollection of scene or anecdote, and provided him opportunity to mimic, and these were his happiest moments. He loved to mimic, and like many poets he was good at it. He performed Eliot and Hemingway with special finesse and gusto.

Often he raised objections to my questions, because they dwelt on the past. He accused me of assuming that he had lived his life in order to talk about it. He had not spent his years, he told me, analyzing his own reactions to things. He objected to my questions, but without rancor. He objected to them when he found them difficult. And I floundered in the difficulty of his answers, even when occasional energy thrust him through complete answers. I would ask him a question, perhaps about coming to Italy in 1908, and his answer would begin with an anecdote about the first rotary snowplow, or about assayers in the Philadelphia mint. At first I thought he misunderstood my questions, but when he persisted — when he was able to persist — from initial anecdote to finished answer, I would see the snowplow's or the mint's analogical relevance to Italy in 1908. Often he strung two or three anecdotes or pieces of information together: the ideogramic method of the *Cantos*, by which differing items, juxtaposed, yield a generality nowhere stated. But often he could not persist or develop — he forgot, he lost himself — and I sat in silence across from him, with the fragment of an answer hanging in the air between us, like background landscape in a painting with the foreground undone.

In excuse, when he failed, he sometimes blamed the years at St. Elizabeths. If you get used to the company of nuts, he told me, you get out of the habit of making sense. Depression grew thicker in the room until his accumulated complaints of failure bulked larger than the failures themselves. Gradually I realized that he was convinced of failure not only in the interview; I understood that he doubted the value of everything that he had done in his life.

Remember that this was 1960, that Pound had not yet told reporters that his work was nothing, that I who interviewed him was thirty-one and more innocent than I had any right to be. Pound was an old man, doubting the worth of his life's work. To my astonishment, he leapt to take scraps from my hand. I mentioned to him casually that Henry Moore as a young sculptor had taken comfort from Pound's book on Gaudier-Brzeska, with its insistence on the superiority of carving to modeling. He was moved almost to tears; it was something he had not known before. I didn't have the idea that he knew Moore's work — Pound's years of championing sculptors like Gaudier and Epstein, painters like Picabia, were well behind him — but he knew Moore's reputation and he was touched by evidence that he had done something helpful. He enjoyed the news for a while in silence. Then he spoke. "There is no doubt — that I have been some use — to some people."

One says "there is no doubt" only when one feels doubt. So he doubted even his generosity or his usefulness to others, this man who had discovered or promoted or found publishers and patrons for the best writers of his time. In recent years, in anecdote or interviews, I had heard that Pound abused some of these old friends and protégés. There was, after all, the quoted remark about Frost. I was prepared for an elder who would denounce his peers and followers. But I heard no disparagements from Pound. When I brought up his reported remark about Frost, the recollection depressed him. To me, he spoke of Frost with affection and gratitude, and of the wisecrack with regret and denial; stumblingly, he said he had been misquoted.

When he talked about Eliot, he spoke with relish and laughter, usually to recall some piece of wit that passed between them. His words about Eliot carried a quality that I recognized as the affection an older man feels for a younger. I did not recognize the quality at first, because from my position they were equally Olympian; what is an age difference on Olympus?

When Pound showed anger in our conversations, it was over institutional betrayals. He was especially angry at Harvard; he felt that the Harvard University Press had betrayed him. He had wanted to publish his translations of Confucius's *Classic Anthology* with the Chinese *en face,* an expensive project. New Directions, his usual and long-faithful publisher, had deferred to HUP. Harvard published the book in English only, promising, as Pound understood it, to print an *en face* edition later. Pound lacked the suspicion, or the acumen, to demand a contract that specified how much later. The Chinese-English edition had not appeared by 1960, nor has it since.

He became angry with Harvard again because of something I told him. As I mentioned, he recorded poems for the Poetry Room on his 1939 visit to the United States. On the label of a huge old disc, a note insisted, "Do Not Play Band Six." Naturally enough, when I first played these records as an undergraduate I set the needle on band six. It was a marvelous reading of "Sestina: Altaforte," also known as the Bloody Sestina, where Pound in the mask of Bertrans de Born praises war. The reading began with the shouted line — I jumped in my blue chair — "Damn it all! all this our South stinks peace." (The poem was composed in the breathless quiet of the British Museum Reading Room.) In the 1939 recording, Pound banged a drum as he spoke the poem; because of 1939 low-fidelity, it sounded as if he were kicking a filing cabinet.

That first morning, forgetting that I had defied a handwritten prohibition, I filled a pause by praising his reading of the poem. Pound interrupted his silence with a black look. "So they're letting them listen, are they?" I remembered my lawlessness then, and confessed it. He muttered again about Harvard's promises. I asked him the obvious question: Why had he demanded that the poem be proscribed? He paused a while to find the phrase. "War," he said, "— is no longer — amusing."

We had agreed to work the morning only, and the morning of the next day. As we talked I became convinced of what I had suspected, that he was lonely and eager for company. At some point halfway through the fragmented interviewing, I broke silence to ask if he would have dinner with us that night. He waited to answer, collecting or recollecting. The *next* night, he told me, he was invited to the Chilean embassy; *Tuesday* night. Tonight, *Monday* night, Dadone was expecting him for dinner; but maybe . . . He asked me to wait a moment and left the room to consult his host. When he returned he immediately began to complete a sentence, to answer a question that he had abandoned earlier, leaving my invitation unanswered. When he paused again, exhausted with effort, supine on the sofa with closed eyes, I asked him if he would have dinner with us tonight.

"Oh, yes," he said, opening his eyes. "It's all arranged. Yes. Yes."

When I left him at noon I walked back to the hotel discouraged, with tapes and notes that added up to little. I felt compassion for the old man, but apprehension about the interview and about our evening. I did not know what to expect of Pound, freed from the menace of interview, loosed on the town. After lunch and a nap — this encounter exhausted me also — I began my book review of *Thrones*. I found myself praising it whether I understood it or not, holding it up for praise.

We arranged for a babysitter, left the hotel, and picked up Pound at Dadone's at seven o'clock, driving the Morris Minor through Roman traffic, sedate at this evening hour. We asked him to choose the restaurant. He said in a humorous manner that, well, Crispi's ought to do — as if everyone understood that Crispi's would do more than *do*. He had attended on Crispi's before the war, he told us; just the other night he had returned for the first time, and it wasn't half bad. He implied that everything else in Italian life had declined precipitously.

He worried that he would direct us incorrectly, but led us through Rome without hesitation or error, which cheered him up. As we strolled toward the restaurant door, I looked him over. This was a new Ezra Pound, shirt open at the neck, wearing a light coat and around his neck a great yellow scarf, carrying a stout stick. His large black hat sat back on his head over his abundant gray hair, and he walked with his head thrown back, his beard strutting forth at a jaunty angle. He chatted with the headwaiter in Italian, holding himself as upright as a general, and requested a table by pointing with his stick. When he had consulted the menu he chose osso buco for himself, and recommended it to Kirby and me. Conspiring together we ordered a carafe of house red wine.

We drank little. We conversed, the three of us, with Pound paying special and even flirtatious attention to Kirby, his eyes glinting as he looked at her. He liked to make her laugh. There were pauses and moments of awkwardness also, when he would stop in midsentence forgetting his way, but these lapses were less frequent in Crispi's than in Ugo Dadone's corner room. Once or twice he made confident references in anecdote to an obscure Parisian friend, or to a Washington caller — and when he saw that we did not understand he lapsed into momentary depression, guilty again of mental error. Then he would recover himself with another story.

Mostly, it was grandfather's night out, and he was happy and funny. If he didn't want to talk about the past in the morning, by evening he loved to reminisce. He told more Eliot stories, mimicking Eliot with avuncular, mocking, affectionate accuracy. He remembered a song that he and Eliot made up back in the years just after the Great War. He sang stanzas of "The Yiddisher Charleston Band" in a vaudevillian Jewish accent, and seemed without fear that we would find him anti-Semitic. (The song was perhaps no more anti-Semitic than "McNamara's Band" was anti-Irish, but we cringed at the name of it; Pound's history lent it retrospective nastiness.) When the Yiddisher Charleston Band was playing — the song's burden — *everybody* danced. It was young Pound and younger Eliot doing music hall. King Bolo made his appearance in one verse, the protagonist of a rumored series of pornographic verses by the young Eliot — these verses have never turned up, to my knowledge; various references occur in memorabilia; when I asked Pound about them, he hinted there might be copies in the Pound archives — and King Bolo was dancing the Charleston too. The only couplet I remember went:

> Mistah Cool-idge, de Pres-i-dent,
> He couldn't come but de fam-il-y vent.

In another stanza, Mary Magdalene put in an appearance, as singer or dancer. She was the only biblical figure, as Pound sang it that night.*

When Pound sang this stanza he dropped his voice, perhaps

---

* John Peck tells me that this song was printed by Louis Zukofsky in *An Objectivist's Anthology* in 1932, attributed solely to Pound. The printed version largely coincides with my recollection of Pound's performance. In Zukofsky's anthology, however, it is "Calvin," not "Mistah"; and "Jheezus" and Mary each make an earlier appearance. I leave my version as it was; I will not allow a text to corrupt a recollection.

out of deference to the religious convictions of diners nearby. I found it hard to hear the words, and Kirby couldn't hear them at all. Pound was looking at her — singing to amuse her — and saw her visage assume an expression he misinterpreted. Her face pretended to hear and to enjoy, but it could not sustain the pretense, so that she appeared pained or disapproving. This verse concluded his song, or Pound chose to conclude it there. With a foxy, roguish expression on his face, he leaned toward Kirby, wagging his finger, and said, "Baptist?"

Ezra Pound considered that a postwar American woman would be shocked by the presence of a biblical personage in a comic song. Looking through his eyes at her, I imagined the distorting glasses of his vision: He looked through 1908 eyes: At the church picnic the young ladies wear straw hats over their white collars; they huddle together and giggle; young Ezra Pound approaches, and with a fine sardonic air speaks with a daring levity — about the literalness of the Bible perhaps, or about the sanctity of the Fourth of July. With satisfaction he hears them say, "*Oh*, Mr. Pound! The things you say."

That night at Crispi's, he spoke of the United States with nostalgia and affection, but he did not speak of a United States I knew at first hand. He spoke of my grandparents' America. Leaving the country in 1908, he had returned briefly in 1910 and in 1939. His only lengthy visit had taken place within walls, and many St. Elizabeths callers were neo-Fascist toadies. "The trouble with seeing nobody but visitors," he said apropos his St. Elizabeths socializing, "is that you never talk to the opposition." His visitors told him what they thought he wanted to hear, and his notion of contemporary American life was naïve. You could hear 1908 in his voice, in that eclectic accent which was Pound's version of the village eccentric. You could hear it in his canny guess: "Baptist?"

Pound was a dinosaur, strangely preserved into a later millennium, stretching his long bones out of dinosaur valley into the chrome city — and not noticing that things had altered.

·   ·   ·

He *missed* the United States, he kept telling us. He wanted to return, to see the country outside asylum walls. His wife had been miserable there, he told us, and she did not want to return — but perhaps he could fly over alone for visits. Did we think someone would pay his way over, perhaps to visit a university? I leapt to assure him: Any number of colleges and universities would pay great sums to hear him read his poems.

He asked: Could we help him? He did not know what to do. His friends did not seem to want him to return, and he did not know how to go about it.

Of course we could help him!

I had no doubts — right then and there — but that Pound could handle himself on a reading tour. There need be no pauses in a poetry reading, with the text in front of him. Despite the pauses in our interview, it was clear from our experience tonight that the old man was in decent shape. He could tell good stories, and I had heard nothing of Weinstein Kirchberger or Franklin Delano Rosenfeld.

And *this* was the man who had poured the foundations of modern poetry in English. In America little poets and big ones traveled from campus to campus all year, earning a livelihood reading their poems; why wouldn't the father of us all receive a thousand invitations from a thousand universities? I told him there would be no problem; I told him he could pick and choose among invitations. He was encouraged but I could see that he remained skeptical. I told him that as soon as we returned to England, I would write letters to initiate his career as rider of the poetry circuit; I would be unpaid agent or advance man for his sallies among the professors.

Dinner done, we fought over the check for a moment, I won, and we walked outside into the mild spring night. As we headed for the car, Pound made it obvious that he wanted the evening to continue, that he did not want to return to Dadone's right away. Did we want to walk? Come to think of it, he no longer knew the area. Perhaps we would like to drive around Rome by moonlight? Had we done any sightseeing? No? Well, then, he would show us around from the car, and when we had time we could return for a closer look by daylight.

We drove in directions and over avenues that I cannot remember. We drove past the Forum and the Colosseum, and through a square where, as he told us, "Muss" delivered speeches to the Roman crowds, past walls where the Duce had erected maps of the ancient Roman Empire and his putative Italian imitation. Pound identified public buildings as we cruised by them, on streets in the evening largely without traffic. "There's the synagogue," he said at one point. He never named a Methodist chapel for us; he *did* point out St. Peter's.

Finally we drove by the new railway station and our hotel, into the Via Angelo Poliziano. Halfway down the street, a gelateria showed bright lights among the closed shops. "*Here*," said Pound, before we could get to number 80. "Stop here. I'll buy you an ice cream." So we three stood on the sidewalk dipping wooden spoons into cups of exquisite gelati. American music issued from the ice cream parlor's jukebox. Pound stood in the yellow light, coat flung across his shoulders like a cape, hat angled back on his head, great stick under his arm, scarf draped with flair around his neck. He stalked up and down a few feet, smiling as his wooden spoon delivered its mouthfuls, veering back and forth on his toes, stalking with youthful gait for a moment again.

ROME: TUESDAY

When my wife and I were alone Monday night, we talked over our evening. I had seen a happier man, but she was unconvinced. Pound had been silent and glum when he had not been entertaining us with stories, and she was afraid that he had been bored. Listening, I became half convinced, old preconceptions returning.

I woke early again and finished a longhand draft of my review. I was seeing Pound at ten this morning and would stay with him until one, when he would take an afternoon nap to prepare himself for the Chilean reception tonight. In the afternoon, I thought, I could type another draft of my review, and maybe finish it after supper. Then the phone rang. It was an American novelist, whom I knew through the *Paris Review*. He had heard that we were in town, and invited us to a party that evening.

Well, I decided, at any rate I can type up another draft this afternoon.

When Pound answered the door at ten o'clock, he was strutting with pride and energy. Leading the way back to his room, he bounced on his toes. He handed me sheets of paper on which he had written sentences to fit into yesterday's answers. He had been up for two hours, and he felt *much better* than he had felt the day before. I watched his energy and his buoyancy with delight, but also with reserve: I had seen ups and downs before.

He let me know the source of his elation. For Pound, our evening out had been a social triumph, proof that he was sane and normal, proof that he could function like anybody else. He kept returning to the subject of my wife. He was charmed with her not only for her positive qualities but for what she wasn't: She was neither poet nor Fascist; she was, in Pound's mind, a *normal American* — a phrase he used two or three times in commendation. During the morning he often returned to the subject of the night before, not in conventional thanks but as illustration of his energy or competence. When he asked again about poetry readings, I said — not to discourage him but to help him prepare — that of course they would be tiring, and that he must protect himself from fatigue. "Well," he said with a proud twang, "you saw me last night!"

For him, our night's diversion had been a carnival discovered in the square of a Calvinist town; it was gaiety, it was health. He spoke of it again when he ruminated about returning to America for two months every winter; *that* was what he needed, "more nights like last night. I haven't had a relaxed evening like that since I left America," he said. "I want to be able to talk to

bright, normal people. Europeans don't understand anything."
Eating at Crispi's, buying gelati on the way home, he had be-
haved like bright, normal people, not like the lunatic they said
he was; he ended a lively evening like everyone in America, with
ice cream and a wooden spoon. Again, it was Philadelphia and
1908.

His elation spilled over into the notion of the coming evening.
He was pleased to be invited to the Chilean embassy. Then I
asked him if he could go out with us again the following night,
Wednesday — our last night in Rome. He accepted at once.

Switching on the tape, I asked questions about politics. The day
before I had asked him about literature and his literary associations. Some of his answers had moved toward politics, involving
themselves in monetary policy, but I had not questioned him
about Mussolini and the broadcasts, about treason or anti-Semitism. Now my questions entered the places of nightmare, country of Blackshirts, blitzkrieg, and genocide. He answered by
explaining himself, even excusing himself. He pleaded in his
defense his long friendship with Louis Zukofsky. Later when
Pound, speaking to Allen Ginsberg, disparaged his anti-Semitism as "suburban," I remembered how he had said that some
of his best friends were Jews. Also, he told how St. Elizabeths
psychiatrists informed him of the death camps, about which I
doubt that he had known anything during the war. He said that
the psychiatrists tried to make him feel guilty. Hearing him
excuse himself, I knew that they had succeeded. He let me know,
guardedly and reluctantly, that he doubted what he had done.
Bunting knew more than Ezra Pound, he had told me; now he
said, "I guess I was off base all along." He no longer defended
his actions for themselves; he defended the *sincerity* of his actions. He told me about trying to leave Italy and return to the
United States after the war started, a return blocked by American authorities. He told me he had not committed treason —
his familiar defense — because there can be no treason without
treasonous intent. And his intent, he insisted, was to defend the

Constitution against President Roosevelt, the usurper. (If Mussolini had gone down in his estimation, there was no funicular that elevated Roosevelt.) In his patriotic defense of the Constitution against the Man in the White House, I heard again the accents of an archaic America. He reminded me of my Connecticut grandfather, conservative Republican brought up on Fourth of July oratory.

In response to his self-defense, I said nothing. I could not agree when I didn't agree. The phrasing of the treason law — about giving aid and comfort to the enemy — seemed fairly straightforward. I could not agree that his friendship for Louis Zukofsky made null and void a hundred attacks on Yids and kikes. So I said nothing, only listened and occasionally asked a question, and my silence drove Pound frantic. He demanded exoneration, forgiveness. I was drawn to the old man, but I could not tell him what he wanted to hear. Finally, after an hour of his excuses and my silence, he gathered himself to make an outrageous plea: "Do *you* think they should have shot me?"

He had me there. No, I did not think they should have shot him — and I told him so. He laughed a long time, his face flushing. When he stopped laughing he suggested we take a walk.

Pound wanted to buy a pad and notepaper. When a writer buys paper, it's an optimistic sign. The energy he gathered from his evening out was still upon him. Wearing his yellow scarf, carrying his stick, he led me four or five blocks to a stationery store. Pound extolled the Bic pen to me, widespread in Europe but not yet arrived in Ann Arbor. Then, on the walk back to the apartment, the energy began to drain from him again. I think that the tension of talking politics had sustained him; now that we talked of other things the fatigue rolled over him like a tide. As we waited for the elevator in the hallway his eyes closed, and I worried that he lacked the strength to walk to his room. Then he lay on his sofa bed and shut his eyes. It was eleven-thirty. I suggested that I leave him now and let him rest, but he told me that I had promised to stay until lunchtime. After lunch — he said slowly, as if he were speaking from sleep — he would take a long nap, to be ready for the Chilean party tonight. Now, he said, I should ask him more questions; we must continue our interview.

We did. I returned to some topics of the day before, and completed more answers. I asked a few new ones. Pound remained supine, his eyes closed, and there were long pauses again. I turned off the recorder two or three times. Once I thought he had fallen asleep. Then his eyes opened and caught me studying the face I thought sleeping. His eyes bored into me and would not let me go. "The question is," the voice said after a long vacancy, "whether I give up now — or have another twenty years — to write in."

We continued to gaze at each other. After another pause he said, "All the time — I feel the hands of the clock — moving." Then he swung his legs over the side of his bed and sat up, still looking hard at me, his face now level with mine. "From what — you see of me," he asked, "— do you think — I will be able to go on writing? Do you think — there is enough of me here — to work?"

I who had expected arrogance and contempt was asked to judge Ezra Pound's mental abilities.

From the time I was a small boy, I had loved old people. From my ninth birthday on, I had been aware of the hands of the clock, for myself but also and perhaps originally for the old people I loved, grandmothers and grandfathers and great-uncles and great-aunts in Connecticut and in New Hampshire. When I was a child, I felt closer to octogenarians than to children my own age. Now I felt close to Ezra Pound in his predicament. He stood where we would all stand, if we lived long enough, at the agonizing moment of power's diminishment before its loss, when energy and understanding flash forth only to be overcome, when hope and hopelessness reasonably alternate.

Because I would not lie to him, I said what he already knew: Maybe he *was* too tired (I permitted myself the euphemism that Pound used) to work on *Cantos;* I did not know. For a long time he continued to stare, with an intensity that was almost devouring. Then he sighed, his body loosened its tension, and he remarked that really, all he needed was two months of relaxation like last night; that would fix him up.

Back at the hotel I worked over my review of *Thrones*. If I could not reassure the old man that he would write more *Cantos*, I could praise what he had already written. I wouldn't lie to him but I might lie to others about him. To my surprise, I felt something like devotion for the man. Some people in old age demand or plead for a filial relationship to the young. I felt this plea in Pound, and I responded. By late afternoon, my typescript of the review was chicken-scratched with revisions. Soon the babysitter would arrive and we would leave for the party. I had to get the review in the mail the next day. I wondered where I could find someone in Rome who could type up an English book review. At the desk, two young clerks told me there was no problem at all: They would type it. If it was a matter of the great poet Ezra Pound, the American who preferred to live in Italy, why should they not work late and without sleeping?

When we left to go to the party, one clerk was reading my English aloud to the other, who was hunting and pecking at a typewriter. When we returned at one in the morning a neat typescript of my review, with only a few exotic errors, was rolled in our mailbox.

At the party were all the literary Americans resident in Rome. I talked a good while with the host, and with Moreland and Saskia Hopkinson. It was relaxing to be away from Pound and among Americans my own age. I didn't need to listen so hard, and I did not have to keep on *feeling* all the time. It was the emotion, I realized, that drained me when I was with Pound. Moreland had told the American literary colony about the interview. No one at the party had ever met Pound, and many were curious. I was called upon to testify to his mental condition, and to talk about his politics. I found myself exaggerating on the side of his health, normality, and coherence. Then I found myself in a brief, sharp argument. One tall and aristocratic figure, whom I knew to be an American who lived in Rome translating Italian books, hung at the edge of several conversations without taking part. I noticed a lip that curled with increasing annoyance. Aware as I thought of the reason — and a little drunk — I escalated my praise of Pound and Pound's poetry until finally the translator could resist no longer. He leapt into the conversation, denouncing Pound and denouncing me for praising him, even for talking with him. Pound was a Fascist, an anti-Semite, a lunatic, a bully, and a bad poet.

Having provoked the fight I wanted, quickly I asserted contraries. The people we stood among tried smiling, as if the argument were in good fun; it wasn't. I was angry, and realized that I had been spoiling for a fight with someone who denigrated Pound. Finally, when it seemed as if somebody might hit somebody else, the translator summed up my moral character in a word or two and walked out of the party. It was time to go home. Driving home with Moreland and Saskia, I felt triumphant, as if I had defended my old father against attack. As my heart slowed down its pounding, I was aware that Saskia was proposing another social engagement. She suggested that, since the interview was going so well — I had exaggerated — perhaps tomorrow I could bring Pound to lunch at their house.

In truth, I doubted that I could. Pound would be tired after the Chilean party; whatever energy remained should go to the interview. I told Saskia that I would extend the invitation to Pound and telephone them about it, but that I didn't think it would work out. I lied, saying that Pound had mentioned some errands he had to do; I protected him in his fatigue and distraction; or maybe I tried not to share him with anyone else.

ROME: WEDNESDAY

In the morning the desk clerk weighed my *New Statesman* envelope, I bought the stamps, and my review of *Thrones* took off by the morning mail. Then as we ate breakfast in our room, the telephone rang. It was Pound calling at nine o'clock, an hour before I was scheduled to see him. His voice was vigorous, he sounded happy and strong. He asked if I would bring the car this morning; we could drive to the Circus Maximus and take a walk together; I should bring the tape recorder, and we could continue the interview on foot.

I wondered where he would lie down when the fatigue took him over; but I enjoyed the new confidence of his proposal, and his hostly generosity — he wanted to show me Rome — and I said I would bring the car. Then he asked if I had plans for the rest of the day. I said we still planned to have dinner with him. He knew that, he said quickly, but he wondered about the *rest* of the day. We would be leaving Rome tomorrow, he said, and he wanted to see as much of us today as he could.

We felt the same way, I told him. I remembered Saskia's invitation to lunch, but I didn't mention it on the phone. I hung up and hurried through breakfast. Kirby agreed that I relay the invitation and sound him out. If he liked the idea, I would bring Pound to our hotel about noon, and pick up the family.

After breakfast I drove the car to Dadone's apartment. It was a bright sunny day, light air with a little breeze, perfect Roman spring. Maybe Pound took vigor from the weather. The fragile elevator creaked upward, and when the door slid open I found myself facing him waiting in the hallway outside the apartment. He was pacing, rubbing his hands together, smiling, and looked twenty years younger than he did when I first saw him. He took my arm and led me back to his sunny room, saying that he had something to show me. Scarf, hat, and stick lay together on a chair near the door, ready for our expedition. He shuffled through a clutch of papers — some of them notes toward answers for old questions, which he gave me later in the morning — to find what he wanted, and handed me two sheets of graph paper scrawled over with a blue Bic. "This might help a bit," he said, "in case I konk out." I remembered that while we walked to the stationer's the day before, he complained that someone had sold him a pad of graph paper when he had wanted plain. Now the graph paper looked purposeful, as the big hand spaced out notes toward the conclusion of the *Cantos*, curved over tight squares in the poet's calligraphy of space:

> Provisional ending
> > re nature of sovereignty
> (if I konk out.)
>
> nostos.
> periplum.
>
> vs. paradiso, difficult
> > to find inhabitants
> > > for.
>
> to clarify obscurities.
> > (vers. prosaici
> > > as note.)
>
> > > get clearer
> definite ideas or dissociations already
> > > expressed.
>
> verbal formula to control
> > rise of brutality.
>
> principle of order
> > vs. split atom

Early this morning — I found out later — he had read over his new *Cantos* and fragments. He was vigorous now, and happy with plans for work, as he had not been "since last July." His "Provisional ending . . . (if I konk out)" was a vital sign, not a morbid one: He was able to conceive that he could finish the *Cantos*. The conception carried with it doubts about what he had done — "clarify obscurities" — but it was humorous when it acknowledged his difficulty in finding inhabitants worthy of Paradise; and the note touched again on the old verities of his life and work: "nostos" is home, and "periplum" is the voyage around the world, like Odysseus's around the Mediterranean, that the traveler must endure before returning home. His provisions looked toward the accomplishment of a goal: "verbal formula to control rise of brutality" that Ortega ascribed to the vertical invasion of the barbarians. Then "principle of order vs. split atom" put the controlling mind on the one side, the violent atom with its destructive power on the other; the atom was split "in fragments" and therefore not under control.

He named the enemy, making general or metaphysical what was also private and personal. Finding and maintaining order in the universe is identical to finding and maintaining order in the self. In *Canto XIII*, from the first collection of *Cantos*, he had quoted Confucius:

> If a man have not order within him
> He can not spread order about him;
> And if a man have not order within him
> His family will not act with due order;
> And if the prince have not order within him
> He can not put order in his dominions.

When I had first arrived ("Mr. Hall, you — find me — in fragments") the atom had split, and all the king's horses and all the king's men couldn't put Ezra Pound together again. Now he dared to hope that he had the energy to reassemble both himself and the atom. He spoke with a vigor that made anything seem possible. He settled his hat back on his head, flung his scarf around his neck, and took up his stick. Then he realized, with a short laugh, that he didn't know how to direct me to the Circus Maximus. He sat at the edge of his sofa bed, hat and scarf still on, and studied a map. Then suddenly it happened, horribly in front of my eyes: Again I saw vigor and energy drain out of him. The strong body visibly sagged into old age; he disintegrated in front of me, smashed into a thousand unconnected and disorderly pieces. He took off his hat slowly and let it drop, his scarf slid to the floor; his stick, which had rested in his lap, thudded to the carpet. His long body slid boneless down, until he lay supine, eyes closed, as if all the lights in a tall building went out in a few seconds and the building itself disassembled, returning to the stone and water and sand from which it had come.

For a few minutes he said nothing, only breathing and sighing. If I had not seen similar catastrophes before, I would have thought he suffered a stroke or a heart attack. After some minutes he opened his eyes and looked at me. I said nothing but looked back into the eyes that watched me. After another two or three minutes he mumbled, "I can't do anything right." After another pause he added, "I get you to go to the trouble — of bringing a car over here — and then I crump out on you."

It was no trouble and I said so. But now Pound was as depressed as he had been elevated. He had brought me "all the way down to Rome for nothing." I told him I had the material for the interview. He said, well, he didn't feel like going out now, so maybe I should ask him some more things. I did, and filled in some gaps, but Pound's depression was heavy. When a question reminded him of the *Cantos*, he doubted that he would live to complete them. He spoke again of the difficulty of finding inhabitants for a Paradiso, and now he was complaining of his incompetence. Maybe he was mistaken all along, he mumbled, to put Confucius at the top; maybe it should have been Agassiz. He looked at me as if I could decide.

Gradually, as we talked and I recorded his answers, he recovered a little. He swung his legs over the side of the bed and sat up. He had been invited to visit Chile, he told me with pleasure. He didn't expect he would go there, but he was glad to be asked; now if someone would ask him to the United States . . . He was gathering strength again, to assault the Circus Maximus. He thought he would feel like it in another ten minutes, he told me. I asked if he could sign some books in the meantime. I had brought them from England in the car, not with the idea that Pound would sign them — who would ask a favor from the ogre I had expected? — but in case I needed to consult them for the interview. Now I wanted his signature, and I knew that he would be pleased to do it. He wrote apologies in all the books, along with his name. In the *Selected Poems* he wrote "Roman holiday," by which he implied that there was nothing for me in Rome but a holiday. In his *Classic Anthology* he wrote, "This at least contains horse sense"; in the collection of his letters, "to Hall having mercy"; in *Rock Drill,* "to Hall persisting"; in *Thrones,* "to D. H. attempting consolation." At the back of *Thrones* I later found another note in his hand, repeating his earlier shame about the errors in his text: "as to minor errata gawd help us."

When he finished signing — handing me each book with a smile, looking at me as I read his line — he stood and put on his hat and picked up his scarf. Then he changed his mind, put them down on the bed, visibly deciding to do something else. He strode rapidly across the room and pulled two suitcases from beneath a desk. He opened one and rummaged through it and closed it and opened the other. From the second suitcase he lifted a loose pile of papers and carried it to me where I sat on the sofa across from his bed. He sat down beside me and set the papers between us. The top page began with a roman numeral; I was looking at the drafts of new *Cantos.*

Go ahead, he told me, read them.

These were the *Cantos* that he had worked over "until last July," and which he had read again this morning. These were essentially the passages collected in 1968 as *Drafts and Fragments.* I say "essentially" because he worked on them again in 1960, from March through June, and when I had returned to England mailed me further versions; and he did some further work until 1962; I cannot distinguish, in my memory, the versions I read that morning from the versions I read later. The differences, I believe, were not great. There was a sheet of paper that I remember whenever I think about form in the *Cantos:* It consisted of quotes and lines from earlier *Cantos* and it was headed, "Things to be Stuck in."

I sat reading, rapt. Pound walked up and down, glancing at me, then lay down and closed his eyes. This time he seemed not to collapse but deliberately to rest himself. I read for half an hour, enthusiasm turning into elation. In my review of *Thrones* I had praised him not so much for *Thrones* as for his whole career. Now I loved *new poems;* I loved sounds, images, passages from the typescript in front of me. I interrupted my reading to tell him so — he made it obvious that he wanted to hear my opinion — and he sighed deeply and smiled. I don't remember just what I said to him. But I have a note that I made later that day, which must represent how I felt. These were the best *Cantos* since the *Pisan,* I wrote; they returned to lyricism and to personal vulnerability, his own life and his own concerns surfacing through the details of history. I was moved by the poetry of old age, by the acknowledgment of error or failure shining through a language that gave the lie to failure. I quote from the final versions:

> Can you enter the great acorn of light?
>   But the beauty is not the madness
> Tho' my errors and wrecks lie about me.
> And I am not a demigod,
> I cannot make it cohere.
> If love be not in the house there is nothing.
>   . . .
> i.e. it coheres all right
>   even if my notes do not cohere.
> Many errors,
>   a little rightness,
> to excuse his hell
>   and my paradiso.
>   . . .
> To confess wrong without losing rightness:
> Charity I have had sometimes,
>   I cannot make it flow thru.
> A little light, like a rushlight
>   to lead back to splendour.

There was also — and I remember reading it that morning; I remember the dazzle of it — the fragment of *Canto CXV* that begins:

The scientists are in terror
        and the European mind stops
Wyndham Lewis chose blindness
           rather than have his mind stop.

The operation that might have saved Lewis's sight might have impaired his intelligence. You must accept the punishment of persistent dark if you are to see inwardly and to speak what you see. *Canto CXV* also contains lines I quoted earlier:

A blown husk that is finished
    but the light sings eternal
a pale flare over marshes
    where the salt hay whispers to tide's change

These poems were paradisal, elevated, and ultimately removed from the scene of personal failure, because there is something that persists and survives individual wreckage: "i.e. it coheres all right" and "the light sings eternal." In the note I wrote that afternoon, I said that I felt that the *Cantos* were almost finished, not finished by resolving all issues raised but finished by their ascent; I must have called these fragments paradisal. Sitting on the sofa reading and rereading them, I exclaimed over lines that were especially beautiful. Pound asked me three or four times if I *really* liked them. I don't think he doubted me — he was positively leering with pleasure — but like most of us he could not hear enough praise. After a few moments he tired again. I did not expect it this time. Horribly his body sagged again. He crossed the room to his sofa bed and sat down with his head in his hands. When fatigue took him over, it drowned his hopes, and the higher his hopes had been, the more profound his despair. I heard his old voice moving out from the darkness under his hands, like a voice from a cave. "The question is," he said, and paused a long time, "whether to live or die." I had no comment to make. I looked into his eyes. My heart broke for him, as he sat possessed again by the conviction of impotence or inability to *finish*, impotence intensified by the conviction that he had made huge mistakes, too gross to rectify, mistakes of life and of art. He looked across the room at another poet (for better or worse; he knew nothing of my work), with forty more years in which to put things together. After a long time he said, "There can be such — communication — in silence." Then his irony, that device which protects us when we become vulnerable, rose up and said, "Well, maybe nothing — is being communicated — to you," and the fatigue passed again, and he put on his hat and scarf. "Let's be going," he said.

We never made it to the Circus Maximus. He tried to direct me, using a map, but we circled helplessly in the Roman traffic, and the roads we wanted were never where we wanted them to be. After fifteen or twenty minutes of frustration, we found a place that looked ancient enough, and parked. (When we drove out again we discovered a sign, and learned that we had visited the Baths of Caracalla.) We walked for half an hour. I asked a few interviewer's questions, lifting the recorder so that it hovered between us at mouth level, and he answered me. But he did not want to talk about himself. He was conscious of having exposed himself, conscious of what he had shown. Walking around the ancient stones, he expressed an interest in my work, as he called it; how was it going these days? He was kind enough to wish to appear interested, but I don't believe he retained interest in the poems of anyone as young as I was. He would read his old friends and contemporaries — Eliot, Williams, Cummings, Marianne Moore — but I think he had to strain to be interested in Robert Lowell.

Perhaps it pained him to lose touch — this was the man who had discovered excellence among the young before anyone else did — but it shouldn't have. As an artist grows older, he loses the ability to discriminate among the young. It is inevitable. He grows away, he grows apart; eventually the faces and poems blur together, beginning to look alike. I have known people who lost their ability to read younger poets while they were still in their forties; most lose it by fifty; Eliot held on to it into his sixties, perhaps because he required discrimination for his profession as a publisher. Pound lost interest, and then judgment, in the 1930s when he was about fifty years old. I was touched that he asked me, and answered by speaking briefly of my endeavors in poetry at the moment, while he nodded to show understanding.

It was eleven or eleven-thirty now. Pound's energy held up. By now I realized that it would rise and fall whatever happened, so I asked him if he would like to eat lunch at the Hopkinsons' place, telling him briefly about Moreland: that he was associated with the *Paris Review,* that he was a novelist, that I had known him at Harvard, that he was rich and his wife beautiful. Pound said yes, let's do it; he was going to stick as close to us as possible all day; after lunch he would take a nap, he said, and then if he was up to it we would go back to Crispi's that night.

We drove back to the hotel, parked, and Pound waited in a café across the street while I went upstairs. My wife was beginning to feed the baby, and the process would take forty-five minutes or so. I telephoned the Hopkinsons and told Saskia that we would arrive for lunch in an hour — a baby, a five-year-old boy, two parents, and an aged poet — if the invitation was still in order. It was. I entered the café and found Pound drinking a cup of coffee. When I sat down a waiter walked up to us, to take my order, and wagged his finger back and forth between us, saying a sentence in Italian, addressed to Pound, that ended with the word "*figlio.*" Thinking he recognized a resemblance, the waiter asked Pound to confirm that I was his son. Pound looked at me, laughed lightly, and said, "*Sì. Sì.*" When the waiter left to get my beer, Pound laughed again and said, "Well, now that you're a member of the family . . ."

A moment later, the fatigue washed over him again. With no place to lie down, he propped his head on his fist, elbow on table, and leaned against the wall. His eyes closed occasionally, but he did not sleep. "Keep on talking," he said. I searched my mind for anecdotes that would please him. I asked him if he had heard about the Ezra Pound night at the Institute of Contemporary Arts, London 1953. If he had heard, he did not remember. So I told him the story I have already recounted in "Notes on T. S. Eliot." Pound was amused to hear of the ruckus Graham Greene and John Davenport raised. ("Their asperities diverted me in my green time.") He was pleased to hear of the occasion itself, and of the cable Peter Russell and I addressed to him at St. Elizabeths, which he did not remember receiving.

Also I told him my favorite of all knock-knock jokes. (First I had to explain the genre.) "Knock-knock." "Who's there?" "Ezra Pound." "Ezra Pound who?" *A capella, con molto brio,* "Ezra Pound to get you in a taxi, honey. I'll be there about a quarter of eight." He seemed to enjoy the pun; definitely he enjoyed the evidence the joke afforded him that his name was *au courant.* Yeats took pleasure, in his old age, to hear Dublin urchins singing a poem he wrote when he was young; Pound in exile accepted solace in the monument of a knock-knock joke. Then he told me a story that pleased him. When the jurist Roscoe Pound, no relation, was introduced to a collegiate audience as Ezra Pound, the audience cheered. Clearly Pound understood that they were cheering Ezra. I knew that the applause was ironic, based on the anomaly that a law professor was confused with an accused traitor. I did not disabuse him.

Instead I dredged up another story. In 1956, the year after I published my first book of poems, I was invited to an insane meeting of writers. President Eisenhower had instituted the People-to-People program, in which groups of American professionals — manufacturers, architects, farmers — gathered to recommend courses of action to the executive branch, to promote contact and understanding with people of foreign countries, especially countries of Eastern Europe. William Faulkner was chairman of a writers' group that included most of the prominent names in American letters, from individual literary monuments to best sellers. In addition, he named one young fiction writer (Harold Brodkey) and one young poet. We met at Harvey Breit's apartment in New York. I call the meeting insane because of the group's diversity: Saul Bellow and Edna Ferber,

Pound's old friend William Carlos Williams and Pound's most hysterical detractor Robert Hillyer.

The gathering was drunken, argumentative, and inconclusive. Some of the proposals angered Saul Bellow and he walked out. Steinbeck brought a Hungarian novelist with him, and much discussion centered on the recent rebellion in Hungary. William Carlos Williams — loyal to Pound, though he found Pound's politics anathema — proposed that we recommend releasing Pound from St. Elizabeths, which occasioned some antipathy. The evening ended, amid the debris of a thousand opinions, with Harvey Breit's parliamentary shrewdness. He suggested that a subcommittee meet the next day to consider all these valuable suggestions. He suggested that the subcommittee consist of William Faulkner, John Steinbeck, and Donald Hall. No one could object to Faulkner and Steinbeck because they were Faulkner and Steinbeck. No one could object to me because I was nobody.

Writers staggered into the streets groping for taxis. I remember standing on a curb with William Carlos Williams, who appeared sober, and telling him with sudden fluency how much I admired his work. Because I was known at the time as an iambic reactionary — although I did indeed love his poems — he may not have returned the admiration; he grunted.

We met the next morning in the office of Saxe Commins, Faulkner's editor at Random House. We decided to limit ourselves to a few simply worded recommendations for our President. We agreed quickly to three proposals that had achieved befuddled consensus the night before. Then I proposed that we add a fourth: "Free Ezra Pound from St. Elizabeths Hospital." Steinbeck was quickly negative. I don't think that he cherished antipathy for Pound; he was afraid that the proposition would offend people, congressmen for instance, and that we endangered our other proposals by including this one. Saxe Commins was nodding his head, and I thought my proposal had lost when Faulkner suddenly sided with me, and the fourth proposal passed, two to one.

But it was Faulkner's phraseology that delighted me, not simply his assent. After Steinbeck finished his objection, Faulkner addressed the secretary who was taking down our proposals. "Yes," he said. "Yes!" He had been laconic the night before and so far this morning; now he almost chattered: "Yes! Say it this way. Take it down this way, young lady. 'While the government of Sweden confers its highest honor on the chairman of this committee, the United States keeps its best poet in jail.' "

Telling the story to Pound, I left out the antipathy at the evening meeting and emphasized that Steinbeck's reluctance was strategic. When he heard Faulkner's sentence he smiled, but Faulkner's vanity was not the lesson he took from the story, nor the one I intended him to take. As with Henry Moore, he had found another celebrated artist to count on his side, another piece of praise to warm himself with. After a moment or two he said, with a moved gruffness, "Please thank Faulkner when you see him."

The baby sat in the very back of the Morris Minor station wagon, in her pram top; my wife and son sat in the back seat; Pound and I sat up front and got lost. It wasn't wholly our fault, because a street prominent in our directions was blocked off for repair. We drove in circles for half an hour, trying to climb an inevitable hill that we could see but lacked access to. We stopped pedestrians and Pound interrogated them without success. Everyone was polite, even warm and jolly, but no one succeeded in directing us. Some seemed to have trouble with Pound's Italian. I understood that his Italian was once excellent; perhaps it deteriorated in thirteen years at St. Elizabeths. Then I remembered that I sometimes had trouble with his English.

We arrived late enough for politeness, not so late as rudeness, and ate a glorious lunch on the terrace of a large house on a Roman hill under the mild Roman sun of early March. Pound loved the sun. Before lunch and between courses he sank back in his chair, his head thrown back on a pillow, to soak it in. Sometimes the brightness bothered his eyes, and he had difficulty adjusting his hat to shield his eyelids. We fussed over him, and an amused calm voice emerged from the covered face: "Grandpa can get out of the sun if he wants."

Cold cucumber soup. Vitello tonnato. Salad. A light white wine. Fruit and cheese. Coffee.

After lunch Pound dozed and listened as we talked with Saskia and Moreland; he seemed content or even pleased to stretch out at the periphery of a conversation among "normal Americans." Occasionally he entered the conversation with a mysterious utterance, especially startling to Moreland and Saskia, who had not experienced earlier obscurities. Moreland was master of a polite sound, resembling a laugh of assent, that stood in for response. On several occasions Pound drew himself together to perform an anecdote, complete with mimicry, some story of Yeats or Wyndham Lewis or Joyce or Eliot. One of his own anecdotes upset him. Someone mentioned I Tatti, Bernard Berenson's villa outside Florence. Immediately Pound perked up, reminded of a story. One day at dinner, he told us, Berenson's young grandson had asked a question out of the blue: "Grandfather, what is a Jew?" Pound mimicked Berenson's answer, drawing himself up in severe dignity, turning slowly upon an invisible grandson, enunciating slowly and carefully: "*I'm — one.*"

We laughed at his performance of Berensonian slow dignity, and then I saw Pound crumple again. Now it was not fatigue; he passed his hand over his mouth and his eyes, his face abject with shame and misery. "Oh," he moaned. "How did we get on the subject of race?"

When he sang "The Yiddisher Charleston Band" at Crispi's, and when he pointed out a synagogue, he had brought up the "subject of race" before; and of course in the interview I had heard him boast of his friendship with Louis Zukofsky. Apparently he feared to disgrace himself in front of Moreland and Saskia. When we had drunk our coffee Pound looked tired. The five of us loaded ourselves into the Morris and set out for the Via Angelo Poliziano with new directions. At first Pound sat back with his eyes closed. Then he opened them and spoke, "I hope I didn't hurt you with Mr. Hopkinson." I said he hadn't, not knowing what he had in mind; maybe he was thinking of the Berenson story, maybe of the cryptic remarks. After a moment I asked him what kind of hurt he meant. Hopkinson was a rich man, he told me; we had to be careful with rich men. He mentioned Moreland's "Harvard-man manner." I told him that the remoteness of the rich had always annoyed me. "Yes," said Pound. "I suppose they have to protect themselves." Then he continued, moving from "they" to the singular: "Particularly if he thinks I may look on the *Paris Review* as a source of some of my sustenance." Thinking about Pound's history of living by his wits, I realized: This is how he learned to think, fifty years ago in London.

When we parked in front of Dadone's, Pound turned in the front seat and shook hands with my wife, continuing to clasp her hand after he had shaken it, and spoke as if he might be saying goodbye. He looked terribly tired.

"We might not see you again," I said suddenly. "I hadn't thought of that."

"Well, I had," he said, and got out of the car. I followed him into the building where he pushed the button for the elevator. It was four o'clock in the afternoon. I told him again that we wanted to see him tonight, to return to Crispi's with him. He nodded his head, too tired to speak. I said I would telephone at seven, to see if he was able. He nodded again and clasped both my hands but said nothing, and when the elevator came he entered it silently and ascended out of sight.

At seven his voice was strong. He had slept well, he was ready for Crispi's, how soon could we come?

That night his conversation was steadier and more consistent than it had been before. Perhaps because he knew us better, perhaps because of his social triumphs, perhaps because of his nap, he never sank into a long pause. He talked mostly about the United States, how much he missed it, how much he wanted to return for visits. I assured him vehemently that he could visit as much as he wanted, paid by universities to read his poems. Oh, he told us, he required annual refreshment at that national source. I told him he would have *no trouble,* moving from campus to campus, as a great poet reading his poems. Like Eliot he could read poems to pay for his annual return. Or he could teach each year at some university near us, so that he could stay with us for a week or a month each year. And not only would he visit the United States for his refreshment, I assured him, he would make enough money on a two-month tour to support his family for a year.

We ate well, and drank more wine than we had drunk two nights before. We were excited planning for the future: He would be working on the new *Cantos,* and he would send them to me; perhaps the *Paris Review* might use some of them with the interview. They would be badly typed, he said; could I retype them for him? Of course I could, and of course the *Paris Review* would want them. And as soon as I could put the interview together, and get it typed, I would mail it to him for correction. Perhaps before I had finished assembling it, he told me, he would have a few emendations for it, "things to be stuck in." For that matter, he said, maybe we could work together in England; the BBC was talking about broadcasting his opera *Villon;* maybe he could talk them into paying his fare to London, and he would stay with us in Thaxted. The Priory where we lived had ten rooms, we told him, and he could have *two* rooms of his own, and stay as long as he liked.

Mostly our happy plans were for America. Pound asked questions about living in America, things that bothered him and that he needed to ask about. He could not drive a car; was it impossible, as some Europeans insisted, to live in America without a car? I swore that I knew three young, male, otherwise sane Americans, all of them poets, who could not drive, and who survived without persecution or loss of citizenship. Then in the same tone he asked a different sort of question. "Tell me," he said, "how do you feel the influence of the American Communist party in your daily life?" For a second I thought he was joking. I knew the American Communist party up close, or I had in the past, and I knew that it had no influence at all on my daily life or anyone else's, unless one chose to grant it influence. But he was wholly serious. He had spent all those years in St. Elizabeths talking with people like John Kasper.

"None," I told him. "None at all. No influence at all."

He looked at me curiously, then nodded. Probably he decided to consider me naïve.

"Why do you ask?" I said. "What do you see?"

Oh, he said, little things. For instance, a higher court had just decided that the NAACP did not have to surrender its membership lists to the attorney general of the state of Mississippi.

In my infatuation, I chose not to set him right; I didn't want to quarrel. Nor did I let his convictions about American Communists and the NAACP stop me from assuring him about his visits to the United States. There are things you do not wish to understand.

After our large dinner, we decided to forgo another ice cream, but we prolonged our evening with another tour of Rome. Pound said again, perhaps a little halfheartedly, that he should show us around because, after all, he had brought us all the way from England for this so-called interview. I told him again that the interview would work, that he would be surprised at how much he had told me. As we drove slowly among darkened streets, he named squares and buildings for us. With a quick gesture he pointed to a huge stone building and said, "There's the scene of the crime."

"Where you made the broadcasts?" I said.

He nodded. "Where I handed in the texts."

A few minutes later we parked in front of Dadone's. We walked into the foyer by the elevator and embraced each other. There were tears in Pound's eyes. We swore we would see each other soon, first in London or Thaxted, then in Ann Arbor when Pound was making his reading tours. The elevator arrived, and Pound — his hat cocked defiantly, his scarf over his shoulders, his stick poked ahead of him — marched into it and swiveled his lined, stone, triangular face toward us, and mouthed good-bye as the elevator disappeared upward; and I never saw him again.

THAXTED, ANN ARBOR

In the bustle of leaving Rome — feeding everybody, packing, clearing out the room; farewells to desk clerks who typed book reviews; tips; consulting maps; wheeling with assumed bravado through Roman traffic — I never lost sight of Pound's lined face miming goodbye. As we drove north, bypassing famous cities astride the *autostrada,* and as the children subsided into sleep, my mind went over the last four days detail by detail — not over Pound's words tape-recorded for the *Paris Review,* but over gestures and motions of body, the look of old eyes, *gli occhi onesti e tardi,* and words unspoken in so eloquent a tongue. For the next few days, my mind existed in a place like the landscape of certain dreams, where experience wheels and hovers over one territory and will not go elsewhere — as when you finally slide into sleep after twenty-four hours straight driving across the American plain; slide into sleep only to continue driving past dream grain elevators and dream acres of soybeans; so, motoring through the changing landscape of Europe, I watched Pound's face over and over again, heard him speak in his slow and hesitant voice.

With my family deposited again in Thaxted, I drove to London, turned in the Morris, and left the tapes with a firm called Tape Typing, which had done earlier transcriptions for me. I returned by train and bus, slept twelve hours, and began what I had promised to do: I wrote two dozen letters to the United States, beginning my campaign to provide Pound an annual reading tour of North America. I wrote Pound's publisher James Laughlin; I wrote the Poetry Center in New York; I wrote Pound's connection at Yale, Norman Holmes Pearson; I wrote

Harry Meacham in Richmond, Virginia; I wrote universities from coast to coast that booked poets for readings.

One morning the *New Statesman* arrived at my door, delivered with the newspaper, and the lead book review was my piece about *Thrones*. "Ezra Pound," it began, "is the poet who, a thousand times more than any other man, has made modern poetry possible in English." All right. Commonplace, but all right. Then I started praising *Thrones*, and my tone became shrill: "In a better world, literary men would queue all night to get their copies of *Thrones*." As I read my review that morning, I felt the slack sensation in my body that tells me I have failed again: For whom did I write that sentence? For the readers of the *New Statesman*? No, I wrote that sentence to be read by Ezra Pound. Much of the review in fact did not even bother to praise *Thrones*, but attacked the critics I presupposed to dislike *Thrones*. By this means — I would discover ten years later, in the pastures of psychotherapy — I was able to transfer my own unacknowledged dislike for *Thrones* to other, imagined critics. "In America," I said, "where Pound has been petrified into an industry by the academics, the first reviews have been either condescending or ignorantly respectful. In England they will copy everything but the respect, for England revels in a massive provincialism which must reject all evidence of the European mind." My review was three columns long. At the bottom of the second column — after scolding the English for six paragraphs — I finally claimed that "*Thrones* is a very good book," and for a few sentences I discussed the subject matter Pound had undertaken. But when I quoted a lyric passage and said, "In all, *Canto CVI* is one of the finest achievements of the *Cantos*," the weary book reviewer's cliché gave me away.

When the *New Statesman* arrived the next week I found myself attacked. Philip Toynbee — son of Arnold; Sunday book reviewer and literary journalist — wrote an angry and eloquent letter:

Sir — It is hard to imagine a more stupefyingly useless review than Mr. Donald Hall's peripheral comments on Ezra

Pound's Cantos. My irritation is probably due to my agreeing with Mr. Hall's general position on modern literature, but intensely disliking the snootiness of his self-approbation and his inability to say anything in the least helpful.

We knew about Pound's unique achievement in the past. The question is whether the Cantos — and in particular the later ones — are great poetry, something very close to megalomaniac rubbish, or something in between. Mr. Hall believes that they are great poetry; but I can find nowhere in his three columns any serious attempt to tell us why.

May I ask Mr. Hall a few questions? . . . Can he understand Chinese; and, whether he can or not, does he believe that the understanding of an English poem should depend on the answer to this question? Is he interested in Chinese economics? Does he think it reasonable or insane to believe that the *fundamental* evil of modern western society is the taking of interest on loans?

I did not answer Toynbee's questions.

Meantime I worked each day on the interview. The transcript from Tape Typing provided limited help, nor was it Tape Typing's fault. My tape equipment was primitive, and I had been careless using it. Windows had been open on those warm Roman days; one tape was crowded with children's games from the street outside, another with the repeated cries of a woman seeking a taxi. These noises filled long Poundian silences, and obscured the rare word. There were many holes in recorded sentences. Still, the typescript included whole speeches by Pound, and fragments he welded together over the days, and my own responses, which sometimes repeated Pound's words and reminded me of what he had said. I sat for days with the transcript of the interview — with blank spaces to indicate unintelligibility, its pages looked like the *Cantos* — listening over and over again to the original tapes, supplying here a missing word, there an inflection that provided a question mark; or hearing the one word in a sentence that was mnemonic to the rest, making sense out of what sounded like gargling; or making corrections. When I finally established a text, I assembled the parts into comprehensible order, attaching to the incomplete answer of one day the completed paragraph of the next.

All spring Pound wrote me at least once a week, enclosing revisions of new *Cantos* or old letters or translations the *Paris Review* might want to print; also, he sent me afterthoughts for the interview. Some of the afterthoughts repeated, word for word, phrases I already had on tape; he only *feared* he had not said this favorite sentence. Others varied in phrasing, and allowed me to take my pick. Others were wholly new, and I built them into the interview — as he wanted me to — as if he had said them in Rome. "Also for interview," he would write in his longhand, then continue: "There are epic subjects. The struggle for individual rights is an epic subject, consecutive from jury trial in Athens. Thru Anselm vs Wm. Rufus. To Coke and Adams." I had the sequence — a little different, a little more detailed — on my tape; and he repeated further versions of the same statement in two subsequent letters. "If I am being 'crucified for an idea,' " he wrote another time, "it is probably the idea that European culture ought to survive me: that the best qualities of it ought to survive along with whatever other cultures, in whatever universality." And a footnote — to his word "idea" — continued to protest his new diffidence: "i.e. the coherent idea round which my muddles accumulated." In the interview, I placed the footnote between dashes, after "idea."

Another page came labeled "add to interview as dialog," and read:

> O.K. I am stuck. Question am I dead as
> Messrs A.B.C. etc might wish?
>
> An epic is a poem containing history.
> Modern mind containing heteroclite elements.
>
> Past epos has succeeded when all or a
> gt. many answers were assumed.

At least between author and audience,
or a great mass of audience.

Attempt in an experimental age IS ergo,
rash.

One's temper is bad when asked to give
specific answers prematurely re the as yet
unexplored.

As to obscurity what about the great
example which occasionally mentions 3 authors
at once?

[D.H. can go into that. sounds megalo
for me to do so. And keep hammering.

one wop calls the 2 boiler makers a
moral shock. Or something of that sort.]

Two dabs sent yester—

Question. how much *rest* is one allowed?
Has rigor mortis set in??

I did indeed "add to interview as dialog," or I added much of it,
mixing these lines with lines gathered from the recorder or from
other written sources, letters and notes. I added "the" to the
beginning of sentences where his epistolary style, like Marianne
Moore's, omitted articles he would have used in speech. When I
mailed him the interview, after all, he could change anything he
wanted to.

A recurrent theme of these letters was the struggle to find
material for the *Paris Review* to print. We talked about using
Versi Prosaici, which was dense but fascinating, but he discovered that it had already been printed in an English magazine,
which bewildered and dismayed him.

I don't know where or when they got text.
I have probly/lost the U.S. copyright anyhow = ugh.
gawd hellup all pore sailors.

He ended the letter, "wd the attempt to translate Horace fill the bill?" Then a day or so later, brooding, guilty, he wrote again. He *knew* — true or not — that losing *Versi Prosaici* was his own fault, and he struggled with the notion like a fly stuck in axle grease. Letter after letter chewed over further possibilities, suggesting that we might print *Versi Prosaici* anyway, because the English magazine did not circulate widely, "but yr ed wd probly not think so/". Or maybe the letter to Untermeyer? He had second thoughts about the Horace translations: "Trouble with the Horace is that it was done *not* as best language, but to illustrate DIFFERENCE in style = H. in relation to quality of Catul. or Propert." Ending a chaotic letter — begun on a strange typewriter, continued with a Bic — he protests, "NOT drunk — just physically too weak to move."

But he began gradually to think that new *Cantos* might do it for the *Paris Review*. "Will also see if a bit of new Canto can be released/" he wrote in one letter; his hesitation became not diffident but painstaking: "damn nuisance that on every or almost every page of 110–117 there is something unready or some sign that needs verification//". He began in fact to show some confidence, and he wrote in reference to criticism of the *Cantos*: "you have seen enough to refute Alvarez re. its being no Fugue (? no stretti?) no pulling together of themes. mere free association." The English book reviewer A. Alvarez, writing in a Sunday paper, had called the *Cantos* a "scrapbook," and decided that the "so-called fugal structure . . . has turned into something no more fugal than free-association."

Pound sent me *Cantos* as he worked them over, his typescript corrected in his hand for me to retype and return. His manuscript corrections removed typos and corrected errors: I was to change "God" into "Gold." Some alterations changed the look of the poem on the page; he put a capital A and a capital B on one page, a circle around each, and in a marginal note gave me the direction: "— A is above — B", meaning that two dashes should be directly aligned in the typescript, although three lines and a space separated them; the dashes themselves had been added in ink, so that the visual and emphatic parallelism appeared to be an afterthought, revision by punctuation and typography.

The *Paris Review* ended by printing *Canto CXVI* and the superb fragment of *Canto CXV*. Also, we printed the letter to Untermeyer under the title "An Autobiographical Outline." Also, we included two facsimiles: the first page of the *Pisan Cantos* and a letter written to the censor from the detention camp, in which Pound explained that new *Cantos* put into the mail were not some sort of Fascist code.

My days in England, toward the end of my year there, remained full of Ezra Pound. When I was not typing *Cantos* I was working over the final touches on the interview, removing repetitions, cutting the interviewer's loquaciousness, simplifying structure.

Because I was free-lancing that year, I traveled up to London once a week; wages waited in the West End. Whenever I could manage, I came up on a Wednesday, which was the day John Wain entrained from Reading on *his* free-lancing errands. Wednesday was Wains-day at the Salisbury, a magnificent gin palace on St. Martin's Lane in the theater district; on Wednesdays, from noon until closing time at three, the Salisbury was a floating, crowded, hectic literary salon, with half the poets of England waving pints in smoky air. A. Alvarez usually came, sometimes Ted Hughes, frequently Michael Hamburger and Christopher Middleton. John Wain had met Pound in Washington. (Wain originally met Pound under trying circumstances, at least as Wain tells the story. In the heyday of existentialist jargon, early in the fifties, the London *Observer* flew Wain to the United States to ask famous people about their commitment to one thing or another. Unaware of the American use of the term, Wain approached Pound in St. Elizabeths Hospital and asked him if he was committed.) Wain, and everyone else at the Salisbury, wanted news of Pound, and by quotation and mimicry I brought the news. Among other matters I told how Pound wanted to visit the United States to read his poems. Immediately

Wain was skeptical — skeptical of the wisdom of Pound's notion, skeptical of the reception he would receive from American universities.

Wain was not alone.

When I came up to London I often did some work for the BBC. One of my producers was D. G. Bridson, old friend of Pound's who had done the radio interviews I consulted before I went to Italy. When I told him that Pound wanted to read poems in the United States he shook his head. At the same time I was co-editing an encyclopedia with Stephen Spender, who had known Pound for thirty years and had visited him in St. Elizabeths. Spender thought it was a bad idea for Pound to do American readings. "They would crush him," he said. Then I started to hear from people in the United States, to whom I had written about Poundian reading tours. From universities I received cautious or negative answers. At first I was astonished. American university English departments refused to listen to Ezra Pound read his poems? Then I reminded myself that English departments at American universities had never wanted to listen to Ezra Pound, or to read him for that matter. English departments had become hospitable to poets — hiring them as teachers, flying poets to campuses to read their poems — but Ezra Pound was difficult. Even a simple symbolist poem like "The Return," or his imagist "In a Station of the Metro," frightened teachers who feared looking foolish. At Michigan, the man who taught the course in modern poetry omitted Pound entirely, which was like omitting Saint Paul from the history of Christianity.

More important to these refusals, though usually unexpressed, was Pound's politics, or particularly his anti-Semitism. For me, Pound's politics and prejudice seemed not political at all; he was crazy. Ezra Pound's hatred for Jews was crazy, and when it came to politics and economics, he was as crazy as your Uncle Charlie. It is not always obvious that Uncle Charlie needs to be locked up (Samuel Johnson said he would as lief pray with Kit Smart as any man), although Uncle Charlie is nuts. When

Pound was caged at Pisa he said that if they didn't shoot him he might talk with President Truman and change Truman's mind — doubtless on monetary policy — but Ezra Pound had as much chance of talking with the President as he did of taking Neil Armstrong's place on the moon. He was crazy, and had been crazy for a long time: Before the war, he proposed in all seriousness that the United States should trade territory to Japan in return for five hundred Noh plays on film. We do not take this maniac seriously when he proposes such things; why do we take his "Weinstein Kirchberger" seriously? When he made Winston Churchill and Franklin Roosevelt into Jews, he was bonkers. Shall we call this ridiculous obsession *anti-Semitism?* Doesn't such usage trivialize the notion of anti-Semitism? Do we compare Pound's crazy obsession to blackballing a Jew from a golf club? Or do we compare it to killing six million in the death camps? Pound's virulent anti-Semitism was a mental disease, strangely resembling Henry Adams's, concurrent with the holocaust, at a time when Pound sided with a Fascist dictator politically allied with the author of the holocaust. Pound had nothing to do with the holocaust.

Therefore it would have taken courage to invite Ezra Pound to read his poems in 1960. Courage in a university? Not long before 1960, Senator Joseph McCarthy had found America's campuses trembling and acquiescent. Courage is not epidemic on university campuses.

Letters from Pound's friends and advocates gave me pause, as Wain and Bridson and Spender had given me pause. One came from a man who was Pound's greatest patron in the United States — no coward, obviously a dear friend — who begged me not to promote a visit by Ezra. He mentioned vaguely "the stress" and "the pressures to which he would be exposed." Finally, a political friend of mine, a leftist admirer of Pound, took me to task: "If he comes over, they'll picket him. They'll boo him off the stage. *Don't do it!*"

My enthusiasm and confidence, expressed to Pound in Rome, had been naïve or stupid. Maybe my stupidity was self-seeking, if unconscious, done from the desire to please the old man. I was slow to accept the results, because I didn't want to disappoint him. I wrote him that it seemed hard "to get anything done by letter from here." I had also looked into the possibility that the BBC might bring him to London for *Villon,* and was told that the BBC "doesn't do things like that." So I passed another negative message on. Pound's letters no longer mentioned visiting the United States, nor coming to England. We talked only about *Cantos* and the interview, as I assured him that the typescript was almost ready. Late in spring I had a letter from him like all the others, and I answered it, typing up a portion of a *Canto* for him; after that, he never wrote again. I finished work on the interview, sent it to him on May 30, and wrote a letter to go with it, hoping that he would correct and return it soon. After a couple of weeks I wrote again; I wrote again and again.

Just before leaving England that August, I had a letter from the Poetry Center in New York. When I wrote them suggesting that they invite Pound to read, I was forgetting (how could I?) that the Poetry Center had its quarters in the Young Men's Hebrew Association. Leonard Lyons had printed an item in "The Lyons Den" suggesting that the Poetry Center of the YMHA intended to invite a well-known Fascist and anti-Semite to read his poems. The Center denied the charges, and asked me to be sure I said nothing to contribute to the brouhaha. I have no idea how Lyons heard about my suggestion — maybe from a Poetry Center staffer? — but it seemed clear that his item derived from my campaign.

So I returned to the United States out of touch with Pound, unable to find him readings, author of fatuous praise of *Thrones,* and doubtless the instigator of another small Poundian scandal.

That fall, I taught Pound's poems to undergraduates. I talked about him all the time, to friends and students and to audiences when I read my poems. At the same time, I became gradually convinced that there would never be an interview in the *Paris Review*. No word arrived from Pound. Of course I retained a carbon of the manuscript interview I had sent him, but I would not print it without his revisions. A message came to me indirectly. James Laughlin wrote me saying that Pound had been having a bad time — "acute depression, irritability, etc." — and was in a nursing home. Then Laughlin told me something else:

> His last letter to me appeared to refer to your interview, but I can't really make much sense out of it. He says: "Considerable effort to ruin me. Hall particularly interesting after article on British spectator re brainwash. Interview in state of fatigue when one mutters first thing that comes into head." Can you figure out what this means? I'm sure you wouldn't have written anything in your interview that would be likely to upset him, and I wonder who it is who he thinks is "trying to ruin him."

"Even paranoids have enemies." Pound's remark that considerable effort was being made to ruin him was about as paranoid as Yossarian's notion in *Catch-22* that the Germans were trying to kill him. Did he number me now among his enemies? I don't know. When I read Laughlin's letter, I believed so. Juxtaposition made it sound as if the interview were part of the conspiracy, my devious attempt to discredit him. Later, when I read his manuscript revisions of the interview, it became obvious that he had not read the interview in such a spirit. His letter to Laughlin is confusing. Considering his enemies, perhaps he remembered what I had written in the *New Statesman* about hostility toward him (I think he confused the *New Statesman* with the *Spectator*) and may have intended something like: "Article in British Statesman re brainwash" of the public about Ezra Pound. But then, I wonder: Why should I be "interesting after" such an article? I don't know, unless — after initially reading and correcting the interview in a friendly spirit — he later decided (in irritability, depression, and mental confusion) that by showing him "tired" I revealed myself to be one of the brainwashers disguised as a friend.

A year later, at the end of September 1961, Dorothy Pound wrote me that she had found the corrected interview while cleaning drawers in her husband's writing table. She told me that he had made numerous changes but that apparently he had been unable to concentrate on the last third of the typescript. She asked me to print a footnote to the interview saying that Pound had lacked strength to complete his corrections. She noted that she had found no new *Cantos,* in her desk-cleaning, and added that as a precaution she was showing the interview to a lawyer in Boston.

A week or so later the interview arrived, annotated in Pound's own hand on every page (corrections grew thin toward the end). The changes were mostly further attempts to clarify, to define, or to set ideas in order. I added them to the text, even though they didn't sound like speech, whenever I could understand their position and function. On the second page of the interview, I had quoted Pound saying that he had tried "to make the *Cantos* historic but not fiction." Between "historic" and "but," on the typescript of the interview, Pound inserted a parenthetical example: "(Vid. G. Giovannini, re relation history to tragedy;. 2 articles 10 years apart in some philological periodical, not source material but relevant)." I changed "2" and "10" to "two" and "ten"; I added a comma. Perhaps I should not have added the parenthesis at all, but he appeared to want me to. James Laughlin helped me to understand Pound's hand, and his abbreviations, but I remember at least one clause that I could not follow, and for which I could not find a place.

Occasionally Pound altered the text to soften dogmatism. When in speech he had told me, "Real free verse is . . . ," in revision he made himself say, "I think the best free verse came from . . ." There were moments of fatigue in his corrections. Reading one perfectly clear statement he had made, about judging poets younger than himself, he could not understand what he was getting at. "I don't know what I said," he wrote in the margin. "You can leave this as something needing clarification, that I am too tired to make now." He changed an adverb describing how Ford Madox Ford rolled on the floor — to criticize the young Pound's diction — from "indecently" to "indecorously." Where he had said, "You used to go poking around in the smelting room" of the Philadelphia mint, he substituted the more formal "You could then be taken around in the smelting room." He corrected my misspelling. The X that crossed out an ill-spelled syllable could be large and irritable. (Other misspellings were changed by pencil in Dorothy's hand.) Beside a few statements he put large question marks, as if he doubted that he had made them. At other times he miscorrected. I had him saying "I grew up in Philadelphia," and then revising himself, as we all do in speech, "the suburbs of Philadelphia." In the first sentence, he had changed "in" to "near." This made the first sentence accurate, but left the following clause redundant.

One footnote made an essential change. He had spoken of the advantage of a university where people "control opinion" or "control data"; this verb sounded authoritarian, maybe Fascist; in a note in the margin he wrote that he was using the French "*contrôler*," "to verify." At a political moment in Rome he had said, "I don't know whether I was doing any good or not, whether I was doing any harm. And I probably was." On the manuscript, Pound circled "And I probably was," saying, "Is this on tape? I don't think I said it." It was not on tape; I remembered him saying it. But I cut it out, because the next sentence came as close as Pound wanted to come — at this time in his life — to retracting his politics: "Oh, I was probably offside."

Paris Review number 28, "the Pound issue," was dated "Summer–Fall 1962."

Pound rarely spoke during the ten years that remained to him. When he did speak — sometimes of the silence itself — he spoke eloquently: "I did not enter the silence," he told someone, "silence captured me."

He stopped writing. He spent hours alone in his study, but after the middle of 1962 he wrote nothing substantial, and the final *Drafts and Fragments of Cantos CX–CXVII*, virtually complete in 1960, was finished by 1962. Yet he did not want to publish work he considered "drafts and fragments"; he allowed these lines into print in 1968 only to correct the errors of a pirated edition.

During his last years I read everything written about him; I think I missed nothing. There were a few interviews in the last ten years, especially one long, intense conversation with Grazia Livi, published in *Epoca*. This interview was garbled into a news story that made it known around the world that Pound had recanted, taking back everything he ever said or stood for. It was not so. Pound was depressed when he gave the interview; he said, "a strange day came and I realized that I did not know anything, indeed, that I did not know anything at all. And so words have become empty of all meaning." The old man had lost touch with his own convictions and abilities. But he did not recant; he was convinced only of personal failure. He held hope, if not for himself, then for others' minds and spirits engaged in the endeavors he had undertaken: "there is something in human consciousness that will endure, despite everything," he said, "and that will be capable of withstanding the forces of unconsciousness."

His sense of failure ran deep: "I know nothing at all." Doubting his memory, he said, "I have even forgotten the name of that Greek philosopher who said that nothing exists, and even if it did exist it would be unknowable, and if it were knowable it would be incommunicable." This sentence does not reveal a victim of senile dementia. The interview continues, miserable and lucid:

Is it . . . a truth to which you have come by suffering?

It is something to which I have come by suffering. . . . Yes, by an experience of suffering.

. . .

What is it, now, that holds you to life, from the time that you have acquired a total certainty of uncertainty?

Nothing holds me any longer to life. Simply, I am "immersed in it."

. . .

And do you manage to work still? Or does the great sense of uncertainty possess you to the extent that all creative efforts seem useless?

No, I do not work anymore. . . . I do nothing. I have become illiterate and uneducated. I simply fall into a lethargy, at the beginning of winter, and to my own disgrace I do nothing but cultivate my greediness and laziness. . . . Yes, I fall into a lethargy, and I contemplate.

He speaks with the tragic energy of a defeated king, like Oedipus the victim of his own errors — fallen, lamenting his smallness in the center of a stage that he dominates. He reminds me of Yeats's final vision of man's life, spoken from the mountain in "Lapis Lazuli"; or of the last Freud, daily wracked by cancer of the jaw, writing *Civilization and Its Discontents.*

Later in his despair he came closer to recanting. He told Daniel Cory that the *Cantos* were "a botch," because "I knew too little about so many things. . . . I picked out this and that thing that interested me, and then jumbled them into a bag." As late as 1967, Pound told Allen Ginsberg that "my poems don't make any sense." Ginsberg argued with him. Perhaps Pound wanted to be argued with, but he was adamant and witty in response: "At seventy," he argued back, "I realized that instead of being a lunatic, I was a moron."

It was at the end of this conversation that Pound came to the remarkable conclusion, frequently quoted: "But the worst mistake I made was that stupid, suburban prejudice of anti-Semitism." Sometimes this late remark has been quoted as if it mattered. In *T. S. Eliot and Prejudice,* Christopher Ricks is skeptical. The sentence quoted does not explain or extenuate or end the subject, which will never vanish. There are those who will never read him for hate of him. And there are others, like the Yale graduate students, writing dissertations on Pound, whom I heard at a Pound conference a few years back, reassuring one another that Ezra Pound was of course never, in any sense, an anti-Semite.

Pound's domestic life had been irregular. I mentioned that in the thirties he had alternated between his wife Dorothy and his mistress Olga on a regular schedule. As late as 1959, he asked a handsome young woman to marry him, and traveled with her for a time. It didn't work out; Dorothy wasn't having any divorces. (Dorothy was not only the wife; she was the Committee for Ezra Pound. "Complications re/Committee," Pound wrote Hemingway during this interlude.) In 1962, Olga fetched Ezra from a private clinic near Merano, and for the rest of his life she took care of him. It was not, as I understand it, that Pound chose to leave his wife and live with Olga. Dorothy was too old to take care of him, and he needed care. Olga, Mary, and Dorothy could not get along, much less live in the same house together; Dorothy remained with Mary at Castle Brunnenburg. Only Olga — or a nursing home — could have taken care of the old man.

Summers Ezra and Olga spent at Sant'Ambrogio, where Olga kept a small house; she and Pound had lived there thirty years before. Dorothy spent summers nearby in Rapallo. September to June, Ezra and Olga lived in Venice, in a narrow house on a narrow street behind the Santa Maria della Salute. Pound's study was the top floor, the middle floor was their bedroom, and the ground floor was a small living room and kitchen. Olga Rudge had owned the house since 1928.

In journals I read about their life together. Pound stayed in bed mornings until ten or eleven, and after a late breakfast walked along the Guidecca Canal. Sometimes he spent hours in his study, reading, sometimes recording poems — his own and other people's — into a Grundig tape recorder. In the study he kept his portrait bust that Gaudier-Brzeska carved in 1914. Sometimes he and Olga ate lunch at Raffaelle's, sometimes at Pensione Cici. After lunch they took another walk, perhaps along the Grand Canal. He played long games of chess. Friends stopped by; Pound would not speak, but seemed pleased with the company. Sometimes with a literary visitor Olga filled the silence by playing a record of Pound speaking his own poems, the disembodied voice floating out over the disenvoiced body.

Unknown visitors came also — pilgrims and exploiters — including one who pitched a tent outside the house. (As Ralph Waldo Emerson grew older, he was beset by admirers visiting Concord. He complained of the thousand strangers seeking an audience: "Whom God hath put asunder, why should man put together?") Many would-be visitors, Olga observed, worshiped Pound without knowing his poetry; she told one man that she would procure him a visit if he could recite *one* line of Ezra Pound's; he couldn't. Others wanted to read Pound their own poems and take his praise away with them. Others were academics looking for an imprimatur to their books on Pound. Others were promoters announcing that they had already booked a hall in London for a poetry reading; one flashed airline tickets. An acquaintance of mine, finding himself in Venice, sought out the house and knocked at the door. He expected to meet Olga Rudge and be turned away. To his astonishment, the door opened to reveal Ezra Pound in bathrobe and slippers. In his confusion, the young man burbled, "How are you, Mr. Pound?" Pound looked down at him for a moment, out of the *hauteur* of his silence, and then uttered a single word. "Senile," he said.

If the wit belied the word, Pound, like anyone in his eighties, was beset from time to time by the illnesses of age. He had surgery for cataracts. He underwent treatment, and perhaps surgery, for his prostate. He visited the clinic of Dr. Paul Niehans in Switzerland, where sheep cells were injected into his bloodstream, but he did not feel rejuvenated. Still, for a man of his age he did well. Part of the life with Olga was travel: She had the vigor and Pound had the appetite; both had a little money. Paradoxical checks arrived for Pound from American social security, and increasing royalties were forwarded by the faithful Committee for Ezra Pound to the ménage in Venice.

Ezra and Olga visited Delphi; they visited James Joyce's grave in Zurich, and near Trieste the castle where Rilke wrote the *Duino Elegies;* in Paris they visited the Salle Gaudier-Brzeska of the Musée de l'Art Moderne. In June of 1969, at the age of eighty-five, Pound flew with Olga to New York for a fortnight, surprising his old friends. This trip — nine years after he and I had talked about an annual visit — was his only return to this country after leaving St. Elizabeths in 1958.

He returned to Hamilton at graduation and received an ovation. At the New York Public Library he inspected the manuscript of Eliot's "Waste Land" with his own deletions, corrections, and comments. He saw Marianne Moore and called on Mary Hemingway, widow of his old friend. He walked through Greenwich Village and saw Patchin Place, where E. E. Cummings had lived. In Wyncote he visited the house where he had lived as a boy. He entertained the notion of a trip to Hailey in Idaho, to visit the town of his birth; but time and energy ran low; he returned to Venice.

In Italy he sometimes attended the Spoleto Festival, reading Marianne Moore's poems one year, his own another. Politics spoiled the 1965 Festival for him, as Yevgeny Yevtushenko left the stage rather than share it with Pound. He avoided politics, except for occasional disavowals like his words to Allen Ginsberg about anti-Semitism. One of his last pieces of writing was a change of economic terminology:

> re USURY
>
> I was out of focus, taking a symptom for
> a cause.
>
> The cause is AVARICE.

The old moralist on his deathbed named as the enemy neither the bank nor the Jew but one of the seven deadly sins. Readers of the *Cantos* — with their poetic denunciations of greed and profit, selfishness and exploitation — had long noticed that the author often sounded more anti-capitalist than national social-ist, less Fascist than Old Testament prophet.

But his old politics informed his silent world in a thousand ways. Each year the Nobel was announced, and each year Ezra Pound was passed over. His friends received it — Eliot in 1948, Hemingway in 1954 — and Stalinist poets received it, but not the former acolyte of Benito Mussolini. Perhaps he would never have received it anyway; neither Tolstoy nor Joyce nor Ibsen nor Conrad nor James nor Lawrence nor Proust won a Nobel Prize. Certainly Pound thought about it. Back in 1935 in Ra-pallo, James Laughlin remembers, he used to say that he would use his Nobel Prize money to hire a chef.

Another prize eluded him, and the scandal afflicted his last months. The American Academy of Arts and Sciences awards the Emerson-Thoreau Medal "for outstanding contributions to the broad field of literature over the recipient's entire lifetime." Robert Frost received the medal, T. S. Eliot, John Crowe Ran-som, Archibald MacLeish, Robert Penn Warren, W. H. Auden, William Carlos Williams, Conrad Aiken, and for that matter Carl Sandburg, Stephen Vincent Benét, Edwin Arlington Rob-inson, and (in 1911) James Whitcomb Riley. In January of 1972, the Academy's nominating committee recommended that Pound receive the award; Leon Edel was chairman of the com-mittee, which included John Cheever, Lillian Hellman, James Laughlin, Harry Levin, Louis Martz, and Lewis Mumford. (Lil-lian Hellman did not vote; Lewis Mumford opposed Pound's nomination and suggested Henry Miller instead.) As soon as the nomination was revealed to the Academy at large, opposition gathered strength and eloquence. A Harvard sociologist named Daniel Bell led the way, saying, "We have to distinguish be-tween those who explore hate and those who approve hate." Irving Howe (not an Academy member) concurred, declining to "close the books of twentieth-century history, certainly not as long as any of us remain alive who can remember the days of the mass murder" — thus perpetuating the bad history that con-nects Pound with Hitler's extermination camps.

Meeting in April, the council of the Academy rejected the

nominating committee's advice. Five Academy members there-upon resigned, including Malcolm Cowley and Allen Tate. Katherine Anne Porter returned her medal to the Academy. Harry Levin, who had defended the nomination with energy and anger, wrote after the rejection:

> The majority of the council, in overriding the recommenda-tion, has attempted to rationalize its decision by repeated as-sertions that art cannot be isolated from morality. This is misleading, if not disingenuous, in its implication that Pound and his proponents were irresponsible esthetes. There was never any disagreement over the principle involved. Members of the committee never questioned the assumption that esthet-ics is grounded in ethics. Pound, like his master, Dante, is not only an artist but an impassioned moralist.
>
> The Cantos have a moral vision behind them; but they are uneven and fragmentary as well as ambitious and brilliant; and they are marred by flaws both esthetic and ethical. To assess such work on balance is a delicate problem, which re-quires historical knowledge and critical experience. . . . What remains to be regretted is the lack of cultural perspective, the willingness of educated minds — twenty-three years after the controversy over the Bollingen Prize — to protract a mistaken personal episode at the expense of a creativity which will out-last the rebuff.

Then to Harry Levin came one last comment on the scandal. The summer after the vote had gone against him, Pound met friends of Levin's in Venice. Out of the years of silence, near death, he raised himself to utter a brief message for Levin:

"It matters."

The old poets had been dying for some time — men of 1914 and younger men and women. Wyndham Lewis died in 1957 while Pound was still at St. Elizabeths; Hilda Doolittle died in 1961, the year Hemingway killed himself; Cummings died in 1962; in 1963 Frost died, and Pound's oldest friend, William

Carlos Williams; in January of 1965, T. S. Eliot died, and only Marianne Moore was left of Pound's generation; she died on February 5, 1972, nine months before Pound. He read her poem "What Are Years?" in a memorial service at the Protestant church in Venice. It was Pound who called for the memorial service.

Eliot's death touched Pound the most. He and Olga flew to England for the memorial service at Westminster Abbey. Then he wrote his final words on his old friend:

> His was the true Dantescan voice — not honored enough, and deserving more than I ever gave him. I had hoped to see him in Venice this year for the Dante commemoration at the Giorgio Cini Foundation — instead: Westminster Abbey. But, later, on his own hearth, a flame tended, a presence felt.
>
> Recollections? let some thesis-writer have the satisfaction of "discovering" whether it was 1920 or '21 that I went from Excideuil to meet a rucksacked Eliot. Days of walking — conversation? literary? le papier Fayard was then the burning topic. Who is there now to share a joke with?
>
> Am I to write "about" the poet Thomas Stearns Eliot? Or my friend "the Possum"? Let him rest in peace. I can only repeat, but with the urgency of 50 years ago: READ HIM.

After two days in London, Pound flew to Dublin and saw Yeats's widow Georgie, determined, it seemed, to visit all the islands once more. He lived inside his silence as if silence were the Mediterranean and he the shipwrecked Odysseus of silence. Once a reporter asked him, "Where are you living now?" He answered, "In hell." "Which hell?" the reporter asked. Pound pressed his hand over his heart. "Here," he said. "Here."

When Grazia Livi interviewed him in 1963, just after he went to live with Olga in Venice, Livi began by telling Pound that she had been afraid to meet him. I suppose Livi feared what I had feared — that Pound would be arrogant, Fascistic, intolerable — but Pound misunderstood the fear's provenance. Pound said yes, he understood that fear: "Everything that I touch, I spoil."

Because interviewers asked him about poems and politics — and because Pound in his depressed answers belittled his poems and his politics — people have assumed that Pound's silence derived from his notion that he had spoiled or botched his artistic and intellectual life. Doubtless he felt as much, but there were profounder abysses: He said it was by "touch" that he spoiled everything. "If love be not in the house," he wrote in *Canto CXVI*, "there is nothing."

In 1971 Mary published *Discretions*, a memoir of her father and mother, and of her own growing up. It is a brilliant book — the author devoted to her father, corrosively angry at her mother. The publication shattered Olga, and shattered Ezra as well because of his double devotion to Mary and Olga, assassin and victim. The women around Ezra Pound could not abide each other. Now Dorothy had quarreled with Mary, and no longer lived at Castle Brunnenburg, but summered in England near her son Omar. Winters she returned to Rapallo, but in the last four years of Pound's life, she saw her husband only four times: old gray ghosts of the married couple — Ezra and the Committee for Ezra — past passion and frail in their ninth decade, hardly speaking to each other, hardly able to speak.

One day Pound broke silence, saying to a friend, "I have never made a person happy in my life." Certainly he blamed himself — with an omnipotence like Robert Frost's, like many people's — and he could reread his Confucius of *Canto XIII* with a particular misery:

> If a man have not order within him
> He can not spread order about him;
> And if a man have not order within him
> His family will not act with due order, . . .

The hell in Ezra Pound's chest had to do with Mary, with Dorothy, with Olga; and the hell within Robert Frost's chest, in the middle of triumph and honors denied Pound, had to do with Elinor, Elliott, Carroll, Irma, Marjorie, and Lesley. At the end

of the lives of the poets, the domestic life is a desert of anguish
— perhaps on account of choices made for the sake of the self
and its passion and its poetry, choices that in the retrospect of
old age appear destructive, cruel, and narcissistic. For some
poets — possibly for most poets; possibly for most people —
life's hell is a self-inflicted wound.

As for Eliot? Eliot died without a hell in his chest, having
endured his hell in middle life — tormented by an insane wife
for whose insanity he took responsibility, tormented by her and
by his failure to help. He searched for rectitude and discovered
grace.

Ezra Pound died in his sleep two days after his eighty-seventh
birthday. That week, he had enjoyed his birthday party, drinking and eating with friends; he had attended a Noh play and
Peter Brook's production of *A Midsummer Night's Dream*. The
funeral took place on San Gregorio with Mary and Olga in
attendance; Dorothy was too weak to make the journey from
England. His coffin went by gondola to the island of the dead,
San Michele, where he was buried near Diaghilev and Stravinsky: island of the exiled dead.

When he died I rehearsed in memory my time with him in
Rome. I went to an old drawer where I keep such things and
extracted my little collection — the interview with his corrections, his letters to me, carbons of the typing I had done for him,
letters from other people about him. On the back of the interview I found lines written in Pound's handwriting which I had
forgotten. Lying in his bed in some rest home, or in the Castle;
facing without knowing it ten years of shoreless silence ahead
of him, estrangement from his wife, his daughter's estrangement
from her mother, years of hopeless sailing around the world
("gawd hellup all pore sailors"), the old man — Odysseus without Penelope, without Telemachus — had inscribed three lines
extracted from the first *Canto,* written a half century past,
which spoke to me now from the grave, words at the bottom of
all other words:

> Shall return
>> thru spiteful Neptune,
>> lose all companions

No man completes his life or his Cantos; we are all fragments. But some men sail the seas. He sailed, not to Paradise; he returned to a personal Inferno, a hell constructed by the arrogance and madness of his middle age. At the same time, the vessel of his sailing reached home port: not Dante's Paradise but Homer's Ithaca. By means of the great and noble language of poetry, Ezra Pound assembled the best of himself and of the cultures he loved and studied. We find him forever in this Ithaca.

Interviews with T. S. Eliot, Marianne Moore, and Ezra Pound

T. S. Eliot

INTERVIEWER: Perhaps I can begin at the beginning. Do you remember the circumstances under which you began to write poetry in St. Louis when you were a boy?

ELIOT: I began I think about the age of fourteen, under the inspiration of Fitzgerald's *Omar Khayyam,* to write a number of very gloomy and atheistical and despairing quatrains in the same style, which fortunately I suppressed completely — so completely that they don't exist. I never showed them to anybody. The first poem that shows is one which appeared first in the *Smith Academy Record,* and later in the *Harvard Advocate,* which was written as an exercise for my English teacher and was an imitation of Ben Jonson. He thought it very good for a boy of fifteen or sixteen. Then I wrote a few at Harvard, just enough to qualify for election to an editorship on the *Harvard Advocate,* which I enjoyed. Then I had an outburst during my junior and senior years. I became much more prolific, under the influence first of Baudelaire and then of Jules Laforgue, whom I discovered I think in my junior year at Harvard.

INTERVIEWER: Did anyone in particular introduce you to the French poets? Not Irving Babbitt, I suppose.

ELIOT: No, Babbitt would be the last person! The one poem that Babbitt always held up for admiration was Gray's *Elegy.* And that's a fine poem but I think this shows certain limitations on Babbitt's part, God bless him. I have advertised my source, I think: It's Arthur Symons's book on French poetry,* which I came across in the Harvard Union. In those days the Harvard Union was a meeting place for any undergraduate who chose to belong to it.

---

* *The Symbolist Movement in Literature.*

They had a very nice little library, like the libraries in many Harvard houses now. I liked his quotations and I went to a foreign bookshop somewhere in Boston (I've forgotten the name and I don't know whether it still exists) which specialized in French and German and other foreign books and found Laforgue, and other poets. I can't imagine why that bookshop should have had a few poets like Laforgue in stock. Goodness knows how long they'd had them or whether there were any other demands for them.

INTERVIEWER: When you were an undergraduate, were you aware of the dominating presence of any older poets? Today the poet in his youth is writing in the age of Eliot and Pound and Stevens. Can you remember your own sense of the literary times? I wonder if your situation may not have been extremely different.

ELIOT: I think it was rather an advantage not having any living poets in England or America in whom one took any particular interest. I don't know what it would be like but I think it would be a rather troublesome distraction to have such a lot of dominating presences, as you call them, about. Fortunately we weren't bothered by each other.

INTERVIEWER: Were you aware of people like Hardy or Robinson at all?

ELIOT: I was slightly aware of Robinson because I read an article about him in *The Atlantic Monthly* which quoted some of his poems, and that wasn't my cup of tea at all. Hardy was hardly known to be a poet at that time. One read his novels, but his poetry only really became conspicuous to a later generation. Then there was Yeats, but it was the early Yeats. It was too much Celtic twilight for me. There was really nothing except the people of the nineties who had all died of drink or suicide or one thing or another.

INTERVIEWER: Did you and Conrad Aiken help each other with your poems, when you were co-editors on the *Advocate*?

ELIOT: We were friends but I don't think we influenced each other at all. When it came to foreign writers, he was more interested in Italian and Spanish, and I was all for the French.

INTERVIEWER: Were there any other friends who read your poems and helped you?

ELIOT: Well, yes. There was a man who was a friend of my brother's, a man named Thomas H. Thomas who lived in Cambridge and who saw some of my poems in the *Harvard Advocate*. He wrote me a most enthusiastic letter and cheered me up. And I wish I had his letters still. I was very grateful to him for giving me that encouragement.

INTERVIEWER: I understand that it was Conrad Aiken who introduced you and your work to Pound.

ELIOT: Yes it was. Aiken was a very generous friend. He tried to place some of my poems in London, one summer when he was over, with Harold Monro and others. Nobody would think of publishing them. He brought them back to me. Then in 1914, I think, we were both in London in the summer. He said, "You go to Pound. Show him your poems." He thought Pound might like them. Aiken liked them, though they were very different from his.

INTERVIEWER: Do you remember the circumstances of your first meeting with Pound?

ELIOT: I think I went to call on him first. I think I made a good impression, in his little triangular sitting room in Kensington. He said, "Send me your poems." And he wrote back, "This is as good as anything I've seen. Come around and have a talk about them." Then he pushed them on Harriet Monroe, which took a little time.

INTERVIEWER: In an article about your *Advocate* days, for the book in honor of your sixtieth birthday, Aiken quotes an early letter from England in which you refer to Pound's verse as "touchingly incompetent." I wonder when you changed your mind.

ELIOT: Hah! *That* was a bit brash, wasn't it? Pound's verse was first shown me by an editor of the *Harvard Advocate*, W. G. Tinckom-Fernandez, who was a crony of mine and Conrad Aiken's and the other Signet * poets of the period. He showed me those little things of Elkin Mathews, *Exultations* and *Personae*.† He said, "This is up your street; you ought to like this." Well, I didn't, really. It seemed to me rather fancy old-fashioned romantic stuff, cloak-and-dagger kind of stuff. I wasn't very much impressed by it. When I went to see Pound, I was not particularly an admirer of his work, and though I now regard the work I saw then as very accomplished, I am certain that in his later work is to be found the grand stuff.

---

* Harvard's literary club.
† Early books of Pound, published by Elkin Mathews in 1909.

INTERVIEWER: You have mentioned in print that Pound cut "The Waste Land" from a much larger poem into its present form. Were you benefited by his criticism of your poems in general? Did he cut other poems?

ELIOT: Yes. At that period, yes. He was a marvelous critic because he didn't try to turn you into an imitation of himself. He tried to see what you were trying to do.

INTERVIEWER: Have you helped to rewrite any of your friends' poems? Ezra Pound's, for instance?

ELIOT: I can't think of any instances. Of course I have made innumerable suggestions on manuscripts of young poets in the last twenty-five years or so.

INTERVIEWER: Does the manuscript of the original, uncut "Waste Land" exist?

ELIOT: Don't ask me. That's one of the things I don't know. It's an unsolved mystery. I sold it to John Quinn. I also gave him a notebook of unpublished poems, because he had been kind to me in various affairs. That's the last I heard of them. Then he died and they didn't turn up at the sale.

INTERVIEWER: What sort of thing did Pound cut from "The Waste Land"? Did he cut whole sections?

ELIOT: Whole sections, yes. There was a long section about a shipwreck. I don't know what that had to do with anything else, but it was rather inspired by the Ulysses canto in *The Inferno*, I think. Then there was another section which was an imitation *Rape of the Lock*. Pound said, "It's no use trying to do something that somebody else has done as well as it can be done. Do something different."

INTERVIEWER: Did the excisions change the intellectual structure of the poem?

ELIOT: No. I think it was just as structureless, only in a more futile way, in the longer version.

INTERVIEWER: I have a question about the poem which is related to its composition. In *Thoughts after Lambeth* you denied the allegation of critics who said that you expressed "the disillusionment of a generation" in "The Waste Land," or you denied that it was your intention. Now F. R. Leavis, I believe, has said that the poem exhibits no progression; yet on the other hand, more recent critics, writing after your later poetry, found "The Waste Land" Christian. I wonder if this was part of your intention.

ELIOT: No, it wasn't part of my conscious intention. I think that in *Thoughts after Lambeth,* I was speaking of intentions more in a negative than in a positive sense, to say what was not my intention. I wonder what an "intention" means! One wants to get something off one's chest. One doesn't know quite what it is that one wants to get off the chest until one's got it off. But I couldn't apply the word "intention" positively to any of my poems. Or to any poem.

INTERVIEWER: I have another question about you and Pound and your earlier career. I have read somewhere that you and Pound decided to write quatrains, in the late teens, because *vers libre* had gone far enough.

ELIOT: I think that's something Pound said. And the suggestion of writing quatrains was his. He put me on to *Émaux et Camées.**

INTERVIEWER: I wonder about your ideas about the relation of form to subject. Would you then have chosen the form before you knew quite what you were going to write in it?

ELIOT: Yes, in a way. One studied originals. We studied Gautier's poems and then we thought, "Have I anything to say in which this form will be useful?" And we experimented. The form gave the impetus to the content.

INTERVIEWER: Why was *vers libre* the form you chose to use in your early poems?

ELIOT: My early *vers libre,* of course, was started under the endeavor to practice the same form as Laforgue. This meant merely rhyming lines of irregular length, with the rhymes coming in irregular places. It wasn't quite so *libre* as much *vers,* especially the sort which Ezra called "Amygism." † Then, of course, there were things in the next phase which were freer, like "Rhapsody on a Windy Night." I don't know whether I had any sort of model or practice in mind when I did that. It just came that way.

INTERVIEWER: Did you feel, possibly, that you were writing against something, more than from any model? Against the poet laureate perhaps?

ELIOT: No, no, no. I don't think one was constantly trying to reject things, but just trying to find out what was right for oneself. One really ignored poet laureates as such, the Robert Bridges. I

---

* Poems by Théophile Gautier.
† A reference to Amy Lowell, who captured and transformed imagism.

don't think good poetry can be produced in a kind of political attempt to overthrow some existing form. I think it just supersedes. People find a way in which they can say something. "I can't say it that way, what way can I find that will do?" One didn't really *bother* about the existing modes.

INTERVIEWER: I think it was after "Prufrock" and before "Gerontion" that you wrote the poems in French which appear in your *Collected Poems*. I wonder how you happened to write them. Have you written any since?

ELIOT: No, and I never shall. That was a very curious thing which I can't altogether explain. At that period I thought I'd dried up completely. I hadn't written anything for some time and was rather desperate. I started writing a few things in French and found I *could*, at that period. I think it was that when I was writing in French I didn't take the poems so seriously, and that, not taking them seriously, I wasn't so worried about not being able to write. I did these things as a sort of tour de force to see what I could do. That went on for some months. The best of them have been printed. I must say that Ezra Pound went through them, and Edmond Dulac, a Frenchman we knew in London, helped with them a bit. We left out some, and I suppose they disappeared completely. Then I suddenly began writing in English again and lost all desire to go on with French. I think it was just something that helped me get started again.

INTERVIEWER: Did you think at all about becoming a French symbolist poet like the two Americans of the last century?

ELIOT: Stuart Merrill and Viélé-Griffin. I only did that during the romantic year I spent in Paris after Harvard. I had at that time the idea of giving up English and trying to settle down and scrape along in Paris and gradually write French. But it would have been a foolish idea even if I'd been much more bilingual than I ever was, because, for one thing, I don't think that one can be a bilingual poet. I don't know of any case in which a man wrote great or even fine poems equally well in two languages. I think one language must be the one you express yourself in in poetry, and you've got to give up the other for that purpose. And I think that the English language really has more resources in some respects than the French. I think, in other words, I've probably done better in English than I ever would have in French even if I'd become as proficient in French as the poets you mentioned.

INTERVIEWER: Can I ask you if you have any plans for poems now?

ELIOT: No, I haven't any plans for anything at the moment, except that I think I would like, having just got rid of *The Elder Statesman* (I only passed the final proofs just before we left London), to do a little prose writing of a critical sort. I never think more than one step ahead. Do I want to do another play or do I want to do more poems? I don't know until I find I want to do it.

INTERVIEWER: Do you have any unfinished poems that you look at occasionally?

ELIOT: I haven't much in that way, no. As a rule, with me an unfinished thing is a thing that might as well be rubbed out. It's better, if there's something good in it that I might make use of elsewhere, to leave it at the back of my mind than on paper in a drawer. If I leave it in a drawer it remains the same thing but if it's in the memory it becomes transformed into something else. As I have said before, "Burnt Norton" began with bits that had to be cut out of *Murder in the Cathedral*. I learned in *Murder in the Cathedral* that it's no use putting in nice lines that you think are good poetry if they don't get the action on at all. That was when Martin Browne was useful. He would say, "There are very nice lines here, but they've nothing to do with what's going on on stage."

INTERVIEWER: Are any of your minor poems actually sections cut out of longer works? There are two that sound like "The Hollow Men."

ELIOT: Oh, those were the preliminary sketches. Those things were earlier. Others I published in periodicals but not in my collected poems. You don't want to say the same thing twice in one book.

INTERVIEWER: You seem often to have written poems in sections. Did they begin as separate poems? I am thinking of "Ash Wednesday," in particular.

ELIOT: Yes, like "The Hollow Men," it originated out of separate poems. As I recall, one or two early drafts of parts of "Ash Wednesday" appeared in *Commerce* and elsewhere. Then gradually I came to see it as a sequence. That's one way in which my mind does seem to have worked throughout the years poetically — doing things separately and then seeing the possibility of fusing them together, altering them, and making a kind of whole of them.

INTERVIEWER: Do you write anything now in the vein of *Old Possum's Book of Practical Cats* or *King Bolo*?

ELIOT: Those things do come from time to time! I keep a few notes of such verse, and there are one or two incomplete cats that probably will never be written. There's one about a glamour cat. It turned out too sad. This would never do. I can't make my children weep over a cat who's gone wrong. She had a very questionable career, did this cat. It wouldn't do for the audience of my previous volume of cats. I've never done any dogs. Of course dogs don't seem to lend themselves to verse quite so well, collectively, as cats. I may eventually do an enlarged edition of my cats. That's more likely than another volume. I did add one poem, which was originally done as an advertisement for Faber and Faber. It seemed to be fairly successful. Oh, yes, one wants to keep one's hand in, you know, in every type of poem, serious and frivolous and proper and improper. One doesn't want to lose one's skill.

INTERVIEWER: There's a good deal of interest now in the process of writing. I wonder if you could talk more about your actual habits in writing verse. I've heard you composed on the typewriter.

ELIOT: Partly on the typewriter. A great deal of my new play, *The Elder Statesman,* was produced in pencil and paper, very roughly. Then I typed it myself first before my wife got to work on it. In typing myself I make alterations, very considerable ones. But whether I write or type, composition of any length, a play for example, means for me regular hours, say ten to one. I found that three hours a day is about all I can do of actual composing. I could do polishing perhaps later. I sometimes found at first that I wanted to go on longer, but when I looked at the stuff the next day, what I'd done after the three hours were up was never satisfactory. It's much better to stop and think about something else quite different.

INTERVIEWER: Did you ever write any of your nondramatic poems on schedule? Perhaps the *Four Quartets*?

ELIOT: Only "occasional" verse. The *Quartets* were not on schedule. Of course the first one was written in '35, but the three which were written during the war were more in fits and starts. In 1939 if there hadn't been a war I would probably have tried to write another play. And I think it's a very good thing I didn't have the opportunity. From my personal point of view, the one good thing the war did was to prevent me from writing another play too soon. I saw some of the things that were wrong with *Family Reunion,* but I think it was much better that any possible play was blocked for five years or so to get up a head of steam. The form of the *Quartets* fitted in very nicely to the conditions under which I was writing, or could write at all. I could write them in sections and I didn't have to have quite the same continuity: It didn't matter if a day or two elapsed when I did not write, as they frequently did, while I did war jobs.

INTERVIEWER: We have been mentioning your plays without talking about them. In *Poetry and Drama* you talked about your first plays. I wonder if you could tell us something about your intentions in *The Elder Statesman.*

ELIOT: I said something, I think, in *Poetry and Drama* about my ideal aims, which I never expect fully to realize. I started, really, from *The Family Reunion,* because *Murder in the Cathedral* is a period piece and something out of the ordinary. It is written in rather a special language, as you do when you're dealing with another period. It didn't solve any of the problems I was interested in. Later I thought that in *The Family Reunion* I was giving so much attention to the versification that I neglected the structure of the play. I think *The Family Reunion* is still the best of my plays in the way of poetry, although it's not very well constructed.

In *The Cocktail Party* and again in *The Confidential Clerk,* I went further in the way of structure. *The Cocktail Party* wasn't altogether satisfactory in that respect. It sometimes happens, disconcertingly, at any rate with a practitioner like myself, that it isn't always the things constructed most according to plan that are the most successful. People criticized the third act of *The Cocktail Party* as being rather an epilogue, so in *The Confidential Clerk* I wanted things to turn up in the third act which were fresh events. Of course, *The Confidential Clerk* was so well constructed in some ways that people thought it was just meant to be farce.

I wanted to get to learn the technique of the theater so well that I could then forget about it. I always feel it's not wise to violate rules until you know how to observe them.

I hope that *The Elder Statesman* goes further in getting more poetry in, at any rate, than *The Confidential Clerk* did. I don't feel that I've got to the point I aim at and I don't think I ever will, but I would like to feel I was getting a little nearer to it each time.

INTERVIEWER: Do you have a Greek model behind *The Elder Statesman*?

ELIOT: The play in the background is the *Oedipus at Colonnus*. But I wouldn't like to refer to my Greek originals as models. I have always regarded them more as points of departure. That was one of the weaknesses of *The Family Reunion;* it was rather too close to the *Eumenides*. I tried to follow my original too literally and in that way led to confusion by mixing pre-Christian and post-Christian attitudes about matters of conscience and sin and guilt.

So in the subsequent three I have tried to take the Greek myth as a sort of springboard, you see. After all, what one gets essential and permanent, I think, in the old plays, is a situation. You can take the situation, rethink it in modern terms, develop your own characters from it, and let another plot develop out of that. Actually you get further and further away from the original. *The Cocktail Party* had to do with Alcestis simply because the question arose in my mind, what would the life of Admetus and Alcestis be, after she'd come back from the dead; I mean if there'd been a break like that, it couldn't go on just as before. Those two people were the center of the thing when I started and the other characters only developed out of it. The character of Celia, who came to be really the most important character in the play, was originally an appendage to a domestic situation.

INTERVIEWER: Do you still hold to the theory of levels in poetic drama (plot, character, diction, rhythm, meaning) which you put forward in 1932?

ELIOT: I am no longer very much interested in my own theories about poetic drama, especially those put forward before 1934. I have thought less about theories since I have given more time to writing for the theater.

INTERVIEWER: How does the writing of a play differ from the writing of poems?

ELIOT: I feel that they take quite different approaches. There is all the difference in the world between writing a play for an audience and writing a poem, in which you're writing primarily for yourself — although obviously you wouldn't be satisfied if the poem didn't mean something to other people afterward. With a poem you can say, "I got my feeling into words for myself. I now have the equivalent in words for that much of what I have felt." Also in a poem you're writing for your own voice, which is very important. You're thinking in terms of your own voice, whereas in a play from the beginning you have to realize that you're preparing something which is going into the hands of other people, unknown at the time you're writing it. Of course I won't say there aren't moments in a play when the two approaches may not converge, when I think ideally they *should*. Very often in Shakespeare they do, when he is writing a poem and thinking in terms of the theater and the actors and the audience all at once. And the two things are one. That's wonderful when you can get that. With me it only happens at odd moments.

INTERVIEWER: Have you tried at all to control the speaking of your verse by the actors? To make it seem more like verse?

ELIOT: I leave that primarily to the producer. The important thing is to have a producer who has the feeling of verse and who can guide them in just how emphatic to make the verse, just how far to depart from prose or how far to approach it. I only guide the actors if they ask me questions directly. Otherwise I think that they should get their advice through the producer. The important thing is to arrive at an agreement with him first, and then leave it to him.

INTERVIEWER: Do you feel that there's been a general tendency in your work, even in your poems, to move from a narrower to a larger audience?

ELIOT: I think that there are two elements in this. One is that I think that writing plays (that is *Murder in the Cathedral* and *The Family Reunion*) made a difference to the writing of the *Four Quartets*. I think that it led to a greater simplification of language and to speaking in a way which is more like conversing with your reader. I see the later *Quartets* as being much simpler and easier to understand than "The Waste Land" and "Ash Wednesday." Sometimes the thing I'm trying to say, the subject matter, may be difficult, but it seems to me that I'm saying it in a simpler way.

The other element that enters into it, I think, is just experience and maturity. I think that in the early poems it was a question of not being able to — of having more to say than one knew how to say, and having something one wanted to put into words and rhythm which one didn't have the command of words and rhythm to put in a way immediately apprehensible.

That type of obscurity comes when the poet is still at the stage of learning how to use language. You have to say the thing the difficult way. The only alternative is not saying it at all, at that stage. By the time of the *Four Quartets*, I couldn't have written in the style of "The Waste Land." In "The Waste Land," I wasn't even bothering whether I understood what I was saying. These things, however, become easier to people with time. You get used to having "The Waste Land," or *Ulysses,* about.

INTERVIEWER: Do you feel that the *Four Quartets* are your best work?

ELIOT: Yes, and I'd like to feel that they get better as they go on. The second is better than the first, the third is better than the second, and the fourth is the best of all. At any rate, that's the way I flatter myself.

INTERVIEWER: This is a very general question, but I wonder if you could give advice to a young poet about what disciplines or attitudes he might cultivate to improve his art.

ELIOT: I think it's awfully dangerous to give general advice. I think the best one can do for a young poet is to criticize in detail a particular poem of his. Argue it with him if necessary, give him your opinion, and if there are any generalizations to be made, let him do them himself. I've found that different people have different ways of working, and things come to them in different ways. You're never sure when you're uttering a statement that's generally valid for all poets or when it's something that only applies to yourself. I think nothing is worse than to try to form people in your own image.

INTERVIEWER: Do you think there's any possible generalization to be made about the fact that all the better poets now, younger than you, seem to be teachers?

ELIOT: I don't know. I think the only generalization that can be made of any value will be one which will be made a generation later. All you can say at this point is that at different times there are different possibilities of making a living, or different limitations on making a living. Obviously a poet has got to find a way of making a living apart from his poetry. After all, artists do a great deal of teaching, and musicians too.

INTERVIEWER: Do you think that the optimal career for a poet would involve no work at all but writing and reading?

ELIOT: No, I think that would be — but there again one can only talk about oneself. It is very dangerous to give an optimal career for everybody, but I feel quite sure that if I'd started by having independent means, if I hadn't had to bother about earning a living and could have given all my time to poetry, it would have had a deadening influence on me.

INTERVIEWER: Why?

ELIOT: I think that for me it's been very useful to exercise other activities, such as working in a bank, or publishing even. And I think also that the difficulty of not having as much time as I would like has given me a greater pressure of concentration. I mean it has prevented me from writing too much. The danger, as a rule, of having nothing else to do is that one might write too much rather than concentrating and perfecting smaller amounts. That would be *my* danger.

INTERVIEWER: Do you consciously attempt, now, to keep up with the poetry that is being written by young men in England and America?

ELIOT: I don't now, not with any conscientiousness. I did at one time when I was reading little reviews and looking out for new talent as a publisher. But as one gets older, one is not quite confident in one's own ability to distinguish new genius among younger men. You're always afraid that you are going as you have seen your elders go. At Faber and Faber now I have a younger colleague who reads poetry manuscripts. But even before that, when I came across new stuff that I thought had real merit, I would show it to younger friends whose critical judgment I trusted and get their opinion. But of course there is always the danger that there is merit when you don't see it. So I'd rather have younger people to look at things first. If they like it, they will show it to me, and see whether I like it too. When you get something that knocks over younger people of taste and judgment and older people as well, then that's likely to be something important. Sometimes there's a lot of resistance. I shouldn't like to feel that I was resisting, as my work was resisted when it was new, by people who thought that it was imposture of some kind or other.

INTERVIEWER: Do you feel that younger poets in general have repudiated the experimentalism of the early poetry of this century? Few poets now seem to be resisted the way you were resisted, but some older critics like Herbert Read believe that poetry after you has been a regression to outdated modes. When you talked about Milton the second time, you spoke of the function of poetry as a retarder of change, as well as a maker of change, in language.

ELIOT: Yes, I don't think you want a revolution every ten years.

INTERVIEWER: But is it possible to think that there has been a counterrevolution rather than an exploration of new possibilities?

ELIOT: No, I don't see anything that looks to me like a counterrevolution. After a period of getting away from the traditional forms, comes a period of curiosity in making new experiments with traditional forms. This can produce very good work if what has happened in between has made a difference: when it's not merely going back, but taking up an old form, which has been out of use for a time, and making something new with it. That is not counterrevolution. Nor does mere regression deserve the name. There is a tendency in some quarters to revert to Georgian scenery and sentiments; and among the public there are always people who prefer mediocrity, and when they get it, say, "What a relief! Here's some real poetry again." And there are also people who like poetry to be modern but for whom the really creative stuff is too strong — they need something diluted.

What seems to me the best of what I've seen in young poets is not reaction at all. I'm not going to mention any names, for I don't like to make public judgments about younger poets. The best stuff is a further development of a less revolutionary character than what appeared in earlier years of the century.

INTERVIEWER: I have some unrelated questions that I'd like to end with. In 1945 you wrote, "A poet must take as his material his own language as it is actually spoken around him." And later you wrote, "The music of poetry, then, will be a music latent in the common speech of his time." After the second remark, you disparaged "standardized BBC English." Now isn't one of the changes of the last fifty years, and perhaps even more of the last five years, the growing dominance of commercial speech through the means of communication? What you referred to as "BBC English" has become immensely more powerful through the ITA and BBC television, not to speak of CBS, NBC, and ABC. Does this development make the problem of the poet and his relationship to common speech more difficult?

ELIOT: You've raised a very good point there. I think you're right, it does make it more difficult.

INTERVIEWER: I wanted *you* to make the point.

ELIOT: Yes, but you wanted the point to be *made*. So I'll take the responsibility of making it: I do think that where you have these modern means of communication and means of imposing the speech and idioms of a small number on the mass of people at large, it does complicate the problem very much. I don't know to what extent that goes for film speech, but obviously radio speech has done much more.

INTERVIEWER: I wonder if there's a possibility that what you mean by common speech will disappear.

ELIOT: That is a very gloomy prospect. But very likely indeed.

INTERVIEWER: Are there other problems for a writer in our time which are unique? Does the prospect of human annihilation have any particular effect on the poet?

ELIOT: I don't see why the prospect of human annihilation should affect the poet differently from men of other vocations. It will affect him as a human being, no doubt in proportion to his sensitiveness.

INTERVIEWER: Another unrelated question: I can see why a man's criticism is better for his being a practicing poet, better although subject to his own prejudices. But do you feel that writing criticism has helped you as a poet?

ELIOT: In an indirect way it has helped me somehow as a poet — to put down in writing my critical valuation of the poets who have influenced me and whom I admire. It is merely making an influence more conscious and more articulate. It's been a rather natural impulse. I think probably my best critical essays are essays on the poets who had influenced me, so to speak, long before I thought of writing essays about them. They're of more value, probably, than any of my more generalized remarks.

INTERVIEWER: G. S. Fraser wonders, in an essay about the two of you, whether you ever met Yeats. From remarks in your talk about him, it would seem that you did. Could you tell us the circumstances?

ELIOT: Of course I had met Yeats many times. Yeats was always very gracious when one met him and had the art of treating younger writers as if they were his equals and contemporaries. I can't remember any one particular occasion.

INTERVIEWER: I have heard that you consider that your poetry belongs in the tradition of American literature. Could you tell us why?

ELIOT: I'd say that my poetry has obviously more in common with my distinguished contemporaries in America than with anything written in my generation in England. That I'm sure of.

INTERVIEWER: Do you think there's a connection with the American past?

ELIOT: Yes, but I couldn't put it any more definitely than that, you see. It wouldn't be what it is, and I imagine it wouldn't be so good; putting it as modestly as I can, it wouldn't be what it is if I'd been born in England, and it wouldn't be what it is if I'd stayed in America. It's a combination of things. But in its sources, in its emotional springs, it comes from America.

INTERVIEWER: One last thing. Seventeen years ago you said, "No honest poet can ever feel quite sure of the permanent value of what he has written. He may have wasted his time and messed up his life for nothing." Do you feel the same now, at seventy?

ELIOT: There may be honest poets who do feel sure. I don't.

Marianne Moore

1960

INTERVIEWER: Miss Moore, I understand that you were born in St. Louis only about ten months before T. S. Eliot. Did your families know each other?

MOORE: No, we did not know the Eliots. We lived in Kirkwood, Missouri, where my grandfather was pastor of the First Presbyterian Church. T. S. Eliot's grandfather — Dr. William Eliot — was a Unitarian. We left when I was about seven, my grandfather having died in 1894, February 20th. My grandfather like Dr. Eliot had attended ministerial meetings in St. Louis. Also, at stated intervals, various ministers met for luncheon. After one of these luncheons my grandfather said, "When Dr. William Eliot asks the blessing and says 'and this we ask in the name of our Lord Jesus Christ,' he is Trinitarian enough for me." The Mary Institute, for girls, was endowed by him as a memorial to his daughter Mary, who had died.

INTERVIEWER: How old were you when you started to write poems?

MOORE: Well, let me see, in Bryn Mawr. I think I was eighteen when I entered Bryn Mawr. I was born in 1887, I entered college in 1906. Now how old would I have been? Can you deduce my probable age?

INTERVIEWER: Eighteen or nineteen.

MOORE: I had no literary plans, but I was interested in the undergraduate monthly magazine, and to my surprise (I wrote one or two little things for it) the editors elected me to the board. It was my sophomore year — I am sure it was — and I stayed on, I believe. And then when I had left college I offered contributions (we weren't paid) to the *Lantern,* the alumnae magazine. But I didn't feel that my product was anything to shake the world.

INTERVIEWER: At what point did poetry become world-shaking for you?

MOORE: Never! I believe I was interested in painting then. At least I said so. I remember Mrs. Otis Skinner asking at commencement time, the year I was graduated, "What would you like to be?"

"A painter," I said.

"Well, I'm not surprised," Mrs. Skinner answered. I had something on that she liked, some kind of summer dress. She commended it — said, "I'm not at all surprised."

I like stories. I like fiction. And — this sounds rather pathetic, bizarre as well — I think verse perhaps was for me the next best thing to it. Didn't I write something one time, "Part of a Poem, Part of a Novel, Part of a Play"? I think I was all too truthful. I could visualize scenes, and deplored the fact that Henry James had to do it unchallenged. Now, if I couldn't write fiction, I'd like to write plays. To me the theater is the most pleasant, in fact my favorite, form of recreation.

INTERVIEWER: Do you go often?

MOORE: No. Never. Unless someone invites me. Lillian Hellman invited me to *Toys in the Attic,* and I am very happy that she did. I would have no notion of the vitality of the thing, have lost sight of her skill as a writer if I hadn't seen the play; would like to go again. The accuracy of the vernacular! That's the kind of thing I am interested in, am always taking down little local expressions and accents. I think I should be in some philological operation or enterprise, am really much interested in dialect and intonations. I scarcely think of any that comes into my so-called poems at all.

INTERVIEWER: I wonder what Bryn Mawr meant for you as a poet. You write that most of your time there was spent in the biological laboratory. Did you like biology better than literature as a subject for study? Did the training possibly affect your poetry?

MOORE: I had hoped to make French and English my major studies, and took the required two-year English course — five hours a week — but was not able to elect a course until my junior year. I did not attain the requisite academic stand of eighty until that year. I then elected seventeenth-century imitative writing — Fuller, Hooker, Bacon, Bishop Andrewes, and others. Lectures in French were in French, and I had had no spoken French.

Did laboratory studies affect my poetry? I am sure they did. I

found the biology courses — minor, major, and histology — exhil-
arating. I thought, in fact, of studying medicine. Precision, econ-
omy of statement, logic employed to ends that are disinterested,
drawing and identifying, liberate — at least have some bearing on
— the imagination, it seems to me.

INTERVIEWER: Whom did you know in the literary world,
before you came to New York? Did you know Bryher and H.D.?

MOORE: It's very hard to get these things seriatim. I met Bryher
in 1921 in New York. H.D. was my classmate at Bryn Mawr. She
was there, I think, only two years. She was a nonresident and I did
not realize that she was interested in writing.

INTERVIEWER: Did you know Ezra Pound and William Carlos
Williams through her? Didn't she know them at the University of
Pennsylvania?

MOORE: Yes. She did. I didn't meet them. I had met no writers
until 1916 when I visited New York, when a friend in Carlisle
wanted me to accompany her.

INTERVIEWER: So you were isolated really from modern poetry
until 1916?

MOORE: Yes.

INTERVIEWER: Was that your first trip to New York, when
you went there for six days and decided that you wanted to live
there?

MOORE: Oh, no. Several times my mother had taken my brother
and me sightseeing and to shop; on the way to Boston, or Maine,
and to Washington and Florida. My senior year in college in 1909,
I visited Dr. Charles Spraguesmith's daughter Hilda, at Christmas-
time in New York. And Louis Anspacher lectured in a very orna-
mental way at Cooper Union. There was plenty of music at
Carnegie Hall, and I got a sense of what was going on in New
York.

INTERVIEWER: And what was going on made you want to
come back?

MOORE: It probably did, when Miss Cowdrey in Carlisle invited
me to come with her for a week. It was the visit in 1916 that made
me want to live there. I don't know what put it into her head to do
it, or why she wasn't likely to have a better time without me. She
was most skeptical of my venturing forth to bohemian parties. But
I was fearless about that. In the first place, I didn't think anyone

would try to harm me, but if they did I felt impervious. It never occurred to me that chaperones were important.

INTERVIEWER: Do you suppose that moving to New York, and the stimulation of the writers whom you found there, led you to write more poems than you would otherwise have written?

MOORE: I'm sure it did — seeing what others wrote, liking this or that. With me it's always some fortuity that traps me. I certainly never intended to write poetry. That never came into my head. And now, too, I think each time I write that it may be the last time; then I'm charmed by something and seem to have to say something. Everything I have written is the result of reading or of interest in people, I'm sure of that. I had no ambition to be a writer.

INTERVIEWER: Let me see. You taught at the Carlisle Indian School, after Bryn Mawr. Then after you moved to New York in 1918 you taught at a private school and worked in a library. Did these occupations have anything to do with you as a writer?

MOORE: I think they hardened my muscles considerably, my mental approach to things. Working as a librarian was a big help, a tremendous help. Miss Leonard of the Hudson Park branch of the New York Public Library opposite our house came to see me one day. I wasn't in, and she asked my mother did she think I would care to be on the staff, work in the library, because I was so fond of books and liked to talk about them to people. My mother said no, she thought not; the shoemaker's children never have shoes, I probably would feel if I joined the staff that I'd have no time to read. When I came home she told me, and I said, "Why, certainly. Ideal. I'll tell her. Only I couldn't work more than half a day." If I had worked all day and maybe evenings or overtime, like the mechanics, why, it would *not* have been ideal.

As a free service we were assigned books to review and I did like that. We didn't get paid but we had the chance to diagnose. I reveled in it. Somewhere I believe I have carbon copies of those "P-slip" summaries. They were the kind of things that brought the worst-best out. I was always wondering why they didn't honor me with an art book or medical book or even a history, or criticism. But no, it was fiction, silent-movie fiction.

INTERVIEWER: Did you travel at this time? Did you go to Europe at all?

MOORE: In 1911. My mother and I went to England for about

two months, July and August probably. We went to Paris and we stayed on the left bank, in a pension in the rue Valette, where Calvin wrote his *Institutes,* I believe. Not far from the Panthéon and the Luxembourg Gardens. I have been much interested in Sylvia Beach's book — reading about Ezra Pound and his Paris days. Where was I and what was I doing? I think, with the objective, an evening stroll — it was one of the hottest summers the world has ever known, 1911 — we walked along to 12, rue de l'Odéon, to see Sylvia Beach's shop. It wouldn't occur to me to say, "Here am I, I'm a writer, would you talk to me a while?" I had no feeling at all like that. I wanted to observe things. And we went to every museum in Paris, I think, except two.

INTERVIEWER: Have you been back since?

MOORE: Not to Paris. Only to England in 1935 or 1936. I like England.

INTERVIEWER: You have mostly stayed put in Brooklyn, then, since you moved here in 1929?

MOORE: Except for four trips to the West: Los Angeles, San Francisco, Puget Sound, and British Columbia. My mother and I went through the canal previously, to San Francisco, and by rail to Seattle.

INTERVIEWER: Have you missed the Dodgers here, since *they* went west?

MOORE: Very much, and I am told that they miss us.

INTERVIEWER: I am still interested in those early years in New York. William Carlos Williams, in his *Autobiography,* says that you were "a rafter holding up the superstructure of our uncompleted building," when he talks about the Greenwich Village group of writers. I guess these were people who contributed to *Others.*

MOORE: I never was a rafter holding up anyone! I have his *Autobiography* and took him to task for his misinformed statements about Robert McAlmon and Bryher. In my indignation I missed some things I ought to have seen.

INTERVIEWER: To what extent did the *Others* contributors form a group?

MOORE: We did foregather a little. Alfred Kreymborg was editor, and was married to Gertrude Lord at the time, one of the loveliest persons you could ever meet. And they had a little apartment somewhere in the Village. There was considerable unanimity about the group.

INTERVIEWER: Someone called Alfred Kreymborg your American discoverer. Do you suppose this is true?

MOORE: It could be said, perhaps; he did all he could to promote me. Miss Monroe and the Aldingtons had asked me simultaneously to contribute to *Poetry* and *The Egoist* in 1917 at the same time. Alfred Kreymborg was not inhibited. I was a little different from the others. He thought I might pass as a novelty, I guess.

INTERVIEWER: What was your reaction when H.D. and Bryher brought out your first collection, which they called *Poems,* in 1921 without your knowledge? Why had you delayed to do it yourself?

MOORE: To issue my slight product — conspicuously tentative — seemed to me premature. I disliked the term "poetry" for any but Chaucer's or Shakespeare's or Dante's. I do not now feel quite my original hostility to the word, since it is a convenient, almost unavoidable term for the thing (although hardly for me — my observations, experiments in rhythm, or exercises in composition). What I write, as I have said before, could only be called poetry because there is no other category in which to put it. For the chivalry of the undertaking — issuing my verse for me in 1921, certainly in format choicer than the content — I am intensely grateful. Again, in 1925, it seemed to me not very self-interested of Faber and Faber, and simultaneously of the Macmillan Company, to propose a *Selected Poems* for me. Desultory occasional magazine publications seemed to me sufficient, conspicuous enough.

INTERVIEWER: Had you been sending poems to magazines before *The Egoist* printed your first poem?

MOORE: I must have. I have a little curio, a little wee book about two by three inches, or two and a half by three inches, in which I systematically entered everything sent out, when I got it back, if they took it, and how much I got for it. That lasted about a year, I think. I can't care as much as all that. I don't know that I submitted anything that wasn't extorted from me.

I have at present three onerous tasks, and each interferes with the others, and I don't know how I am going to write anything. If I get a promising idea I set it down, and it stays there. I don't make myself do anything with it. I've had several things in *The New Yorker*. And I said to them, "I might never write again," and not

to expect me to. I never knew anyone who had a passion for words
who had as much difficulty in saying things as I do and I very
seldom say them in a manner I like. If I do it's because I don't
know I'm trying. I've written several things for *The New Yorker*
— and I did want to write *them*.

INTERVIEWER: When did you last write a poem?

MOORE: It appeared in August. What was it about? Oh . . .
Carnegie Hall. You see, anything that really rouses me . . .

INTERVIEWER: How does a poem start for you?

MOORE: A felicitous phrase springs to mind — a word or two,
say — simultaneous usually with some thought or object of equal
attraction: "Its leaps should be *set* / to the flageo*let*"; "Katydid-
wing subdivided by *sun* / till the nettings are *legion*." I like light
rhymes and unpompous conspicuous rhymes: Gilbert and Sullivan:

> Yet, when the danger's near,
> We manage to appear
> As insensible to fear
> As anybody here.

I have a passion for rhythm and accent, so blundered into versi-
fying. Considering the stanza the unit, I came to hazard hyphens at
the end of the line, but found that readers are distracted from the
content by hyphens, so I try not to use them. My interest in La
Fontaine originated entirely independent of content. I then fell a
prey to that surgical kind of courtesy of his.

> I fear that appearances are worshiped throughout France
>   Whereas pre-eminence perchance
>   Merely means a pushing person.

I like the unaccented syllable and accented near-rhyme:

> By love and his blindness
> Possibly a service was done,
> Let lovers say. A lonely man has no criterion.

INTERVIEWER: What in your reading or your background led
you to write the way you do write? Was imagism a help to you?

MOORE: No. I wondered why anyone would adopt the term.

INTERVIEWER: The descriptiveness of your poems has nothing
to do with them, you think?

MOORE: No; I really don't. I was rather sorry to be a pariah, or at least that I had no connection with anything. But I *did* feel gratitude to *Others*.

INTERVIEWER: Where do you think your style of writing came from? Was it a gradual accumulation, out of your character? Or does it have literary antecedents?

MOORE: Not so far as I know. Ezra Pound said, "Someone has been reading Laforgue, and French authors." Well, sad to say, I had not read any of them until fairly recently. Retroactively I see that Francis Jammes's titles and treatment are a good deal like my own. I seem almost a plagiarist.

INTERVIEWER: And the extensive use of quotations?

MOORE: I was just trying to be honorable and not to steal things. I've always felt that if a thing had been said in the *best* way, how can you say it better? If I wanted to say something and some-body had said it ideally, then I'd take it but give the person credit for it. That's all there is to it. If you are charmed by an author, I think it's a very strange and invalid imagination that doesn't long to share it. Somebody else should read it, don't you think?

INTERVIEWER: Did any prose stylists help you in finding your poetic style? Elizabeth Bishop mentions Poe's prose in connection with your writing, and you have always made people think of Henry James.

MOORE: Prose stylists, very much. Doctor Johnson on Richard Savage: "He was in two months illegitimated by the Parliament, and disowned by his mother, doomed to poverty and obscurity, and launched upon the ocean of life only that he might be swal-lowed by its quicksands, or dashed upon its rocks. . . . It was his peculiar happiness that he scarcely ever found a stranger whom he did not leave a friend; but it must likewise be added, that he had not often a friend long without obliging him to become a stranger." Or Edmund Burke on the colonies: "You can shear a wolf; but will he comply?" Or Sir Thomas Browne: "States are not governed by Ergotisms." He calls a bee "that industrious flie," and his home his "hive." His manner is a kind of erudition-proof sweetness. Or Sir Francis Bacon: "Civil War is like the heat of fever; a foreign war is like the heat of exercise." Or Cellini: "I had by me a dog black as a mulberry. . . . I swelled up in my rage like an asp." Or Caesar's *Commentaries*, and Xenophon's *Cynegeticus:* the gusto and interest in every detail! In Henry James it is the essays and letters especially that affect me. In Ezra Pound, *The Spirit of Romance:* his definiteness, his indigenously unmistakable accent. Charles Norman says in his biography of Ezra Pound that he said to a poet, "Nothing, *nothing,* that you couldn't in some circumstance, under stress of some emotion, *actually say.*" And Ezra said of Shakespeare and Dante, "Here we are with the masters; of neither can we say, 'He is the greater'; of each we must say, 'He is unexcelled.'"

INTERVIEWER: Do you have in your own work any favorites and unfavorites?

MOORE: Indeed, I do. I think the most difficult thing for me is to be satisfactorily lucid, yet have enough implication in it to suit myself. That's a problem. And I don't approve of my "enigmas," or as somebody said, "the not ungreen grass." I said to my mother one time, "How did you ever permit me to let this be printed?" And she said, "You didn't ask my advice."

INTERVIEWER: One time I heard you give a reading, and I think you said that you didn't like "In Distrust of Merits," which is one of your most popular poems.

MOORE: I do like it; it is sincere but I wouldn't call it a poem. It's truthful; it is testimony — to the fact that war is intolerable, and unjust.

INTERVIEWER: How can you call it not a poem, on what basis?

MOORE: Haphazard; as form, what has it? It is just a protest — disjointed, exclamatory. Emotion overpowered me. First this thought and then that.

INTERVIEWER: Your mother said that you hadn't asked her advice. Did you ever? Do you go for criticism to your family or friends?

MOORE: Well, not friends, but my brother if I get a chance. When my mother said "You didn't ask my advice" must have been years ago, because when I wrote "A Face," I had written something first about "the adder and the child with a bowl of porridge," and she said "It won't do." "All right," I said, "but I have to produce something." Cyril Connolly had asked me for something for *Horizon.* So I wrote "A Face." That is one of the few things I ever set down that didn't give me any trouble. She said, "I like it." I remember that.

Then, much before that, I wrote "The Buffalo." I thought it would probably outrage a number of persons because it had to me a kind of pleasing jerky progress. I thought, "Well, if it seems bad my brother will tell me, and if it has a point he'll detect it." And he said, with considerable gusto, "It takes my fancy." I was happy as could be.

INTERVIEWER: Did you ever suppress anything because of family objections?

MOORE: Yes, "the adder and the child with a bowl of porridge." I never even wanted to improve it. You know, Mr. Saintsbury said that Andrew Lang wanted him to contribute something on Poe, and he did, and Lang returned it. Mr. Saintsbury said, "Once a thing has been rejected, I would not offer it to the most different of editors." That shocked me. I have offered a thing, submitted it thirty-five times. Not simultaneously, of course.

INTERVIEWER: A poem?

MOORE: Yes. I am very tenacious.

INTERVIEWER: Do people ever ask you to write poems for them?

MOORE: Continually. Everything from on the death of a dog to a little item for an album.

INTERVIEWER: Do you ever write them?

MOORE: Oh, perhaps; usually quote something. Once when I was in the library we gave a party for Miss Leonard, and I wrote a line or two of doggerel about a bouquet of violets we gave her. It has no life or point. It was meant well but didn't amount to anything. Then in college, I had a sonnet as an assignment. The epitome of weakness.

INTERVIEWER: I'm interested in asking about the principles, and the methods, of your way of writing. What is the rationale behind syllabic verse? How does it differ from free verse in which the line length is controlled visually but not arithmetically?

MOORE: It never occurred to me that what I wrote was something to define. I am governed by the pull of the sentence as the pull of a fabric is governed by gravity. I like the end-stopped line and dislike the reversed order of words; like symmetry.

INTERVIEWER: How do you plan the shape of your stanzas? I am thinking of the poems, usually syllabic, which employ a repeated stanza form. Do you ever experiment with shapes before you write, by drawing lines on a page?

MOORE: Never, I never "plan" a stanza. Words cluster like chromosomes, determining the procedure. I may influence an arrangement or thin it, then try to have successive stanzas identical with the first. Spontaneous initial originality — say, impetus — seems difficult to reproduce consciously later. As Stravinsky said about pitch, "If I transpose it for some reason, I am in danger of losing the freshness of first contact and will have difficulty in recapturing its attractiveness."

No, I never "draw lines." I make a rhyme conspicuous, to me at a glance, by underlining with red, blue, or other pencil — as many colors as I have rhymes to differentiate. However, if the phrases recur in too incoherent an architecture — as print — I notice that the words as a tune do not sound right. I may start a piece, find it obstructive, lack a way out, and not complete the thing for a year, or years, am thrifty. I salvage anything promising and set it down in a small notebook.

INTERVIEWER: I wonder if the act of translating La Fontaine's *Fables* helped you as a writer.

MOORE: Indeed it did. It was the best help I've ever had. I suffered frustration. I'm so naïve, so docile, I *tend* to take anybody's word for anything the person says, even in matters of art. The publisher who had commissioned the *Fables* died. I had no publisher. Well, I struggled on for a time and it didn't go very well. I thought, I'd better ask if they don't want to terminate the contract; then I could offer it elsewhere. I thought Macmillan, who took an interest in me, might like it. *Might*. The editor in charge of translations said, "Well, I studied French at Cornell, took a degree in French, I love French, and . . . well, I think you'd better put it away for a while." "How long?" I said. "About ten years; besides, it will hurt your own work. You won't write so well afterward."

"Oh," I said, "that's one reason I was undertaking it; I thought it would train me and give me momentum." Much dejected, I asked, "What is wrong? Have I not a good ear? Are the meanings not sound?"

"Well, there are conflicts," the editor reiterated, as it seemed to me, countless times. I don't know yet what they are or were. (A little "editorial.")

I said, "Don't write me an extenuating letter, please. Just send back the material in the envelope I put with it." I had submitted it in January and this was May. I had had a kind of uneasy hope that all would be well; meanwhile had volumes, hours, and years of work yet to do and might as well go on and do it, I had thought. The ultimatum was devastating.

At the same time Monroe Engel of the Viking Press wrote to me and said that he had supposed I had a commitment for my *Fables*, but if I hadn't would I let the Viking Press see them? I feel an everlasting gratitude to him.

However, I said, "I can't offer you something which somebody else thinks isn't fit to print. I would have to have someone to stabilize it and guarantee that the meanings are sound."

Mr. Engel said, "Who do you think could do that? Whom would you like?"

I said, "Harry Levin," because he had written a cogent, very shrewd review of Edna St. Vincent Millay's and George Dillon's translation of Baudelaire. I admired its finesse.

Mr. Engel said, "I'll ask him. But you won't hear for a long time. He's very busy. And how much do you think we ought to offer him?"

"Well," I said, "not less than ten dollars a book; there would be no incentive in undertaking the bother of it, if it weren't twenty."

He said, "That would reduce your royalties too much on an advance."

I said, "I don't want an advance, wouldn't even consider one."

And then Harry Levin said, quite soon, that he would be glad to do it as a "refreshment against the chores of the term," but of course he would accept no remuneration. It was a very dubious refreshment, let me tell you. (He is precise, and not abusive, and did not "resign.")

INTERVIEWER: I've been asking you about your poems, which is of course what interests me most. But you were editor of *The Dial*, too, and I want to ask you a few things about that. You were editor from 1925 until it ended in 1929, I think. How did you first come to be associated with it?

MOORE: Let me see. I think I took the initiative. I sent the editors a couple of things and they sent them back. And Lola Ridge had a party — she had a large apartment on a ground floor somewhere — and John Reed and Marsden Hartley, who was very confident with the brush, and Scofield Thayer, editor of *The Dial*, were there. And much to my disgust, we were induced each to read something we had written. And Scofield Thayer said of my piece, "Would you send that to us at *The Dial*?"

"I did send it," I said.

And he said, "Well, send it again." That is how it began, I think. Then he said, one time, "I'd like you to meet my partner, Sibley Watson," and invited me to tea at 152 West 13th Street. I was impressed. Dr. Watson is rare. He said nothing, but what he did say was striking and the significance would creep over you because unanticipated. And they asked me to join the staff, at *The Dial*.

INTERVIEWER: I have just been looking at that magazine, the years when you edited it. It's an incredible magazine.

MOORE: *The Dial*? There *were* good things in it, weren't there?

INTERVIEWER: Yes. It combined George Saintsbury and Ezra Pound in the same issue. How do you account for it? What made it so good?

MOORE: Lack of fear, for one thing. We didn't care what other people said. I never knew a magazine which was so self-propulsive. Everybody liked what he was doing, and when we made grievous mistakes we were sorry but we laughed over them.

INTERVIEWER: Louise Bogan said that *The Dial* made clear "the obvious division between American avant-garde and American conventional writing." Do you think this kind of division continues or has continued? Was this in any way a deliberate policy?

MOORE: I think that individuality was the great thing. We were not conforming to anything. We certainly didn't have a policy, except I remember hearing the word "intensity" very often. A thing must have intensity. That seemed to be the criterion.

The thing applied to it, I think, that should apply to your own writing. As George Grosz said, at that last meeting he attended at the National Institute, "How did I come to be an artist? Endless curiosity, observation, research — and a great amount of joy in the thing." It was a matter of taking a liking to things. Things that were in accordance with your taste. I think that was it. And we didn't care how unhomogeneous they might seem. Didn't Aristotle say that it is the mark of a poet to see resemblances between apparently incongruous things? There was any amount of attraction about it.

INTERVIEWER: Do you think there is anything in the change of literary life in America that would make *The Dial* different if it existed today under the same editors? Were there any special conditions in the twenties that made the literary life of America different?

MOORE: I think it is always about the same.

INTERVIEWER: I wonder, if it had survived into the thirties, if it might have made that rather dry literary decade a little better.

MOORE: I think so. Because we weren't in captivity to anything.

INTERVIEWER: Was it just finances that made it stop?

MOORE: No, it wasn't the Depression. Conditions changed. Scofield Thayer had a nervous breakdown, and he didn't come to meetings. Doctor Watson was interested in photography — was studying medicine; is a doctor of medicine, and lived in Rochester. I was alone. I didn't know that Rochester was about a night's journey away, and I would say to Doctor Watson, "Couldn't you come in for a makeup meeting, or send us these manuscripts and say what you think of them?" I may, as usual, have exaggerated my enslavement and my preoccupation with tasks — writing letters and reading manuscripts. Originally I had said I would come if I didn't have to write letters and didn't have to see contributors. And presently I was doing both. I think it was largely chivalry — the decision to discontinue the magazine — because I didn't have time for work of my own.

INTERVIEWER: I wonder how you worked as an editor. Hart Crane complains, in one of his letters, that you rearranged "The Wine Menagerie" and changed the title. Do you feel that you were justified? Did you ask for revisions from many poets?

MOORE: No. We had an inflexible rule: Do not ask changes of so much as a comma. Accept it or reject it. But in that instance I felt that in compassion I should disregard the rule. Hart Crane complains of me? Well, I complain of *him*. He liked *The Dial* and we liked him — friends, and with certain tastes in common. He was in dire need of money. It seemed careless not to so much as ask if he might like to make some changes ("like" in quotations). His gratitude was ardent and later his repudiation of it commensurate — he perhaps being in both instances under a disability with which I was not familiar. (Penalizing us for compassion?) I say "us," and should say "me." Really I am not used to having people in that bemused state. He was so *anxious* to have us take that thing, and so *delighted*. "Well, if you would modify it a little," I said, "we would like it better." I never attended "their" wild parties, as Lachaise once said. It was lawless of me to suggest changes; I disobeyed.

INTERVIEWER: Have you had editors suggest changes to you? Changes in your own poems, I mean?

MOORE: No, but my ardor to be helped being sincere, I sometimes *induce* assistance: the *Times,* the *Herald Tribune, The New Yorker,* have a number of times had to patch and piece me out. If you have a genius of an editor, you are blessed: e.g., T. S. Eliot and Ezra Pound, Harry Levin, and others; Irita Van Doren and Miss Belle Rosenbaum.

Have I found "help" helpful? I certainly have; and in three instances, when I was at *The Dial,* I hazarded suggestions the results of which were to me drama. Excoriated by Herman George Schefauer for offering to suggest a verbal change or two in his translation of Thomas Mann's *Disorder and Early Sorrow,* I must have posted the suggestions before I was able to withdraw them. In any case, his joyous subsequent retraction of abuse, and his pleasure in the narrative, were not unwelcome. Gilbert Seldes strongly commended me for excisions proposed by me in his "Jonathan Edwards" (for *The Dial*); and I have not ceased to marvel at the overrating by Mark Van Doren of editorial conscience on my reverting (after an interval) to keeping some final lines I had wished he would omit. (Verse! but not a sonnet.)

We should try to judge the work of others by the most that it is, and our own, if not by the least that it is, take the least into consideration. I feel that I would not be worth a button if not grateful to be preserved from myself, and informed if what I have written is not to the point. I think we should feel free, like La Fontaine's captious critic, to say, if asked, "Your phrases are too long, and the content is not good. Break up the type and put it in the font." As Kenneth Burke says in *Counter-Statement:* "[Great] artists feel as opportunity what others feel as a menace. This ability does not, I believe, derive from an exceptional strength, it probably arises purely from professional interest the artist may take in his difficulties."

Lew Sarett says, in the *Poetry Society Bulletin,* we ask of a poet: Does this mean something? Does the poet say what he has to say and in his own manner? Does it stir the reader?

Shouldn't we replace vanity with honesty, as Robert Frost rec-

ommends? Annoyances abound. We should not find them lethal —
a baffled printer's emendations for instance (my "elephant with
frog-colored skin" instead of "fog-colored skin," and "the power
of the invisible is the invisible," instead of "the power of the visible
is the invisible") sounding like a parody on my meticulousness, a
"glasshopper" instead of a "grasshopper."

INTERVIEWER: Editing *The Dial* must have acquainted you
with the writers of the day whom you did not know already. Had
you known Hart Crane earlier?

MOORE: Yes, I did. You remember *Broom*? Toward the beginning of that magazine, in 1921, Lola Ridge was very hospitable,
and she invited to a party — previous to my work on *The Dial* —
Kay Boyle and her husband, a French soldier, and Hart Crane,
Elinor Wylie, and some others. I took a great liking to Hart Crane.
We talked about French bindings, and he was diffident and modest
and seemed to have so much intuition, such a feel for things, for
books — really a bibliophile — that I took special interest in him.
And Dr. Watson and Scofield Thayer liked him — felt that he was
one of our talents, that he couldn't fit himself into an IBM position
to find a livelihood; that we ought to, whenever we could, take
anything he sent us.

I know a cousin of his, Joe Nowak, who is rather proud of him.
He lives here in Brooklyn, and is * at the Dry Dock Savings Bank
and used to work in antiques. Joe was very convinced of Hart's
sincerity and his innate love of all that I have specified. Anyhow,
The Bridge is a grand theme. Here and there I think he could have
firmed it up. A writer is unfair to himself when he is unable to be
hard on himself.

INTERVIEWER: Did Crane have anything to do with *Others*?

MOORE: *Others* antedated *Broom*. *Others* was Alfred Kreymborg and Skipwith Cannéll, Wallace Stevens, William Carlos Williams. Wallace Stevens — odd; I nearly met him a dozen times
before I did meet him in 1941 at Mount Holyoke, at the college's
Entretiens de Pontigny of which Professor Gustav Cohen was
chairman. Wallace Stevens was Henry Church's favorite American
poet. Mr. Church had published him and some others, and me, in
Mésure, in Paris. Raymond Queneau translated us.

---

* *Was;* killed; his car run into by a reckless driver in April 1961. — M.M.

During the French program at Mount Holyoke one afternoon Wallace Stevens had a discourse, the one about Goethe dancing on a packet boat in black wool stockings. My mother and I were there; and I gave a reading with commentary. Henry Church had an astoundingly beautiful Panama hat — a sort of porkpie with a wide brim, a little like Bernard Berenson's hats. I have never seen as fine a weave, and he had a pepper-and-salt shawl which he draped about himself. This lecture was on the lawn.

Wallace Stevens was extremely friendly. We should have had a tape recorder on that occasion, for at lunch they seated us all at a kind of refectory table and a girl kept asking him questions such as, "Mr. Stevens have you read the — *Four — Quartets?*"

"Of course, but I can't read much of Eliot or I wouldn't have any individuality of my own."

INTERVIEWER: Do you read new poetry now? Do you try to keep up?

MOORE: I am always seeing it — am sent some every day. Some, good. But it does interfere with my work. I can't get much done. Yet I would be a monster if I tossed everything away without looking at it; I write more notes, letters, cards in an hour than is sane.

Although everyone is penalized by being quoted inexactly, I wonder if there is anybody alive whose remarks are so often paraphrased as mine — printed as verbatim. It is really martyrdom. In his book *Ezra Pound,* Charles Norman was very scrupulous. He got several things exactly right. The first time I met Ezra Pound, when he came here to see my mother and me, I said that Henry Eliot seemed to me more nearly the artist than anyone I had ever met. "Now, now," said Ezra. "Be careful." Maybe that isn't exact, but he quotes it just the way I said it.

INTERVIEWER: Do you mean Henry Ware Eliot, T. S. Eliot's brother?

MOORE: Yes. After the Henry Eliots moved from Chicago to New York to — is it 68th Street? It's the street on which Hunter College is — to an apartment there, they invited me to dinner, I should think at T. S. Eliot's suggestion, and I took to them immediately. I felt as if I'd known them a great while. It was some time before I felt that way about T. S. Eliot.

About inaccuracies — when I went to see Ezra Pound at St. Elizabeths, about the third time I went, the official who escorted me to the grounds said, "Good of you to come to see him," and I said, "Good? You have no idea how much he has done for me, and others." This pertains to an early rather than final visit.

I was not in the habit of asking experts or anybody else to help me with things that I was doing, unless it was a librarian or someone whose business it was to help applicants; or a teacher. But I was desperate when Macmillan declined my *Fables*. I had worked about four years on them and sent Ezra Pound several — although I hesitated. I didn't like to bother him. He had enough trouble without that; but finally I said, "Would you have time to tell me if the rhythms grate on you? Is my ear not good?"

INTERVIEWER: He replied?

MOORE: Yes, said, "The least touch of merit upsets these blighters."

INTERVIEWER: When you first read Pound in 1916, did you recognize him as one of the great ones?

MOORE: Surely did. *The Spirit of Romance*. I don't think anybody could read that book and feel that a flounderer was writing.

INTERVIEWER: What about the early poems?

MOORE: Yes. They seemed a little didactic, but I liked them.

INTERVIEWER: I wanted to ask you a few questions about poetry in general. Somewhere you have said that originality is a byproduct of sincerity. You often use moral terms in your criticism. Is the necessary morality specifically literary, a moral use of words, or is it larger? In what way must a man be good if he is to write good poems?

MOORE: If emotion is strong enough, the words are unambiguous. Someone asked Robert Frost (is this right?) if he was selective. He said, "Call it passionate preference." Must a man be good to write good poems? The villains in Shakespeare are not illiterate, are they? But rectitude *has* a ring that is implicative, I would say. And with *no* integrity, a man is not likely to write the kind of book I read.

INTERVIEWER: Eliot, in his introduction to your *Selected Poems*, talks about your function as poet relative to the living language, as he calls it. Do you agree that this is a function of a poet? How does the poetry have the effect on the living language? What's the mechanics of it?

MOORE: You accept certain modes of saying a thing. Or

strongly repudiate things. You do something of your own, you modify, invent a variant or revive a root meaning. Any doubt about that?

INTERVIEWER: I want to ask you a question about your correspondence with the Ford Motor Company, those letters which were printed in *The New Yorker*. They were looking for a name for the car they eventually called the Edsel, and they asked you to think of a name that would make people admire the car —

MOORE: Elegance and grace, they said it would have —

INTERVIEWER: ". . . some visceral feeling of elegance, fleetness, advanced features and design. A name, in short, which flashes a dramatically desirable picture in people's minds."

MOORE: Really?

INTERVIEWER: That's what they said, in their first letter to you. I was thinking about this in connection with my question about language. Do you remember Pound's talk about expression and meaning? He says that when expression and meaning are far apart, the culture is in a bad way. I was wondering if this request doesn't ask you to remove expression a bit further from meaning.

MOORE: No, I don't think so. At least, to exposit the irresistibleness of the car. I got deep in motors and turbines and recessed wheels. No. That seemed to me a very worthy pursuit. I was more interested in the mechanics. I am interested in mechanisms, mechanics in general. And I enjoyed the assignment, for all that it was abortive. Dr. Pick at Marquette University procured a young demonstrator of the Edsel to call for me in a black one, to convey me to the auditorium. Nothing was wrong with that Edsel! I thought it was a very handsome car. It came out the wrong year.

INTERVIEWER: Another thing: in your criticism you make frequent analogies between the poet and the scientist. Do you think this analogy is helpful to the modern poet? Most people would consider the comparison a paradox, and assume that the poet and the scientist are opposed.

MOORE: Do the poet and scientist not work analogously? Both are willing to waste effort. To be hard on himself is one of the main strengths of each. Each is attentive to clues, each must narrow the choice, must strive for precision. As George Grosz says, "In art there is no place for gossip and but a small place for the satirist." The objective is fertile procedure. Is it not? Jacob Bronowski says in *The Saturday Evening Post* that science is not a mere collection of discoveries, but that science is the process of discovering. In any case it's not established once and for all; it's evolving.

INTERVIEWER: One last question. I was intrigued when you wrote that "America has in Wallace Stevens at least one artist whom professionalism will not demolish." What sort of literary professionalism did you have in mind? And do you find this a feature of America still?

MOORE: Yes. I think that writers sometimes lose verve and pugnacity, and he never would say "frame of reference" or "I wouldn't know." A question I am often asked is: "What work can I find that will enable me to spend my whole time writing?" Charles Ives, the composer, says, "You cannot set art off in a corner and hope for it to have vitality, reality, and substance. The fabric weaves itself whole. My work in music helped my business and my work in business helped my music." I am like Charles Ives. I guess Lawrence Durrell and Henry Miller would not agree with me.

INTERVIEWER: But how does professionalism make a writer lose his verve and pugnacity?

MOORE: Money may have something to do with it, and being regarded as a pundit; Wallace Stevens was really very much annoyed at being catalogued, categorized, and compelled to be scientific about what he was doing — to give satisfaction, to answer the teachers. He wouldn't do that. I think the same of William Carlos Williams. I think he wouldn't make so much of the great American language if he were plausible, and tractable. That's the beauty of it; he is willing to be reckless; if you can't be that, what's the point of the whole thing?

Marianne Moore

1965

INTERVIEWER: Was your mother a literary woman, Miss Moore?

MISS MOORE: She really was, but never conscious of being expert.

INTERVIEWER: Did she ever write poetry?

MISS MOORE: No. And I rather resisted the idea of it myself. I disliked poetry, anything partly true and improbably lengthened out to *sound* true. As a child, I had no use for it. We had to recite things in school, learn them by heart, and my mother would rehearse us. My brother memorized for school Bayard Taylor's "The Buffalo Hunt" — "Strike the tent, the sun has risen." And I had to learn something called "The Little Red Hen." The hen's cackle was imitated: "Cut-cut-cut-cudaw-cut." That — well — had no verisimilitude for me. I thought, Anything but awkward fictitiousness.

INTERVIEWER: When you left St. Louis for Carlisle, it must have been very upsetting for you. Did you leave a lot of friends behind?

MISS MOORE: Was too young. Journeys always had followed funerals, and as we started for Pittsburgh, I said to my mother, "Is this a funeral?" And she said, "No, no. We're going to visit your cousin Henry and cousin Annie."

INTERVIEWER: Did you know your father?

MISS MOORE: No. My father was an engineer, with his brother as consulting engineer — both graduates of Stevens Institute. Our mother lost him early, and we never saw him.

INTERVIEWER: But your mother and your brother and you were extremely close?

MISS MOORE: Yes, always were. And my grandfather was a most affectionate person.

INTERVIEWER: I remember you once said something about loneliness.

MISS MOORE: Did I?

INTERVIEWER: "The cure for loneliness is solitude."

MISS MOORE: I saw that in a French paper somewhere — in an essay a boy wrote that won a prize. I get plenty of recreation from books. I could keep you here weeks, talking about Augustus Buell's life of John Paul Jones and Kenneth Robinson's *Wilkie Collins,* and Thomas Bewick's *Memoir.* You don't have to have anyone with you — have the best company when reading those books.

INTERVIEWER: Did you ever come close to marriage?

MISS MOORE: No, but our butter-and-egg man, also our milk-man, persistently affected an admiration for me. The egg man was British and expressed things very well; had wonderful cheese, besides butter and eggs. He said one day, "Miss Moore, did you ever think of getting married?" "Of course," I said. "It's brought to your attention from time to time." "And you don't think well of it?" "Why certainly," I said. "It's the proper thing for everyone — but *me.*"

He said, "Why not?" I said, "I'm taking care of my mother. Am a little old, too, set in some ways, a little rigid and tyrannical." He said, "I don't like to say it, but your mother won't live forever." I said, "Well, I'm doing everything I can to help her to."

He said, "May I ask how old you are?" "Oh — fifty to sixty." He said, "You're not." I said, "I have no reason to deceive you." He sighed. "Well, you're a writer. You wouldn't need much, would you, but a desk and a certain amount of quiet?" I said, "I wouldn't need even that. Mr. X, you don't marry for practical reasons but for *im*practical reasons." He looked at the ceiling, paused and said, "I guess you're right."

Well, I think anyone aiming to marry can do it. I said to a college friend once, "What degree is it, Elsie, that you're working for now?" She said, with a smile, "M.R.S.," and achieved it almost simultaneously. I'm not matrimonially ambitious and am called a variety of things — a pterodactyl, said to "lead an enclosed life," diagnosed as "a case of arrested emotional development, but seeming to haunt places full of potential victims." Once I stopped a porter on the Canadian Pacific from folding my coat inside out, said, "The other way, porter. It's the *inside* I want clean. I'm a terrible old maid about my clothes." He said, "Well, if you are, Miss, it's your own fault."

I was arrested by some idealistic quixotry a while ago — and good sense on the part of my Gladys, my houseworker.

She said, "Mr. de G" — a widower she worked for, who has died — "asked me if I thought you would ever marry, and I said, 'No.' He said, 'Why not?' I said I didn't think you would ever leave your mother, and he said, 'I'd be glad to have her, too,' "

"*Generous*, trustful, idealistic man!" I said. "He doesn't know what he's escaping. He might find me a terrible disappointment."

Gladys: "Not with *your* disposition."

"And without even seeing me!"

Gladys: "He saw your picture — just now in the paper. He asked me the same thing once before, but I knew what you'd say — that it would just bother you — so I didn't tell you."

I said, "I so *thank* you for that."

Gladys said, "If you did want to marry him, it would be ideal for me. He's a wonderful man, everybody thinks so, and he's very easy to work for. He has a vacuum cleaner on every floor and cedar-lined closets, has just got a new Buick. He has a house in Vermont and goes to Buck Hills Falls in September. Every time he gives a party, he has the best caterer in Brooklyn, for I don't know about the drinks and the 'or dooves' — is that the word? What does it mean?"

"It's French. The *hors* means outside or beyond, and *oeuvre*, the main course."

"He has a gardener and Japanese lanterns when he's giving a party. I know you would like him."

I said, "Would never do, Gladys. He's formal. I cut corners — use my oldest dishes, am almost a miser, gobble my food at times. It's a wonder you work for me."

Gladys: "I'd work for you even if you didn't pay me. I've learned a great deal from you. Mrs. de G was fancier than you are, but I think you're happier."

INTERVIEWER: I am thinking of the passage in your poem "The Arctic Ox":

> While not incapable
> of courtship, they may find its
> servitude and flutter, too much
> like Procrustes' bed;
> so some decide to stay unwed.

MISS MOORE: David Seabury, the psychologist, said marriage could be a success if each is willing to contribute sixty percent and expect forty percent.

INTERVIEWER: Were any of your teachers, in high school and college, especially important to you?

MISS MOORE: Very, very; especially an art teacher, Miss Foster, who became Mrs. Beitzel. She taught German and drawing; made us think we liked teasels and milkweed pods, jointed grasses and twigs with buds that had died on the stem. We painted apples and onions and things like that. I would get a prize or two at the county fair and call for the money at the courthouse — a dollar or two dollars. We drew from plaster casts of famous subjects, the Discobolus, Saint Cecilia in low relief, a bunch of grapes, a fox's head. Miss Foster was delightful. She also taught us German. I failed it when I entered college, passed later.

There was Miss MacAllen, with a Latin class of two — Anna Hammond and me. I thought I was being killed with twenty lines of Latin as an assignment. When I got to college, it was pages — the most unjust thing I'd ever known, I felt; dogged along and then did fairly well.

Dr. Wheeler, at Bryn Mawr, gave me *one* credit — equivalent to about eighty in a standard of one hundred — but I didn't have a stand high enough in English entitling me to choose electives until my senior year. Then all that was left for me to elect was seventeenth-century imitative writing, with Georgiana Goddard King — Bishop Andrewes, Francis Bacon, Jeremy Taylor, and others. People say, "How terrible." It wasn't at all, was the very thing for me. Somewhat as Mr. Churchill acquired a love of well-shaped sentences from Gibbon and Macaulay. I was really fond of those sermons and the antique sentence structure.

INTERVIEWER: Do you have any idea of the contrast between schools when you were a girl and schools now?

MISS MOORE: Well, I was hand reared. I got almost too much individual attention. We weren't made to take enough responsibility. But lonely? If anyone ever was homesick, *I* was in college. I didn't know how to work. I liked to discuss everything with someone and be corrected, phrase by phrase. It was very painful. I was at sea two years. All I could do was elect courses in biology — the professors in that department were very humane, also exacting, detailed and pertinacious. Dr. Warren, head of the department and secretary of the faculty, favored me with terrifying advice. He said, "You have to stop going away on weekends and cutting classes." I said, "Why, Dr. Warren, I'm in deadly fear of missing something, never have been away for a weekend, never yet cut a class, *ever*. I'm just not grown up enough for these assignments; everyone is ahead of me. I seem a kind of juvenile."

I failed Italian twice, in fact, which I had thought would enable me to read Dante. I was contending with a psychological obstacle. I think the instructor distrusted my linguistic apperception, and well might. He had a little pointed beard and very black eyes, an expressionless, not very compassionate face, and intimidated me, scared me — but passed me. If I had failed again, I wouldn't have got a degree — have been demolished — a pariah.

Dr. Ashley came over from Columbia to give courses in law. I took torts, just because he was giving the course, as a relief from some of the more ferocious instructors. He was compassion itself. I seemed to need very humane handling, mothering by everyone — the case all my life, I think.

INTERVIEWER: Do you get humane handling here? My taxi driver called this part of Brooklyn "the jungle" and said he wouldn't even stop for a stop sign at night, with all his doors locked.

MISS MOORE: Violence! Until 1947, I didn't know what it was to be timid. I would come home from New York at one or two o'clock, if by chance I was as wild as that, come out of the subway and home without a fear. Once I was amazed when someone said, "Do you want me to go in with you to see if anyone might be in the house?" What a neurotic question! Someone in the house!

And now Gladys Berry, my houseworker, will say, "Never open the door without asking, 'Who is it?' Look through that little peephole and see who's there." Well, I've at last schooled myself to say, "Who is it?" And I feel so craven and degraded when they say, "Oh, it's Grace" or "This is your neighbor."

INTERVIEWER: What do you suppose is causing this violence?

MISS MOORE: I think it's a lack of sacrifice on the part of parents in bringing children up. A very lovely person doesn't attend the church I go to, but was at our Maundy Thursday dinner, and I was sitting beside her. We got to talking about danger, and she said she went out to mail a letter, and before she could get to the mailbox, seven or eight twelve-year-old boys surrounded her, then eight more from the other direction. And the ringleader said, "We want money."

She said, "Look at me. I have no pocketbook. I'm just mailing a letter."

He said, "Do you know I could slit your throat?"

She said, "But you aren't going to! What is the matter with you, talking like this? Do you want candy? What do you want *money* for?"

And then one of the group gave a whistle, a little shrill police whistle, and they all disappeared, vanished. That *is* frightening. Young boys not more than twelve years old.

INTERVIEWER: Do you ever think of moving away from this neighborhood?

MISS MOORE: No, I don't, although urged to nearly every day.

INTERVIEWER: Do you think the church is doing what it can about violence?

MISS MOORE: *Our* church is. Our pastor, George Litch Knight, is, and we have phenomenal young people in our educational center — "cultural center," they call it.

INTERVIEWER: What is your church?

MISS MOORE: Lafayette Avenue Presbyterian. Mr. Knight can stabilize the fabric of this neighborhood if anyone can. He has had mercury lights installed round the streets, and instead of a nest of drug addicts quite near, we have a rehabilitation center, like an Alcoholics Anonymous. Mr. Knight is found fault with for not marching with the Negroes at Selma; but he does mammoth work here for Negroes, Puerto Ricans, and Spanish that no one would be doing if he didn't.

INTERVIEWER: I know your St. Louis grandfather was a Presbyterian minister. Have you ever departed from Christian doctrine?

MISS MOORE: A big question! I would say no. I like what President Pusey said at Harvard commencement in 1957, was it? He said, "The quest for learning is not enough. . . . The university seeks to 'know' . . . but its concern is not only for widened knowledge. It cannot be produced by methodical thinking alone. . . . Beyond the intellectual quest there is another, where one steps out on the venture of faith." True, isn't it?

INTERVIEWER: Do you read the Bible very much?

MISS MOORE: I might say yes. I *think* I read it every day, but I don't. I have certain favorite portions of the Bible. I once attempted to learn by heart that chapter on faith in Hebrews (*picking up her Bible*): "Now faith is the substance of things hoped for, the evidence of things not seen." And at the end of Jude, the benediction: "Now unto him that is able to keep you from falling, and to present you faultless before the presence of his glory with exceeding joy, To the only wise God our Saviour, be glory and majesty, dominion and power, both now and forever." It *says* something.

INTERVIEWER: You found your Bible to hand, but with all the books around you, you must have trouble finding things. Yet it seems to me your apartment has changed since I was here four years ago.

MISS MOORE: Last year, my two nieces renovated it. I was going mad, had books piled up as tall as I am. I had no file case, had ancestral dishes all along the plate rail. The walls were very nearly the color of that bag. And I irresponsibly went off to England and Ireland with two friends.

In the first place, they thinned it. And my Gladys, as a present for me, took the dark varnish off the floors with steel wool and wood alcohol, let the floors stand a week, and then varnished them again. She looked quite radiant when I came in and saw it.

An arm of my French armchair had been weakened. One of my nieces took it away, had it mended and bought me a file case. The other put my strewn-about garments, that were crowded together or lay in boxes, in garment bags in my bedroom and in my little room. Now I'm a different person.

INTERVIEWER: How long were you in England and Ireland?

MISS MOORE: A good while. In England a month.

INTERVIEWER: Did you see T. S. Eliot before his death?

MISS MOORE: Yes, and it was an ideal visit. Dinner with Theresa Eliot, T. S. Eliot's sister-in-law, who was staying at an adjacent hotel as the Eliots' guest, and Peter and Mrs. du Sautoy. The Eliots had a driver, Ellis, and had him come for me and then for Theresa Eliot — Mrs. Henry Ware Eliot. For dinner there were individual little round yellow melons with green stripes, sweet like Cranshaw melons. The roast — lamb — was carved at a serving table by Valerie Eliot. For dessert there was a chocolate in ramekins — slightly bitter — of an ancestral recipe, with marzipan candies in the shapes of flowers and tiny vegetables, coffee and liqueurs in the drawing room. Among various souvenirs was a stout gray jug with a pair of jolly sailors depicted, arm in arm, ribbons flying from their caps — an anniversary gift to T. S. Eliot from Faber, of the publishing firm:

> If you loves me as I loves you,
> What a happy pair, we two.

Nothing somber about this dinner — punctuated by esprit such as "Wensleydale is not the Mozart of cheeses."

INTERVIEWER: You went to Ireland?

MISS MOORE: Yes. And my friends, Frances and Norvelle Browne, had friends in Ireland, who took me on trust — Mr. and Mrs. Austen Boyd. I was very perturbed, really was, about this; was told, "They specially want you, are crazy to have you." Perhaps said it more handsomely.

INTERVIEWER: Were you in Dublin?

MISS MOORE: Yes, at the Shelbourne. It seemed a kind of Anthony Trollope, romantic, leisurely town to me, Dublin. And what was that shop? Hodges Figgis and Company? Well, one of the best bookshops I've ever been in.

INTERVIEWER: Had you ever been in Ireland before?

MISS MOORE: No, I never had. My great-grandfather lived at Eleven Merrion Square. And we saw it. After we'd been to Trinity College, I looked at the map, and I saw that Merrion Square is just round the curve. So I led the way and exhausted my poor friends. We should have had a taxi.

INTERVIEWER: Let me go way back for a bit. You and your mother lived together in New York City, after Carlisle, Pennsylvania. What was your life like?

MISS MOORE: The perfect thing. I worked at the library diagonally across from the house. St. Luke's Place is part of Leroy Street, and it was a simple, unself-conscious part of town then. The Barbers — a classmate of mine and her sister — lived a few houses away, a prizefighter next door, and Genevieve Taggard lived there — other writers a little farther away.

INTERVIEWER: Did you ever see Edna St. Vincent Millay?

MISS MOORE: Yes, I knew her. She lived on — I forget. Houston Street? And then she moved to a little house in Bedford Street. She gave beautiful parties on the ground floor of this little house, and dressed picturesquely. I wasn't devoted enough to her work to press myself on her attention. Then she gave a program here in the Brooklyn Academy. I went to see her. And she was very romantic, had a long velvet cloak and gold slippers. Did it well. Then she read her piece about that dead kitten in a shoebox, covered with fleas. I was quite dismayed, felt affronted. In St. Louis, I was given an alligator, called him Tibby, and tended him as if he were a little deity, caught flies for him, could hardly bear it when he died. We had some cats and kittens, cloth ones and sometimes real ones. I put oval stones along the fence where they were buried, which had roses growing on the wire between our yard and the neighbor's. And white clematis. They had fragrant graves certainly and plenty of flowers. I couldn't bear that shoebox.

INTERVIEWER: What did you and your mother do for entertainment?

MISS MOORE: Every Wednesday afternoon, we went to City College to hear remarkable Dr. Baldwin, the organist. I would take *The Spectator* for my mother and me to read before the recital, Proust in French. I thought I understood it. We'd go very early, sit there in the great hall and listen to Dr. Baldwin. He gave a lecture once on early music — Pachelbel, Frescobaldi, Bach, and Handel — not Händl — and how organs were made. I was delighted with him. And we went now and then to the theater.

INTERVIEWER: What did you see that you liked especially?

MISS MOORE: I think one of the best things was *Love for Love*, by Congreve. They had a splendid cast. And we heard some music at Carnegie Hall. Paul Rosenfeld [a well-known music critic] was very thoughtful and kind, often would give us tickets. I remember we were painting our black floor; some boards were worn a little bare. Two tickets for the Rachmaninoff concert were telegraphed us. We were tired to death, but immediately renovated ourselves and went to the concert. The seats, I think, were in the third row, right under the keyboard, as it were. And we came home exhilarated — extremely refreshed. I'll never forget that.

INTERVIEWER: Have you ever played an instrument yourself?

MISS MOORE: I took piano lessons for years. My mother also had me take singing lessons — in Carlisle — not because I had a good voice, but because I didn't. She wanted me to know about it at least. I've given to Colby College in Maine some Abbott books that I'd been given as prizes. One "for faithfulness in practicing"! We had a Steinway, on which my mother had practiced ten hours a day. We gave it to a young girl when we moved to New York.

INTERVIEWER: When you worked in the library, was there at that time any anomaly in being a working woman?

MISS MOORE: Not to us. Some of my elegant English friends — not T. S. Eliot — looked on my library tasks as menial work; felt I ought to be secretary to a potentate or doing something rather enviable, instead of charging books and answering reference questions. Actually, I never did reference work — I was completely incompetent. How many women garment workers are there? In what year was so-and-so mayor? To find things like that, I consulted the assistant librarian.

We did many things. William Rose Benét and Elinor Wylie were prominent in our lives. And as for New York hospitalities, I didn't keep a record until 1921; but I have little diaries, about the width of three postage stamps, from 1921 until now. And I wrote down the names of friends we saw and of museums and galleries we went to.

INTERVIEWER: You were painting then, were you, for fun?

MISS MOORE: Well, always I'd done a little of it. Recently, my sister-in-law's sister invited us into the country in Connecticut, and I did some petunias, pink ones, on rather poor paper; but they were really accurate. They are somewhere. I'll find them, I know, when my nieces sort me out again. Yes, I love to paint and draw. I almost spoiled a vacation by trying to record things — draw a turtle and a sailboat, and copy drawings by Leonardo da Vinci. When a ship is tacking, you know, the sails take a beautiful slant.

INTERVIEWER: I know you have a number of diverse fascinations. Have you been going to baseball games at all lately?

MISS MOORE: No, a Mets and Pirates game in the spring of 1964 is the last thing I saw. Oh, yes, on television I saw Warren Spahn. It's wonderful what confidence he inspires. And he's not just a child, either.

INTERVIEWER: He's forty-three years old.

MISS MOORE: Yes. And I was delighted when the Cardinals won the World Series, because of Ken Boyer. He has shown great fortitude, I think. He had only *dreamed* of playing *in* the World Series, let alone hoped to *win*. I thought that rather touching. Cletis and he ought to be on the same team.

INTERVIEWER: Do you like to fly?

MISS MOORE: Oh, yes. Until I got timid when the large plane exploded in Brooklyn a year or two back. And there were several other freak accidents. I went to British Columbia by plane — my last long trip. And to San Francisco and Los Angeles three times — three or four times.

INTERVIEWER: What do you like about it?

MISS MOORE: Well, I like to sit close to the window, and if the plane flies below the clouds, you can see the fields, meadows, and so on. I like the conciseness of things in miniature.

INTERVIEWER: Have you had any more adventures like the time when the Ford Motor Company asked you to help name the Edsel?

MISS MOORE: No, but I seem embedded like a mosaic in "projects." I was invited this year to the Ford pavilion at the world's fair and received a little light-blue leather packet holding an admission to the Ford pavilion — nothing else.

INTERVIEWER: Do you like the Mustang — that name they've got for their new line?

MISS MOORE: I think it's a little ostentatious.

INTERVIEWER: As a car or as a name?

MISS MOORE: Oh, as a name.

INTERVIEWER: What's your favorite car on the road now?

MISS MOORE: Well, a Humber or a Cadillac! A small one — runabout.

INTERVIEWER: Do you like a Rolls-Royce?

MISS MOORE: Yes, but I've never driven one.

INTERVIEWER: You do drive, do you?

MISS MOORE: I have a license, no car.

INTERVIEWER: Let me make another backward jump. Did you go to many parties when you were a girl?

MISS MOORE: We had most scintillating parties at the home of Mrs. E. P. Howard, who was my mother's favorite classmate at the Mary Institute in St. Louis. She had any amount of imagination and would give parties with spun-sugar candy and favors.

INTERVIEWER: Did you have parties at Christmas?

MISS MOORE: I can remember when we moved to Carlisle. At Christmas, my mother would buy a little hemlock tree with tiny cones, and ground pine, and decorate the house. My brother was about eight or ten at the time and said, "Now it will never *grow* anymore." That weakened the romance of the little hemlock for our mother. We never had another, but plenty of holly and ground pine.

Mrs. Howard, who had the romantic parties, would take us out in a brougham with two horses with cropped tails, and we used to see swan boats on the lake in the park, like the ones there are in Boston. Well, she sent us to Carlisle at Christmas boxes that were almost like a party — a piece of jewelry for each, something to wear, pralines and fruitcake.

INTERVIEWER: What kind of food do you like, by the way?

MISS MOORE: Regular food.

INTERVIEWER: Do you remember the great meals of your life?

MISS MOORE: Oh, yes! Especially in Carlisle at the Norcrosses' — dinners and Thanksgivings. I don't remember ingenious dinners in St. Louis, although "Uncle Mermod" — Augustus S. Mermod, an elder in my grandfather's church — had beautiful meals.

INTERVIEWER: Do you like to cook?

MISS MOORE: Yes and no. I don't like to cook for myself, but I'll exert myself to exhaustion to cook a decent meal for someone who will really like it.

INTERVIEWER: What are your specialties?

MISS MOORE: Chops, browned potatoes, a funny kind of fruit and lemon and orange gelatin, with whipped cream. Silver and gold, I think it's called. Simple things like that. And I can stew fruit so it's rather appetizing. I rather think I *am* a good cook. I've never made a pie or layer cake. Can you make a pie?

INTERVIEWER: No, I'm afraid not.

MISS MOORE: Applesauce, sour apples. Oh, and I can do fish, smelts. I can't get scallops right. I can make a wonderful corn pudding; grate the corn and just let it congeal — a kind of corn custard, I suppose it is. You have to grate it with a sharp grater. I can brown apples and peaches — braise them on top of the stove.

INTERVIEWER: You're a fruit cook.

MISS MOORE: Yes. Pears in vinegar and spice, and green peaches. And tomatoes, pickled. Unnecessary things. I can make good scrambled eggs that don't toughen. I think the secret is water and milk, a little water and milk, and turn the heat off almost right away, so it can't get leathery. I've some remarkable dishes of thin steel, a broiler, a frying pan, a baking dish. They have an interstitial layer between the outside and the bottom, so that the things don't burn; like a fireless frying pan.

INTERVIEWER: Do you do most of your own cooking?

MISS MOORE: Yes, but I try to persuade my Gladys to assemble enough things on Tuesdays and Thursdays so I don't have to. She is very ambitious to provide me food ahead; will say, "You have *nothing* in the icebox. What would you like?" I'm fond of carrot juice. I have a juice-extracting machine, a blender and juice mixer. I can cook most vegetables — young spinach, zucchini, carrots. Carrots we used to hate, but very small ones — not cooked to death, either boiled or roasted — are very dainty, I think.

INTERVIEWER: I believe you like boxing, don't you?

MISS MOORE: On occasion. George Plimpton took me to the fight between Floyd Patterson and Chuvalo, had invited about twelve others, and we ate at the Coffee House Club and went from there to the fight. There were George Brown, the trainer, who gave George Plimpton and Ernest Hemingway lessons, and several others. And then Norman Mailer invited us to sit at his table at Toots Shor's. But there were so many of us we couldn't crowd the table and went to the back. The fight turned out just the way I wanted it to, though one of the guests was in sympathy with Chuvalo's wife, because she had kept her finger on the starter of the car — which didn't work — all the way across the country, so they could get there. There was nobody to fix it. She had to do something mechanical that should have been automatic. The guest thought the husband of any woman who'd do that ought to prevail.

I've written about Floyd Patterson twice, about *Victory over Myself,* his book. He's so honest. He said he wasn't in favor of boxing, but it was "a way out for my family." His mother had never had a new dress until he got to be a champion in the Olympics.

INTERVIEWER: You admire athletic dexterity so much. I wonder if you admire the dexterity of a dancer equally?

MISS MOORE: With reservations. Nureyev won me over almost entirely here in Brooklyn. He seemed automatically to just float through the air without effort. And I, like Arthur Mitchell, wrote a little piece about him. He's like an Egyptian — with legs in an A shape, the kind of scissor-legged Nubian we see incised on tombs — so clean-cut and decisive.

INTERVIEWER: Do you go to the circus when it comes to town?

MISS MOORE: I haven't been for some time.

INTERVIEWER: You used to like it, didn't you?

MISS MOORE: I do still. Paul Rosenfeld said, "I don't see how you can like anything so cruel," but animal anatomy is for me an irresistible study.

INTERVIEWER: What else is it about the circus you like?

MISS MOORE: Acrobats. Timing.

INTERVIEWER: Dexterity again?

MISS MOORE: Yes, but not the endurance marathons.

INTERVIEWER: How do you like going to universities to read your poems?

MISS MOORE: Well, I always have misgivings, for fear I'll be a disappointment. Am in dread of experts, at Harvard, say — or Johns Hopkins, Bryn Mawr, and Radcliffe — because they know so much. It oughtn't to be that way. One thing does impress me: People who have a whole cosmos in their heads seem to have an equiforce that doesn't hurry you or themselves, take lots of time for things, becoming lost in the topic. They aren't tied in knots; appear very gentle.

When I got home from St. John's University, I found in my briefcase this note, not signed: "How do you remain in the peaceable kingdom in an age of tigers in tanks and violence on the streets?" It was considerate not to sign it. I would say it's the excellent mentalities I mentioned, that come out of all I read.

One doesn't have to think every minute about sleuths and malefactors. One time on the Bowery, I saw a man with a knife creeping up on another. That's the only time I've ever seen Madame Tussaud in person. The car was going pretty fast, and I don't know what the end was. If I seem like those people who see a girl murdered and don't lift a finger, I am not. I think these books that I read are antidotes, in the absolute aptitudes for life shown; being lost in *things*, instead of in strained exhibitionism. That seems to me the peaceable kingdom of Insights.

INTERVIEWER: Are there things in the world around you that irritate you especially?

MISS MOORE: Yes. Verbal affectations and indirectness. My mother disliked "so," "such," and "very." But for naturalness, you have to use them a little. I tire of exaggeration and overemphasis, denigration and vaunted obscenity. Gratuitous insults in books and magazines.

INTERVIEWER: Do you read a newspaper every day?

MISS MOORE: Yes, indeed. I'm very dejected when I can't get my *Times;* was annoyed when the papers threatened to strike. I have to go out for it, too. I suppose I could have it delivered; but then I'd have to give someone the key, and am always going away.

Recently a boy *lit* one, set it on fire in the lobby downstairs. People don't notice the bell at the door — a telegram and so on — and he put a match to a lady's paper and also to our chair in the front. It's nothing of a lobby — it's a kind of sad entrance I have there — but we *had* a chair with upholstery.

INTERVIEWER: Do you get magazines regularly?

MISS MOORE: I've subscribed for *Encounter,* a British magazine — just for this year, but like it and may keep on. Stephen Spender, the co-editor, went to a great deal of trouble for me when we were in London last year — my friends the Brownes and I. He chanced to say, "Have you seen Dame Edith?" Edith Sitwell, you know.

And I said, "No, wish I *could* see her."

He said, "Well, I don't know just where she is, but I can find out and shall let you know."

He did several things of that sort. But before he let me know, Dame Edith wrote to me saying she was not at all well but knew of my being in town and wanted to see me if I could come. It was not like Walter Sickert, who told Denton Welch, as Dame Edith says, "Come again when you have a little less time!"

It was arranged that I come about four o'clock on Sunday afternoon. The taximan I chanced to get had worked in the Keats Museum, Hampstead, diagonally across from Twenty Keats Grove, Dame Edith's somewhat newly acquired house and garden, surrounded by a white picket fence. I persuaded my young taximan to wait, ring for me after ten minutes, or fifteen at most, and take me home — the route to Keats Grove being circuitous — strongly determined not to be hospitably persuaded to overstay.

I unlatched the gate and, passing a tall rose in bloom and some small white bells, saw a blue-gray door between a glossy-leafed laurestinus on the left and a tall, exceedingly prickly holly bush on the right. Presently I rang the bell, and Miss Farquhar, Dame Edith's nurse, graciously cordial, seated me in a small front drawing room beside calf-bound books. At right angles, more similar sets were at the left of the fireplace, over which hung a three-quarter portrait in oil of Dame Edith, which had been rescued from where it had been hidden behind a panel in a house during war days in Paris, a careful profile in pale tones, contrasting handsomely with Dame Edith's pale-gold hair and chiseled features.

A large orange cat slowly appeared from the further room, examined me, but before I could more than lay my hand on his head, returned to seclusion. He was followed by a thin black cat — less curious — who sauntered toward stairs opening at the right, to which Miss Farquhar soon conducted me. There was a Helen Hokinson cartoon on the stair wall — of ladies fearlessly social — which Miss Farquhar said Dame Edith thought accurately inane.

I entered a large, square room with two windows on the garden I had seen and a round table with a rose on it, by which Dame Edith, in bed, was sitting erect and greeted me with warmth that had the emphasis of health, and her customary firm accents of interest and unself-pity.

After she had inquired if my friends and I were comfortable at Durrant's, our hotel, and I had inquired the meaning of adhesive tape on her left forefinger, she explained that pneumonia, which settled in the finger, "had been induced by a reception fortissimo, unduly prolonged." This infirmity had been a scourge for months.

I inquired about Sir Osbert's summer address. Dame Edith said Renishaw and encouraged me to send him my "Arctic Ox," which I had not known where to send. We talked about Montegufoni, the Sitwells' castle near Florence, and I referred to the benevolent Guido, who had taken my friends and me about the castle when we were in Italy during Sir Osbert's absence, and had shown us a Book of Hours distant view of blue hills and yellow harvest fields, a promenade of lemon pots of terra-cotta leading to a frog grotto. They were man-size frogs, conversing — one was seated on an ottoman — in stone. I recalled for Dame Edith how Guido, having escorted us to our car, said as I got in, "Signora, may the Blessed Virgin watch over you wherever you are and in all that you do" — the words in Italian were enunciated with true messianic solemnity.

Miss Salter, Dame Edith's secretary, came in and regretted not having arrived in time to show me the garden. She did, however, as I left, saying she hoped Dame Edith would be able before long to get the sun in a little shelter at the far end of the walk.

I rose to go, but Dame Edith detained me for tea, which Miss Farquhar got. Dame Edith did not drink her own while I drank mine. She then said firmly, "I'll see you in New York," as the young taximan rang again. After my glimpse of the garden, I entered the little black taxi — *grateful* that valiant Dame Edith had with her the ministrants I had met, and that her nephew Francis steadied her courage as isolated visits from affectionate friends cannot do — are mere tests of stamina.

INTERVIEWER: Have you a favorite person in history?

MISS MOORE: I believe I have. Leonardo da Vinci, and I like Sir Isaac Newton.

INTERVIEWER: Have you a favorite statesman?

MISS MOORE: Well, I wrote a piece — I'm ashamed to mention it; I don't know that it's anything but platitudes — on Mr. Churchill, Sir Winston. I got very excited reading *My Early Life*. Perhaps my hero is feminine — Clementine Churchill — in winning "the Battle for Britain of her husband's health."

INTERVIEWER: Do you find yourself thinking about death much?

MISS MOORE: No. Do you?

INTERVIEWER: I sometimes do.

MISS MOORE: I would like to be cremated, whatever comes. My brother says that on my mother's birthday years ago, he remembered asking her, "Do you feel well?" And she said, "Yes, very well, but I don't want to live to a great old age." I feel that way, too. I can't imagine complete helplessness. I'm not thought likely to die of a heart attack. I rather wish I could, but my heart is supposed to be good.

I really *have* been near death a couple of times and was disgusted because it was my own fault. I got myself exhausted from overwork. You sent me a plant. Do you remember it? With little oblong yellow freckles on bright green leaves. It's alive and thriving. I let Gladys take it to her daughter, who wanted one. I couldn't care for it and sun it then. I ought never to have been in the hospital, but I got enteritis and thought, to cure it, I wouldn't drink water, got dehydrated, and then I had no appetite. I thought I knew everything about hygiene — *thought* I did. But, no! And one day, Doctor Laf Loofy, my Syrian doctor, said, "Now, I've been telling you I wanted you in the hospital. You're going today. How soon can you be ready?" And then, "Three o'clock? In an hour?"

"No," I said. "I'll have to have three hours to get things together." I was too weak to get ready. If I hadn't been really determined, I could have died right then, I was so devitalized. A disgrace.

INTERVIEWER: You're fortunate to have continued as an active poet. So many stop.

MISS MOORE: Yes? People study my face and say, "Do *you* still *write?*" Of course I do. Why not?

INTERVIEWER: Don't you have difficulty in getting down to it? Writing? Your phone must ring a good deal.

MISS MOORE: Every other minute, and I don't like to insult people. My brother says, "Sometimes you have to have paws and teeth and know when to use them." Well, I am accused of never knowing how to say no. I *beg* to be neglected — but everyone with an objective is ruthless. And one thing I don't like is to have them *think* for me, to be overreached and boxed in, so that "no" is without meaning.

INTERVIEWER: Yet the quality of being without fear, you said once, helped you all when you edited *The Dial.*

MISS MOORE: I did? Weston McDaniel said to me one time, "You must be a very timid person, you're so brave." True or not, I can tremble and shrink.

One of my neighbors asked, "Before you give a program, are you nervous?" And her sister said, "Why, of course she is. Caruso said he wouldn't be any good if he didn't feel nervous before every concert."

INTERVIEWER: Have you a favorite poem of your own?

MISS MOORE: Perhaps. I like my "Arctic Ox" as well as anything.

INTERVIEWER: Have you other poems you could name that come to mind?

MISS MOORE: I think "What Are Years?" is one of my solider compositions. I like "His Shield" and "The Buffalo" — the managing of the rhythms. I think "What Are Years?" is the best done, best written.

INTERVIEWER: Does anyone ever ask you to define poetry?

MISS MOORE: The art teacher at St. John's did. I couldn't answer. But afterward I wrote for Professor Galassi to give the lady: "I would say that it's words used with a sense of heightened consciousness." Answering a pedant, Stephen Spender said, "In prose, you might say a thing seven different ways. In poetry, the words are not replaceable." I liked that.

In a poem, the words should be as pleasing to the ear as the meaning is to the mind.

Ezra Pound

INTERVIEWER: You are nearly through the *Cantos* now, and this sets me to wondering about their beginning. In 1916 you wrote a letter in which you talked about trying to write a version of Andreas Divus in *Seafarer* rhythms. This sounds like a reference to *Canto I*. Did you begin the *Cantos* in 1916?

POUND: I began the *Cantos* about 1904, I suppose. I had various schemes, starting in 1904 or 1905. The problem was to get a form — something elastic enough to take the necessary material. It had to be a form that wouldn't exclude something merely because it didn't fit. In the first sketches, a draft of the present first *Canto* was the third.

Obviously you haven't got a nice little road map such as the Middle Ages possessed of Heaven. Only a musical form would take the material, and the Confucian universe as I see it is a universe of interacting strains and tensions.

INTERVIEWER: Had your interest in Confucius begun in 1904?

POUND: No, the first thing was this: You had six centuries that hadn't been packaged. It was a question of dealing with material that wasn't in the *Divina Commedia*. Hugo did a *Légende des Siècles* that wasn't an evaluative affair but just bits of history strung together. The problem was to build up a circle of reference — taking the modern mind to be the medieval mind with wash after wash of classical culture poured over it since the Renaissance. That was the psyche, if you like. One had to deal with one's own subject.

INTERVIEWER: It must be thirty or thirty-five years since you have written any poetry outside the *Cantos,* except for the Alfred Venison poems. Why is this?

POUND: I got to the point where, apart from an occasional lighter impulse, what I had to say fitted the general scheme. There has been a good deal of work thrown away because one is attracted to an historic character and then finds that he doesn't function within my form, doesn't embody a value needed. I have tried to make the *Cantos* historic (Vid. G. Giovannini, re relation history to tragedy. Two articles ten years apart in some philological periodical, not source material but relevant) but not fiction. The material one wants to fit in doesn't always work. If the stone isn't hard enough to maintain the form, it has to go out.

INTERVIEWER: When you write a *Canto* now, how do you plan it? Do you follow a special course of reading for each one?

POUND: One isn't necessarily reading. One is working on the life vouchsafed, I should think. I don't know about method. The *what* is so much more important than how.

INTERVIEWER: Yet when you were a young man, your interest in poetry concentrated on form. Your professionalism, and your devotion to technique, became proverbial. In the last thirty years, you have traded your interest in form for an interest in content. Was the change on principle?

POUND: I think I've covered that. Technique is the test of sincerity. If a thing isn't worth getting the technique to say, it is of inferior value. All that must be regarded as exercise. Richter in his *Treatise on Harmony,* you see, says, "These are the principles of harmony and counterpoint; they have nothing whatever to do with composition, which is quite a separate activity." The statement, which somebody made, that you couldn't write Provençal canzoni forms in English, is false. The question of whether it was advisable or not was another matter. When there wasn't the criterion of natural language without inversion, those forms were natural, and they realized them with music. In English the music is of a limited nature. You've got Chaucer's French perfection, you've got Shakespeare's Italian perfection, you've got Campion and Lawes. I don't think I got around to this kind of form until I got to the choruses in the *Trachiniae.* I don't know that I got to anything at all, really, but I thought it was an extension of the gamut. It may be a delusion. One was always interested in the implication of change of pitch in the union of *motz et son,* of the word and melody.

INTERVIEWER: Does writing the *Cantos,* now, exhaust all of your technical interest, or does the writing of translations, like the *Trachiniae* you just mentioned, satisfy you by giving you more fingerwork?

POUND: One sees a job to be done and goes at it. The *Trachi-*

niae came from reading the Fenollosa Noh plays for the new edition, and from wanting to see what would happen to a Greek play, given that same medium and the hope of its being performed by the Minorou company. The sight of Cathay in Greek, looking like poetry, stimulated crosscurrents.

INTERVIEWER: Do you think that free verse is particularly an American form? I imagine that William Carlos Williams probably does, and thinks of the iambic as English.

POUND: I like Eliot's sentence: "No verse is *libre* for the man who wants to do a good job." I think the best free verse comes from an attempt to get back to quantitative meter.

I suppose it may be *un-English* without being specifically *American*. I remember Cocteau playing drums in a jazz band as if it were a very difficult mathematical problem.

I'll tell you a thing that I think *is* an American form, and that is the Jamesian parenthesis. You realize that the person you are talking to hasn't got the different steps, and you go back over them. In fact the Jamesian parenthesis has immensely increased now. That I think is something that is definitely American. The struggle that one has when one meets another man who has had a lot of experience to find the point where the two experiences touch, so that he really knows what you are talking about.

INTERVIEWER: Your work includes a great range of experience, as well as of form. What do you think is the greatest quality a poet can have? Is it formal, or is it a quality of thinking?

POUND: I don't know that you can put the needed qualities in hierarchic order, but he must have a continuous curiosity, which of course does not make him a writer, but if he hasn't got that he will wither. And the question of doing anything about it depends on a persistent energy. A man like Agassiz is never bored, never tired. The transit from the reception of stimuli to the recording, to the correlation, that is what takes the whole energy of a lifetime.

INTERVIEWER: Do you think that the modern world has changed the ways in which poetry can be written?

POUND: There is a lot of competition that never was there before. Take the serious side of Disney, the Confucian side of Disney. It's in having taken an ethos, as he does in *Perri*, that squirrel film, where you have the values of courage and tenderness asserted in a way that everybody can understand. You have got an absolute genius there. You have got a greater correlation of nature than you have had since the time of Alexander the Great. Alexander gave orders to the fishermen that if they found out anything about fish that was interesting, a specific thing, they were to tell Aristotle. And with that correlation you got ichthyology to the scientific point where it stayed for two thousand years. And now one has got with the camera an *enormous* correlation of particulars. That capacity for making contact is a tremendous challenge to literature. It throws up the question of what needs to be done and what is superfluous.

INTERVIEWER: Maybe it's an opportunity, too. When you were a young man in particular, and even through the *Cantos*, you changed your poetic style again and again. You have never been content to stick anywhere. Were you consciously looking to extend your style? Does the artist *need* to keep moving?

POUND: I think the artist *has* to keep moving. You are trying to render life in a way that won't bore people and you are trying to put down what you see.

INTERVIEWER: I wonder what you think of contemporary movements. I haven't seen remarks of yours about poets more recent than Cummings, except for Bunting and Zukofsky. Other things have occupied you, I suppose.

POUND: One can't read everything. I was trying to find out a number of historic facts, and you can't see out of the back of your head. I do not think there is any record of a man being able to criticize the people that come after him. It is a sheer question of the amount of reading one man can do.

I don't know whether it is his own or whether it is a gem that he collected, but at any rate one of the things Frost said in London in 19— whenever it was — 1912, was this: "Summary of prayer: 'Oh God, pay attention to *me*.' " And that is the approach of younger writers — not to divinity exactly! — and in general one has to limit one's reading to younger poets who are recommended by at least one other younger poet, as a sponsor. Of course a routine of that kind could lead to conspiracy, but at any rate . . .

As far as criticizing younger people, one has not the time to make a *comparative* estimate. People one is learning from, one does measure one against the other. I see a stirring now, but . . . For *general* conditions there is undoubtedly a *liveliness*. And Cal [Robert] Lowell is very good.

INTERVIEWER: You have given advice to the young all your life. Do you have anything special to say to them now?

POUND: To improve their curiosity and not to fake. But that is not enough. The mere registering of bellyache and the mere dumping of the ashcan is not enough. In fact the University of Pennsylvania student *Punchbowl* used to have as its motto, "Any damn fool can be spontaneous."

INTERVIEWER: You once wrote that you had four useful hints from living literary predecessors, who were Thomas Hardy, William Butler Yeats, Ford Madox Ford, and Robert Bridges. What were these things?

POUND: Bridges' was the simplest. Bridges' was a warning against homophones. Hardy's was the degree to which he would concentrate on the subject matter, not on the manner. Ford's in general was the *freshness* of language. And Yeats you say was the fourth? Well, Yeats by 1908 had written simple lyrics in which there were no departures from the natural order of words.

INTERVIEWER: You were secretary to Yeats in 1913 and 1914. What sort of thing did you do for him?

POUND: Mostly reading aloud. Doughty's *Dawn in Britain*, and so on. And wrangling, you see. The Irish like contradiction. He tried to learn fencing at forty-five, which was amusing. He would thrash around with the foils like a whale. He sometimes gave the impression of being even a worse idiot than I am.

INTERVIEWER: There is an academic controversy about your influence on Yeats. Did you work over his poetry with him? Did you cut any of his poems in the way you cut "The Waste Land"?

POUND: I don't think I can remember anything like that. I am sure I objected to particular expressions. Once out at Rapallo I tried for God's sake to prevent him from printing a thing. I told him it was rubbish. All he did was print it with a preface saying that I *said* it was rubbish.

I remember when Tagore had taken to doodling on the edge of his proofs, and they told him it was art. There was a show of it in Paris. "Is this art?" Nobody was very keen on these doodlings, but of course so many people lied to him.

As far as the change in Yeats goes, I think that Ford Madox Ford might have some credit. Yeats never would have taken advice from Ford, but I think that Fordie helped him, via me, in trying to get toward a natural way of writing.

INTERVIEWER: Did anyone ever help you with your work as extensively as you have helped others? I mean by criticism or cutting.

POUND: Apart from Fordie, rolling on the floor undecorously and holding his head in his hands, and groaning on one occasion, I don't think anybody helped me through my manuscripts. Ford's stuff appeared too loose then, but he led the fight against tertiary archaisms.

INTERVIEWER: You have been closely associated with visual artists — Gaudier-Brzeska and Wyndham Lewis in the vorticist movement, and later Picabia, Picasso, and Brancusi. Has this had anything to do with you as a writer?

POUND: I don't believe so. One looked at paintings in galleries and one might have found out something. "The Game of Chess" poems shows the effect of modern abstract art, but vorticism from my angle was a renewal of the sense of construction. Color went dead and Manet and the impressionists revived it. Then what I would call the sense of form was blurred, and vorticism, as distinct from cubism, was an attempt to revive the sense of form — the form you had in Piero della Francesca's *De Prospettive Pingendi*, his treatise on the proportions and composition. I got started on the idea of comparative forms before I left America. A fellow named Poole did a book on composition. I did have *some* things in my head when I got to London, and I *had* heard of Catullus before I heard about modern French poetry. There's a bit of biography that might be rectified.

INTERVIEWER: I have wondered about your literary activities in America before you came to Europe. When did you first come over, by the way?

POUND: In 1898. At the age of twelve. With my great-aunt.

INTERVIEWER: Were you reading French poetry then?

POUND: No, I suppose I was reading Grey's "Elegy in a Country Churchyard" or something. No, I wasn't reading French poetry. I was starting Latin next year.

INTERVIEWER: You entered college at fifteen, I believe?

POUND: I did it to get out of drill at military academy.

INTERVIEWER: How did you get started being a poet?

POUND: My grandfather on one side used to correspond with the local bank president in verse. My grandmother on the other side and her brothers used verse back and forth in their letters. It was taken for granted that anyone would write it.

INTERVIEWER: Did you learn anything in your university studies which helped you as a poet? I think you were a student for seven or eight years.

POUND: Only six. Well, six years and four months. I was writing all the time, especially as a graduate student. I started in freshman year studying Layamon's *Brut* and Latin. I got into college on my Latin; it was the only reason they *did* take me in. I did have the idea, at fifteen, of making a general survey. Of course whether I was or wasn't a poet was a matter for the gods to decide, but at least it was up to me to find out what had been done.

INTERVIEWER: You taught for four months only, as I remember. But you know that now the poets in America are mostly teachers. Do you have any ideas on the connection of teaching in the university with writing poetry?

POUND: It is the economic factor. A man's got to get in his rent somehow.

INTERVIEWER: How did you manage all the years in Europe?

POUND: Oh, God. A miracle of God. My income gained from October 1914 to October 1915 was £42.10.0. That figure is clearly engraved on my memory. . . .

I was never too good a hand at writing for the magazines. I once did a satirical article for *Vogue*, I think it was. On a painter whom I did not admire. They thought I had got just the right tone and then Verhaeren died and they asked me to do a note on Verhaeren. And I went down and said, "You want a nice bright snappy obituary notice of the gloomiest man in Europe."

"What, gloomy cuss, was he?"

"Yes," I said. "He wrote about peasants."

"Peasants or pheasants?"

"Peasants."

"Oh, I don't think we ought to touch it."

That is the way I crippled my earning capacity by not knowing enough to keep quiet.

INTERVIEWER: I read somewhere — I think you wrote it — that you once tried to write a novel. Did that get anywhere?

POUND: It got, fortunately, into the fireplace at Langham Place. I think there were two attempts, before I had any idea whatever of what a novel ought to be.

INTERVIEWER: Did they have anything to do with "Hugh Selwyn Mauberley"?

POUND: These were long before "Mauberley." "Mauberley" was later, but it *was* the definite attempt to get the novel cut down to the size of verse. It really is "Contacts and Life." Wadsworth seemed to think "Propertius" difficult because it was about Rome, so one applied the same thing to the contemporary outside.

INTERVIEWER: You said it was Ford who helped you toward a natural language, didn't you? Let's get back to London again.

POUND: One was hunting for a simple and natural language, and Ford was ten years older, and accelerated the process toward it. It was a continual discussion of that sort of thing. Ford knew the best of the people who were there before him, you see, and he had nobody to play with until Wyndham and I and my generation came along. He was definitely in opposition to the dialect, let us say, of Lionel Johnson and Oxford.

INTERVIEWER: You were for two or three decades at least in contact with all of the leading writers in English of the day and a lot of the painters, sculptors, and musicians. Of all these people, who were the most stimulating to you as an artist?

POUND: I saw most of Ford and Gaudier, I suppose. I should think that the people that I have written about were the most important to me. There isn't much revision to make there.

I may have limited my work, and limited the interest in it, by concentrating on the particular intelligence of particular people, instead of looking at the complete character and personality of my friends. Wyndham Lewis always claimed that I never *saw* people because I never noticed how wicked they were, what SOBs they were. I wasn't the least interested in the vices of my friends, but in their intelligence.

INTERVIEWER: Was James a kind of a standard for you in London?

POUND: When he died one felt there was no one to ask about anything. Up to then one felt someone knew. After I was sixty-five

I had great difficulty in realizing that I was older than James had been when I met him.

INTERVIEWER: Did you know Remy de Gourmont personally? You've mentioned him frequently.

POUND: Only by letter. There was one letter, which Jean de Gourmont also considered important, where he said, *"Franche-ment d'écrire ce qu'on pense, seul plaisir d'un écrivain."*

INTERVIEWER: It is amazing that you could come to Europe and quickly associate yourself with the best living writers. Had you been aware of any of the poets writing in America before you left? Was Robinson anything to you?

POUND: Aiken tried to sell me Robinson and I didn't fall. This was in London too. I then dragged it out of him that there was a guy at Harvard doing funny stuff. Mr. Eliot turned up a year or so later.

No, I should say that about 1900, you had Carman and Hovey, Carwine and Vance Cheney. The impression then was that the American stuff wasn't *quite* as good as the English at any point. And you had Mosher's pirated editions of the English stuff. No, I went to London because I thought Yeats knew more about poetry than anybody else. I made my life in London by going to see Ford in the afternoons and Yeats in the evenings. By mentioning one to the other one could always start a discussion. That was the exercise. I went to study with Yeats and found that Ford disagreed with him. So then I kept on disagreeing with *them* for twenty years.

INTERVIEWER: In 1942, you wrote that you and Eliot disagreed by calling each other protestants. I wonder when you and Eliot diverged.

POUND: Oh, Eliot and I started diverging from the beginning. The fun of an intellectual friendship is that you diverge on something or other and agree on a few points. Eliot, having had the Christian patience of tolerance all his life and so forth, and working very hard, must have found me very trying. We started disagreeing about a number of things from the time we met. We also agreed on a few things and I suppose both of us must have been right about something or other.

INTERVIEWER: Well, was there a point at which poetically and intellectually you felt further apart than you had been?

POUND: There's the whole problem of the relation of Christianity to Confucianism, and there's the whole problem of the different brands of Christianity. There is the struggle for orthodoxy — Eliot for the Church, me gunning round for particular theologians. In one sense Eliot's curiosity would appear to have been focused on a smaller number of problems. Even that is too much to say. The actual outlook of the experimental generation was all a question of the private ethos.

INTERVIEWER: Do you think that as poets you felt a divergence on technical grounds, unrelated to your subject matter?

POUND: I should think the divergence was first a difference in subject matter. He has undoubtedly got a natural language. In the language in the plays, he seems to me to have made a very great contribution. And in being able to make contact with an extant milieu, and an extant state of comprehension.

INTERVIEWER: That reminds me of the two operas — *Villon* and *Cavalcanti* — which you wrote. How did you come to compose music?

POUND: One wanted the word *and* the tune. One wanted great poetry *sung,* and the technique of the English opera libretto was not satisfactory. One wanted, with the quality of the texts of Villon and of Cavalcanti, to get something more extended than the single lyric. That's all.

INTERVIEWER: I suppose your interest in words to be sung was especially stimulated by your study of Provence. Do you feel that the discovery of Provençal poetry was your greatest breakthrough? Or perhaps the Fenollosa manuscripts?

POUND: The Provençal began with a very early interest, so that it wasn't really a discovery. And the Fenollosa was a windfall and one struggled against one's ignorance. One had the inside knowledge of Fenollosa's notes and the ignorance of a five-year-old child.

INTERVIEWER: How did Mrs. Fenollosa happen to hit upon you?

POUND: Well, I met her at Sarojini Naidu's and she said that Fenollosa had been in opposition to all the profs and academes, and she had seen some of my stuff and said I was the only person who could finish up these notes as Ernest would have wanted them done. Fenollosa saw what needed to be done but he didn't have time to finish it.

INTERVIEWER: Let me change the subject now, and ask you

some questions which are more biographical than literary. I have read that you were born in Hailey, Idaho, in 1885. I suppose it must have been pretty rough out there then?

POUND: I left at the age of eighteen months and I don't remember the roughness.

INTERVIEWER: You did not grow up in Hailey?

POUND: I did not grow up in Hailey.

INTERVIEWER: What was your family doing there when you were born?

POUND: Dad opened the Government Land Office out there. I grew up near Philadelphia. The suburbs of Philadelphia.

INTERVIEWER: The wild Indian from the West then was not . . . ?

POUND: The wild Indian from the West is apocryphal, and the assistant assayer of the mint was not one of the most noted bandits of the frontier.

INTERVIEWER: I believe it's *true* that your grandfather built a railroad. What was the story of that?

POUND: Well, he got the railroad into Chippewa Falls, and they ganged up on him and would not let him buy any rails. That's in the *Cantos*. He went up to the north of New York State and found some rails on an abandoned road up there, bought them and had them shipped out, and then used his credit with the lumberjacks to get the road going to Chippewa Falls. What one learns in the home one learns in a way one doesn't learn in school.

INTERVIEWER: Does your particular interest in coinage start from your father's work at the mint?

POUND: You can go on for a long time on that. The government offices were more informal then, though I don't know that any other kids got in and visited. Now the visitors are taken through glass tunnels and see things from a distance, but you could then be taken around in the smelting room and see the gold piled up in the safe. You were offered a large bag of gold and told you could have it if you could take it away with you. You couldn't lift it.

When the Democrats finally came back in, they recounted all the silver dollars, four million dollars in silver. All the bags had rotted in these enormous vaults, and they were heaving it into the counting machines with shovels bigger than coal shovels. This spectacle of coin being shoveled around like it was litter — these fellows naked to the waist shoveling it around in the gas flares — things like that strike your imagination.

Then there's the whole technique of making metallic money. First, the testing of the silver is much more tricky than testing gold. Gold is simple. It is weighed, then refined and weighed again. You can tell the grade of the ore by the relative weights. But the test for silver is a cloudy solution; the accuracy of the eye in measuring the thickness of the cloud is an aesthetic perception, like the critical sense. I like the idea of the *fineness* of the metal, and it moves by analogy to the habit of testing verbal manifestations. At that time, you see, gold bricks, and specimens of iron pyrites mistaken for gold, were brought up to Dad's office. You heard the talk about the last guy who bought a gold brick and it turned out to be fool's gold.

INTERVIEWER: I know you consider monetary reform the key to good government. I wonder by what process you moved from aesthetic problems toward governmental ones. Did the Great War, which slaughtered so many of your friends, do the moving?

POUND: The Great War came as a surprise, and certainly to see the English — these people who had never done anything — get hold of themselves, fight it, was immensely impressive. But as soon as it was over they went dead, and then one spent the next twenty years trying to prevent the Second War. I can't say exactly where my study of government started. I think the *New Age* office helped me to see the war not as a separate event but as part of a system, one war after another.

INTERVIEWER: One point of connection between literature and politics which you make in your writing interests me particularly. In the *ABC of Reading* you say that good writers are those who keep the language efficient, and that this is their function. You disassociate this function from party. Can a man of the wrong party use language efficiently?

POUND: Yes. That's the whole trouble! A gun is just as good, no matter who shoots it.

INTERVIEWER: Can an instrument which is orderly be used to create disorder? Suppose good language is used to forward bad government? Doesn't bad government make bad language?

POUND: Yes, but bad language is *bound* to make in addition bad government, whereas good language is *not* bound to make bad government. That again is clear Confucius: If the orders aren't clear they can't be carried out. Lloyd George's laws were such a mess, the lawyers never knew what they meant. And Talleyrand proclaimed that they changed the meaning of words between one conference and another. The means of communication breaks down, and that of course is what we are suffering now. We are enduring the drive to work on the subconscious without appealing to the reason. They repeat a trade name with the music a few times, and then repeat the music without it so that the music will give you the name. I think of the *assault*. We suffer from the use of language to conceal thought and to withhold all vital and direct answers. There is the definite use of propaganda, forensic language, merely to conceal and mislead.

INTERVIEWER: Where do ignorance and innocence end and the chicanery begin?

POUND: There is natural ignorance and there is artificial ignorance. I should say at the present moment the artificial ignorance is about eighty-five percent.

INTERVIEWER: What kind of action can you hope to take?

POUND: The only chance for victory over the brainwash is the right of every man to have his ideas judged one at a time. You never get clarity as long as you have these package words, as long as a word is used by twenty-five people in twenty-five different ways. That seems to me to be the first fight, if there is going to be any intellect left.

It is doubtful whether the individual soul is going to be allowed to survive at all. Now you get a Buddhist movement with everything *except* Confucius taken into it. An Indian Circe of negation and dissolution.

We are up against so many mysteries. There is the problem of benevolence, the point at which benevolence has ceased to be operative. Eliot says that they spend their time trying to imagine systems so perfect that nobody will have to be good. A lot of questions asked in that essay of Eliot's cannot be dodged, like the question of whether there need be any change from the Dantesquan scale of values or the Chaucerian scale of values. If so, how much? People who have lost reverence have lost a great deal. That was where I split with Tiffany Thayer. All these large words fall into clichés.

There is the mystery of the scattering, the fact that the people who presumably understand each other are geographically scattered. A man who fits in his milieu, as Frost does, is to be considered a happy man.

Oh, the luck of a man like Mavrocordato, who is in touch with other scholars, so that there is somewhere where he can verify a point! Now for certain points where I want verification there is a fellow named Dazzi in Venice that I write to and he comes up with an answer, as it might be about the forged Donation of Constantine. But the advantages which were supposed to inhere in the university — where there are other people to *contrôl** opinion or to *contrôl* the data — were very great. It is crippling not to have had them. Of course I have been trying over a ten-year period to get any member of an American faculty to mention any other member of his same faculty, in his own department or outside it, whose intelligence he respects or with whom he will discuss serious matters. In one case the gentleman regretted that someone else had *left* the faculty.

I have been unable to get straight answers out of people on what appeared to me to be vital questions. That may have been due to my violence or obscurity with which I framed the questions. Often, I think, so-called obscurity is not obscurity in the language but in the other person's not being able to make out *why* you are saying a thing. For instance the attack on *Endymion* was complicated because Gifford and company couldn't see why the deuce Keats was doing it.

Another struggle has been the struggle to keep the value of a local and particular character, of a particular culture in this awful maelstrom, this awful avalanche toward uniformity. The whole fight is for the conservation of the individual soul. The enemy is the suppression of history; against us is the bewildering propaganda and brainwash, luxury and violence. Sixty years ago, poetry was the poor man's art: a man off on the edge of the wilderness, or Frémont, going off with a Greek text in his pocket. A man who wanted the best could have it on a lonely farm. Then there was the cinema, and now television.

---

* Pound indicates that he is using the French *contrôler:* "to verify, check information, a fact."

INTERVIEWER: The political action of yours that everybody remembers is your broadcasts from Italy during the war. When you gave these talks, were you conscious of breaking the American law?

POUND: No, I was completely surprised. You see I had that promise. I was given the freedom of the microphone twice a week. "He will not be asked to say anything contrary to his conscience or contrary to his duty as an American citizen." I thought that covered it.

INTERVIEWER: Doesn't the law of treason talk about "giving aid and comfort to the enemy," and isn't the enemy the country with whom we are at war?

POUND: I thought I was fighting for a constitutional point. I mean to say, I may have been completely nuts, but I certainly *felt* that it wasn't committing treason.

Wodehouse went on the air and the British asked him not to. Nobody asked me not to. There was no announcement until the collapse that the people who had spoken on the radio would be prosecuted.

Having worked for years to prevent war, and seeing the folly of Italy and America being at war — ! I certainly wasn't telling the troops to revolt. I thought I was fighting an internal question of constitutional government. And if any man, any individual man, can say he has had a bad deal from me because of race, creed, or color, let him come out and state it with particulars. The *Guide to Kulchur* was dedicated to Basil Bunting and Louis Zukofsky, a Quaker and a Jew.

I don't know whether you think the Russians ought to be in Berlin or not. I don't know whether I was doing any good or not, whether I was doing any harm. Oh, I was probably offside. But the ruling in Boston was that there is no treason without treasonable intention.

What I was right about was the conservation of individual rights. If, when the executive or any other branch exceeds its legitimate powers, no one protests, you will lose all your liberties. My method of opposing tyranny was wrong over a thirty-year period; it had nothing to do with the Second World War in particular. If the individual, or heretic, gets hold of some essential truth, or sees some error in the system being practiced, he commits so many marginal errors himself that he is worn out before he can establish his point.

The world in twenty years has piled up hysteria — anxiety over a third war, bureaucratic tyranny, and hysteria from paper forms. The immense and undeniable loss of freedoms, as they were in 1900, is undeniable. We have seen the acceleration in efficiency of the tyrannizing factors. It's enough to keep a man worried. Wars are made to make debt. I suppose there's a possible out in space satellites and other ways of making debt.

INTERVIEWER: When you were arrested by the Americans, did you then expect to be convicted? To be hanged?

POUND: At first I puzzled over having missed a cog somewhere. I expected to turn myself in and to be asked about what I learned. I did and I wasn't. I know that I checked myself, on several occasions during the broadcasts, on reflecting that it was not up to me to do certain things, or to take service with a foreign country. Oh, it was paranoia to think one could argue against the usurpations, against the folks who got the war started to get America into it. Yet I hate the idea of obedience to something which is wrong.

Then later I was driven into the courtyard at Chiavari. They had been shooting them, and I thought I was finished then and there. Then finally a guy came in and said he was damned if he would hand me over to the Americans unless I wanted to be handed over to them.

INTERVIEWER: In 1942, when the war started for America, I understand you tried to leave Italy and come back to the United States. What were the circumstances of the refusal?

POUND: Those circumstances were by hearsay. I am a bit hazy in my head about a considerable period, and I think that . . . I know that I had a chance to get as far as Lisbon, and be cooped up there for the rest of the war.

INTERVIEWER: Why did you want to get back to the States at that time?

POUND: I wanted to get back during the election, before the election.

INTERVIEWER: The election was in 1940, wasn't it?

POUND: That would be 1940. I don't honestly remember what happened. My parents were too old to travel. They would have had to stay there in Rapallo. Dad retired there on his pension.

INTERVIEWER: During those years in the war in Italy did you write poetry? The *Pisan Cantos* were written when you were interned. What did you write during those years?

POUND: Arguments, arguments and arguments. Oh, I did some of the Confucius translation.

INTERVIEWER: How was it that you began to write poetry again only after you were interned? You didn't write any *Cantos* at all during the war, did you?

POUND: Let's see — the Adams stuff came out just before the war shut off. No. There was *Oro e Lavoro*. I was writing economic stuff in Italian.

INTERVIEWER: Since your internment, you've published three collections of *Cantos, Thrones* just recently. You must be near the end. Can you say what you are going to do in the remaining *Cantos*?

POUND: It is difficult to write a paradiso when all the superficial indications are that you ought to write an apocalypse. It is obviously much easier to find inhabitants for an inferno or even a purgatorio. I am trying to collect the record of the top flights of the mind. I might have done better to put Agassiz on top instead of Confucius.

INTERVIEWER: Are you more or less stuck?

POUND: Okay, I am stuck. The question is, am I dead, as Messrs. A.B.C. might wish? In case I conk out, this is provisionally what I have to do: I must clarify obscurities; I must make clearer definite ideas or dissociations. I must find a verbal formula to combat the rise of brutality — the principle of order versus the split atom. There was a man in the bughouse, by the way, who insisted that the atom had never been split.

An epic is a poem containing history. The modern mind contains heteroclite elements. The past epos has succeeded when all or a great many of the answers were assumed, at least between author and audience, or a great mass of audience. The attempt in an experimental age is therefore rash. Do you know the story: "What are you drawing, Johnny?"

"God."

"But nobody knows what He looks like."

"They will when I get through!"

That confidence is no longer obtainable.

There *are* epic subjects. The struggle for individual rights is an epic subject, consecutive from jury trial in Athens to Anselm versus William Rufus, to the murder of Becket and to Coke and through John Adams.

Then the struggle appears to come up against a block. The nature of sovereignty is epic matter, though it may be a bit obscured by circumstance. Some of this *can* be traced, pointed; obviously it has to be condensed to get into the form. The nature of the individual, the heteroclite contents of contemporary consciousness. It's the fight for light versus subconsciousness; it demands obscurities and penumbras. A lot of contemporary writing avoids inconvenient areas of the subject.

I am writing to resist the view that Europe and civilization are going to Hell. If I am being "crucified for an idea" — that is, the coherent idea around which my muddles accumulated — it is probably the idea that European culture ought to survive, that the best qualities of it ought to survive along with whatever other cultures, in whatever universality. Against the propaganda of terror and the propaganda of luxury, have you a nice simple answer? One has worked on certain materials trying to establish bases and axes of reference. In writing so as to be understood, there is always the problem of rectification without giving up what is correct. There is the struggle not to sign on the dotted line for the opposition.

INTERVIEWER: Do the separate sections of the *Cantos*, now — the last three sections have appeared under separate names — mean that you are attacking particular problems in particular sections?

POUND: No. *Rock Drill* was intended to imply the necessary resistance in getting a certain main thesis across — hammering. I was not following the three divisions of the *Divine Comedy* exactly. One can't follow the Dantesquan cosmos in an age of experiment. But I have made the division between people dominated by emotion, people struggling upwards, and those who have some part of the divine vision. The thrones in Dante's *Paradiso* are for the spirits of the people who have been responsible for good government. The thrones in the *Cantos* are an attempt to move out from egoism and to establish some definition of an order possible or at any rate conceivable on earth. One is held up by the low percentage of reason which seems to operate in human affairs. *Thrones* concerns the states of mind of people responsible for something more than their personal conduct.

INTERVIEWER: Now that you come near the end, have you made any plans for revising the *Cantos*, after you've finished?

POUND: I don't know. There's need of elaboration, of clarification, but I don't know that a comprehensive revision is in order. There is no doubt that the writing is too obscure as it stands, but I hope that the order of ascension in the Paradiso will be toward a greater limpidity. Of course there ought to be a corrected edition because of errors that have crept in.

INTERVIEWER: Let me change the subject again, if I may. In all those years in St. Elizabeths, did you get a sense of contemporary America from your visitors?

POUND: The trouble with visitors is that you don't get enough of the opposition. I suffer from the cumulative isolation of not having had enough contact — fifteen years living more with ideas than with persons.

INTERVIEWER: Do you have any plans for going back to the States? Do you want to?

POUND: I undoubtedly want to. But whether it is nostalgia for America that isn't there anymore or not I don't know. This is a difference between an abstract Adams–Jefferson–Adams–Jackson America, and whatever is really going on. I undoubtedly have moments when I should like very much to live in America. There are these concrete difficulties against the general desire. Richmond is a beautiful city, but you can't live in it unless you drive an automobile. I'd like at least to spend a month or two a year in the U.S.

INTERVIEWER: You said the other day that as you grew older you felt more American all the time. How does this work?

POUND: It works. Exotics were necessary as an attempt at a foundation. One is transplanted and grows, and one is pulled up and taken back to what one has been transplanted from and it is no longer there. The contacts aren't there and I suppose one reverts to one's organic nature and finds it merciful. Have you ever read Andy White's memoirs? He's the fellow who founded Cornell University. That was the period of euphoria, when everybody thought that all the good things in America were going to function, before the decline, about 1900. White covers a period of history that goes back to Buchanan on one side. He alternated between being ambassador to Russia and head of Cornell.

INTERVIEWER: Your return to Italy has been a disappointment, then?

POUND: Undoubtedly. Europe was a shock. The shock of no

longer feeling oneself in the center of something is probably part of it. Then there is the incomprehension, Europe's incomprehension, of organic America. There are so many things which I, as an American, cannot say to a European with any hope of being understood. Somebody said that I am the last American living the tragedy of Europe.

Index

337

347